www.wadsworth.com

www.wadsworth.com is the World Wide Web site for
Thomson Wadsworth and is your direct source to dozens
of online resources.

At *www.wadsworth.com* you can find out about supple-
ments, demonstration software, and student resources. You
can also send email to many of our authors and preview
new publications and exciting new technologies.

www.wadsworth.com
Changing the way the world learns®

Guide to Criminal Law
for California

Guide to Criminal Law
for California

Third Edition

SANDRA TOZZINI
Attorney at Law

THOMSON

WADSWORTH

Australia • Canada • Mexico • Singapore • Spain • United Kingdom • United States

Executive Editor: Sabra Horne
Development Editor: Julie Sakaue
Assistant Editor: Jana Davis
Editorial Assistant: Elise Smith
Marketing Manager: Terra Schultz
Marketing Assistant: Annabelle Yang

Project Manager, Editorial Production: Jennifer Klos
Print Buyer: Emma Claydon
Permissions Editor: Chelsea Junget
Cover Designer: Yvo Riezebos
Cover Image: Donovan Reese/Getty Images
Text and Cover Printer: Thomson West

For more information about our products,
contact us at:
Thomson Learning Academic Resource Center
1-800-423-0563

For permission to use material from this text or product,
submit a request online at
http://www.thomsonrights.com.

Any additional questions about permissions
can be submitted by email to
thomsonrights@thomson.com.

Library of Congress Control Number: 2004109557

ISBN: 0-534-64414-7

Thomson Wadsworth
10 Davis Drive
Belmont, CA 94002-3098
USA

Asia
Thomson Learning
5 Shenton Way #01-01
UIC Building
Singapore 068808

Australia/New Zealand
Thomson Learning
102 Dodds Street
Southbank, Victoria 3006
Australia

Canada
Nelson
1120 Birchmount Road
Toronto, Ontario M1K 5G4
Canada

Europe/Middle East/South Africa
Thomson Learning
High Holborn House
50/51 Bedford Row
London WC1R 4LR
United Kingdom

Latin America
Thomson Learning
Seneca, 53
Colonia Polanco
11560 Mexico D.F.
Mexico

Spain/Portugal
Paraninfo
Calle/Magallanes, 25
28015 Madrid, Spain

To Mom: the third times the charm
No "Chance" of Re-"Petes"
....

TABLE OF CONTENTS

INTRODUCTION

Welcome to the world of California criminal law! You will soon come face-to-face with actual statutes and cases from California law books. Because our government is based on a concept of federalism, each state has enacted its own criminal laws. In turn, the state courts have interpreted their own criminal law statutes. For this reason, it is important to study the specific laws of the state in which you live or work.

CALIFORNIA IS A LEGAL TRENDSETTER

As you will see, some of California's laws are in keeping with "generic" criminal law throughout the United States. In other instances, you will find that California forges its own path in defining or interpreting its criminal laws. Whether the cases and statutes that you read are consistent with mainstream notions of criminal law or take a bent of their own, these materials bear the unique stamp of California itself. Remember, too, that California has traditionally been considered a legal trendsetter and that lawmakers and legal scholars from other states often look to the "California experience" in fashioning their own laws or advocating changes in existing law.

THE CONCEPTUAL FRAMEWORK OF THIS TEXT

Before you begin reading the supplemental materials, we would like to point out a few things that you should keep in mind before beginning your studies.

First of all, and most importantly, we assume that you understand that California law may differ from general principles of American law. A basic understanding of criminal law principles is critical to laying the foundation for your understanding of California law. Although we briefly summarize basic principles of American Law at the beginning of each chapter or its on the summary. Without a basic foundation underneath you, you will have nothing to build on. If you do not read the background material first, you will simply be learning isolated snippets of information with no real foundation on which to build information in your brain bank.

Second, it is important that you learn to be able to understand "the primary sources" of law, which include statutes, causes and constitutions. "Primary sources" of law are the actual law itself and not someone else's interpretation of the law. The reason that students often times are not given primary sources of law is that they can be very hard to understand. Legislators do not use plain English to write the laws and judges can write forever on a seemingly minute point of law that will add pages to a decision. Our job is to edit this material for you so that it is understandable but at the same time allows you to practice reading primary sources of law that you may need to refer to later on in life. By learning to read these edited sources, you can build your skills in understanding and interpreting the law.

Third, we will provide you with questions to help guide your learning experience. Some of these questions will be geared to checking your general understanding of the area of law. Other questions will help assess your reading comprehension of specific passages. Other types of questions will tap your critical thinking skills, that is, thinking the way that lawyers think. We know that most of you do not want to become lawyers. However, that is not the reason to focus on critical thinking skills that teach you to "think like a lawyer." The real reason for developing these skills is that most legislators and judges are lawyers. Understanding how their minds work will make the law fall more easily into place for you.

HOW THIS TEXT IS ORGANIZED

Introducing you to the organization of the book will help you follow the intellectual garden path on which we will be taking you throughout your studies. One of the key organizational components of this text is the use of columns: double columns signal that the material is primary authority (i.e., the "law"); all other material is in single column format.

Each chapter contains various headings that reflect the major area of study (such as murder, arson, etc.). Within each heading you may find several subheadings. We have placed a symbol under each major area of study to correspond with the following subheadings.

 Constitution

Whenever a constitutional issue is raised, the constitution must be the starting point of any analysis. A constitution places limits on the breadth of criminal laws as well as their enforcement. Although most of the issues in this text do not touch on topics of constitutional magnitude, you will see California constitutional provisions and their application to California criminal law.

 Statutes

With rare exception, each chapter contains both statutes and cases. Whenever we present *both* statutes and cases on a particular topic for your review, we always place the statutory material first. We have placed the statutes first because when researching criminal law, you should *always* read the relevant statutes first before reading the cases that interpret them.

The statutes are often edited, but not paraphrased. This provides you with the opportunity to try reading statutes as the Legislature has drafted them. They are often wordy, complex and (yes!) confusing, but this is a good opportunity to become familiar with the language of the law.

 Cases

Generally speaking, we have edited the cases to highlight the relevant legal point that is the focus of discussion. However, we have tried to keep the original flavor of the cases we have selected for study purposes. In the older cases, you will notice that the language can appear rather stilted and antiquated compared to more modern cases. In addition, spelling has changed a bit since some of the cases first appeared 50 or more years ago. Do not become daunted by some awkward phraseology. By reading the actual language of the cases, you will get a better feel for the judicial decision-making process.

Comments

Comments precede both statutes and cases. We use this section to point out what is important or help explain what you will be reading. Consider this section "roadmap" for the material that follows.

Questions

Questions follow both statutes and cases. We use this section to ask you questions about what you have read and to pose hypothetical questions to further your mastery of the material you have just encountered.

ON WITH THE SHOW!

Now that all of the preliminary remarks are out of the way, you are now ready to begin your study of California criminal law. It is our sincerest hope that you will enjoy reading these materials as much as we have enjoyed preparing them. Best wishes to you in your endeavors in this course and throughout your college and professional careers.

Sandra Tozzini

Guide to Criminal Law
for California

CHAPTER ONE

The Nature, Origins, & Purposes of Criminal Law

Crimes are statutory offenses defined by the Legislature. (Unlike California, many states rely heavily on the Model Penal Code in formulating their criminal laws.) In order to convict a person of a crime, a state must: 1) prove the defendant's act violated an existing criminal law; 2) prove the defendant committed those acts by proof beyond a reasonable doubt; and 3) prove the defendant had the necessary criminal intent.

This book takes your studies beyond general concepts of American criminal law and familiarizes you with California criminal law. As you will learn during your studies, in some ways California follows general principles of American law, but in other ways it forges its own path.

Although all states have incorporated the most serious common law felonies (such as rape and murder) into their laws, the language of these state laws is not always uniform. Each state defines its own crimes and establishes permissible punishments for those crimes. In California, most criminal offenses are contained in the volume of books known as the "California Penal Code." As you will see, California's Penal Code has four major divisions under which all the statutes are organized.

I. THE ORGANIZATIONAL FRAMEWORK OF THE CALIFORNIA PENAL CODE

A. Comments

As Penal Code section 1 demonstrates below, the California Penal Code is divided into four sections. Section 1 of the Penal Code will be the focus of your studies because Section 1 defines crimes and punishments. Although it is not necessary for you to be familiar with all portions of the California Penal Code, it is helpful to see the organizational framework of this statutory scheme. By familiarizing yourself with the organizational framework of the Penal Code, you will gain an insight into what the California State Legislature considers important elements of our criminal justice system.

B. Statutes

Penal Code section 1

1. This Act shall be known as THE PENAL CODE OF CALIFORNIA, and is divided into four parts, as follows:
  I.--OF CRIMES AND PUNISHMENTS.
  II.--OF CRIMINAL PROCEDURE.
  III.--OF THE STATE PRISON AND COUNTY JAILS.
  IV.--OF PREVENTION OF CRIMES AND APPREHENSION OF CRIMINALS.

C. Questions

- ♦ Do you think the Legislature's organizational framework of the Penal Code makes sense?

- ♦ If you do not agree with the Legislature's organization of the Penal Code, how would you restructure it?

II. CLASSIFICATION OF CRIMES

A. Comments

The following statutes (Penal Code sections 16 and 17) are very important. These statutes set forth the classifications of crimes and public offenses that exist under California law. They also set forth the allowable punishment for different classifications of crimes. There is also a category of crimes, which can be punished either as misdemeanors or felonies that is known as "wobblers." We have included an example of a "wobbler" in California, the crime of cruelty to animals.

B. Statutes

Penal Code section 16

Crimes and public offenses include:
1. Felonies;
2. Misdemeanors; and
3. Infractions.

Penal Code section 17

A felony is a crime that is punishable with death or by imprisonment in the state prison.   Every other crime or public offense is a misdemeanor except those offenses that are classified as infractions.

Penal Code section 597

(a) Every person who maliciously and intentionally maims, mutilates, tortures, or wounds a living animal, or maliciously and intentionally kills an animal, is guilty of an offense punishable by imprisonment in the state prison, or by a fine of not more than twenty thousand dollars ($20,000), or by both the fine and imprisonment, or, alternatively, by imprisonment in the county jail for not more than one year, or by a fine of not more than twenty thousand dollars ($20,000), or by both the fine and imprisonment.

(b) Every person who overdrives, overloads, drives when overloaded, overworks, tortures, torments, deprives of necessary sustenance, drink, or shelter, cruelly beats, mutilates, or cruelly kills any animal, or causes or procures any animal to be so overdriven, overloaded, driven when overloaded, overworked, tortured, tormented, deprived of necessary sustenance, drink, shelter, or to be cruelly beaten, mutilated, or cruelly killed; and whoever, having the charge or custody of any animal, either as owner or otherwise, subjects any animal to needless suffering, or inflicts unnecessary cruelty upon the animal, or in any manner abuses any animal, or fails to provide the animal with proper food, drink, or shelter or protection from the weather, or who drives, rides, or otherwise uses the animal when unfit for labor, is, for every such offense, guilty of a crime punishable as a misdemeanor or as a felony or alternatively punishable as a misdemeanor or a felony and by a fine of not more than twenty thousand dollars ($20,000).

***

(f) Upon the conviction of a person charged with a violation of this section by causing or permitting an act of cruelty, all animals lawfully seized and impounded with respect to the violation by a peace officer, officer of a humane society, or officer of a pound or animal regulation department of a public agency shall be adjudged by the court to be forfeited and shall thereupon be awarded to the impounding officer for proper disposition. A person convicted of a violation of this section by causing or permitting an act of cruelty, shall be liable to the impounding officer for all costs of impoundment from the time of seizure to the time of proper disposition.

C. Questions

♦ Why do you think the Legislature authorizes some crimes to be punishable either as misdemeanors or as felonies ("wobblers")?

♦ In an individual case of animal cruelty, what do you think is the critical factor or factors in determining whether the offense is a misdemeanor or a felony? Does the statute make that clear or not?

♦ Assume that you have two criminal defendants before you, both charged with a violation of Penal Code section 597. In one case, the defendant has used an electric cattle prod (a battery-operated electrical stimulus device) on a horse for training purposes. In the other case, the defendant has starved three horses to death. Do you think that criminal justice system will treat these two defendants similarly under Penal Code section 597? If not, which do you think should be punished as a felony and which as a misdemeanor?

III. PUNISHMENTS

A. Comments

The following statutes deal with the punishment provisions for felonies, misdemeanors, and infractions. The special statutory punishment commonly known as the "Three Strikes Law" is also included. Even though the "Three Strikes" statute has been heavily edited, it does provide you with a sense of the magnitude of this law. Finally, among the statutory provisions set forth below is the Penal Code section that authorizes the death penalty in California and the permissible methods of execution.

B. Statutes

Felonies: Penal Code section 18

Except in cases where a different punishment is prescribed by any law of this state, every offense declared to be a felony, or to be punishable by imprisonment in a state prison, is punishable by imprisonment in any of the state prisons for 16 months, or two or three years; provided, however, every offence which is prescribed by any law of the state to be a felony punishable offense which is prescribed by any law of the state to be a felony punishable by imprisonment in any of the state prisons or by a fine, but without an alternate sentence to the county jail, may be punishable by imprisonment in the county jail not exceeding one year or by a fine, or by both.

Misdemeanors: Penal Code section 19

Except in cases where a different punishment is prescribed by any law of this state, every offense declared to be a misdemeanor is punishable by imprisonment in the county jail not exceeding six months, or by fine not exceeding one thousand dollars ($1,000), or by both.

Infractions: Penal Code section 19

An infraction is not punishable by imprisonment. A person charged with an infraction shall not be entitled to a trial by jury. A person charged with an infraction shall not be entitled to have the public defender or other counsel appointed at public expense to represent him or her unless he or she is arrested and not released on his or her written promise to appear, his or her own recognizance, or a deposit of bail.

Where not defined: Penal Code section 19.4

When an act or omission is declared by a statute to be a public offense and no penalty for the offense is proscribed in any statute, the act or omission is punishable as a misdemeanor.

Penal Code section 667, subdivision (e)

(1) If a defendant has one prior felony conviction that has been pled and proved, the determinate term or minimum term for an indeterminate term shall be twice the term otherwise provided as punishment for the current felony conviction.

(2)(A) If a defendant has two or more prior felony convictions as defined in subdivision (d) that have been pled and proved, the term for current felony conviction shall be indeterminate term of life imprisonment as a minimum term of the indeterminate sentence calculated as the greater of.

(i)Three times the term otherwise provided as punishment for each current felony conviction subsequent to the two or more prior felony convictions.

(ii) Imprisonment in the state prison for 25 years.

Penal Code Section 1192.7

"Serious felony" means any of the following.:

(1) Murder or voluntary manslaughter; (2) mayhem; (3) rape; (4) sodomy by force, violence, duress, menace, threat of great bodily injury, or fear of immediate and unlawful bodily injury on the victim or another person; (5) oral copulation by force, violence, duress, menace, threat of great bodily injury, or fear of immediate and unlawful bodily injury on the victim or another person; (6) lewd or lascivious act on a child under the age of 14 years; (7) any felony punishable by death or imprisonment in the state prison for life; (8) any other felony in which the defendant personally inflicts great bodily injury on any person, other than an accomplice, or any felony in which the defendant personally uses a firearm; (9) attempted murder; (10) assault with intent to commit rape or robbery; (11) assault with a deadly weapon or instrument on a peace officer; (12) assault by a life prisoner on a non-inmate; (13) assault with a deadly weapon by an inmate; (14) arson; (15) exploding a destructive device or any explosive with intent to injure; (16) exploding a destructive device or any explosive causing great bodily injury or mayhem; (17) exploding a destructive device or any explosive with intent to murder; (18) burglary of an inhabited dwelling house, or trailer coach as defined by the Vehicle Code, or inhabited portion of any other building; (19) robbery or bank robbery; (20) kidnapping; (21) holding of a hostage by a person confined in a state prison; (22) attempt to commit a felony punishable by death or imprisonment in the state prison for life; (23) any felony in which the defendant personally used a dangerous or deadly weapon; (24) selling, furnishing, administering, giving, or offering to sell, furnish, administer, or give to a minor any heroin, cocaine, phencyclidine (PCP), or any methamphetamine-related drug, or any of the precursors of methamphetamines, (25) any violation where the act is accomplished against the victim's will by

force, violence, duress, menace, or fear of immediate and unlawful bodily injury on the victim or another person; (26) grand theft involving a firearm; (27) carjacking....

Death Penalty: Penal Code section 3604

(a) The punishment of death shall be inflicted by the administration of a lethal gas or by an intravenous injection of a substance or substances in a lethal quantity sufficient to cause death, by standards established under the direction of the Department of Corrections.

(b) Persons sentenced to death prior to or after the operative date of this subdivision shall have the opportunity to elect to have the punishment imposed by lethal gas or lethal injection. This choice shall be made in writing and shall be submitted to the warden pursuant to regulations established by the Department of Corrections. If a person under sentence of death does not choose either lethal gas or lethal injection within 10 days after the warden's service upon the inmate of an execution warrant issued following the operative date of this subdivision, the penalty of death shall be imposed by lethal injection.

(c) Where the person sentenced to death is not executed on the date set for execution and a new execution date is subsequently set, the inmate again shall have the opportunity to elect to have punishment imposed by lethal gas or lethal injection, according to the procedures set forth in subdivision (b).

C. Comments

As you have already seen, the Legislature not only defines crimes, it also determines the punishments for committing crimes. In California, the punishment that a defendant receives depends not only on the crime he or she has committed. Many California statutes contain increased punishments ("enhancements") to augment the usual punishment that a defendant would receive for committing a particular offense. If a defendant commits a crime in an egregious fashion (which meets specific statutory requirements), the defendant's sentence can be enhanced.

The *Andrade* case is an example of an enhanced punishment for a specific crime, the crime of arson. When reading this case, note the court's recitation of the legislative origin of the arson enhancement. The court also remarks on the urgent nature of this enhancement legislation. (If you are unaware of California legislative procedure, here is a thumbnail overview. In California, bills that pass both houses and are signed by the governor become effective on the following January 1. There are two exceptions to the January 1 date. If the Legislature deems the legislation to be an emergency measure, it becomes effective immediately. The second exception to the January 1 date is the initiative process. When voters pass an initiative, it becomes effective the day after approval by the voters.)

D. Case

PEOPLE V. ANDRADE
Court of Appeal, First Appellate District, Division Five
85 Cal. App. 4th 579 (2000)

RICHMAN, J..

Devon Ray Andrade appeals his conviction by jury trial of arson of a structure with use of a device designed to accelerate a fire (Pen. Code, § § 451, subd. (c), 451.1, subd. (a)(5)).

BACKGROUND
***

At approximately 2:30 a.m. on November 29, 1997, defendant smashed the glass front door and entered Impostors, a jewelry store located on the ground floor of a semi-high-rise building on Geary Street in San Francisco. According to eyewitness Victor Zacca, once inside the store defendant shattered two or three glass display cases, pulled a liquid-filled glass beverage bottle with a cloth protruding from it out of his backpack, and lit the cloth, causing flames to quickly erupt on the floor around him. He then threw the bottle against the display case. According to eyewitness Charles Davis, after defendant threw what appeared to be a liquid-filled juice bottle several times, the bottle broke on the floor, after which defendant walked forward and threw a match causing the entire back wall up the ceiling to erupt in flames. Defendant then left the store. Davis and another person used portable fire extinguishers to put out the fires.

Davis and Zacca selected defendant's photograph from a photo lineup as depicting the person they saw damage and set fire to the Impostors store.

San Francisco Fire Captain Thomas Ryan responded to the scene and noted that there had been several fires in different locations inside Impostors, indicating that the fires did not start naturally or accidentally, but were set. Ryan noted scorching, but not charring, on the rear floor, and testified that the floor had "some evidence of burning." He identified a "little bit of charring" on a photograph of the store floor. Ryan opined that a flammable liquid, i.e., an accelerant, had been used in setting the fires in the Impostors store.

Lieutenant Lawrence Wright of the San Francisco Fire Department's Bureau of Fire Investigation arrived at the fire scene shortly after the other firefighters. Wright noticed actual charring of the hardwood floor. There was also charring of the molding around several nearby display cases, indicative of burning associated with an ignitable or flammable liquid such as gasoline. Wright also smelled gasoline and noted a plastic container obviously involved in the fires. Gasoline was present on the hardwood floor and in the remains of the plastic container. Wright, testifying as an expert on the cause and origin of the fires, opined that the fires were incendiary, i.e., deliberately set and initiated and accelerated with gasoline, explaining that an accelerant is defined as any material, often a liquid, used to either enhance or spread a fire, and that gasoline is a known accelerant. Wright also opined that the first origin of fire was the area adjacent to the charred hardwood floor.

***

Defendant contends that the court misinstructed the jury on the factual elements of the section 451.1, subdivision (a)(5), enhancement alleged in conjunction with the count 1 charge of arson of the structure at the Impostors store.

Section 451.1 provides in relevant part: "(a) Notwithstanding any other law, any person who is convicted of a felony violation of Section 451 shall be punished by a three-, four-, or five-year enhancement if one or more of the following circumstances is found to be true: ¶ ... ¶ (5) The defendant committed arson as described in subdivision ... (c) of Section 451 and the arson was *caused by use of a device designed to accelerate the fire* or delay ignition. ¶ (b) The additional term specified in subdivision (a) shall not be imposed unless the existence of any fact required under this section shall be alleged in the accusatory pleading and either admitted by the defendant in open court or found to be true by the trier of fact." (Italics added.)

The court orally instructed the jury as follows: "It is further alleged that at the time of the commission of the crime charged in count 1, that the defendant *used a device to accelerate the fire* or delay ignition. [P] If you find defendant guilty of the crime charged in count 1, you must determine whether or not the truth of this allegation has been proved. [P] The People have the burden of proving the truth of this allegation. If you have a reasonable doubt that it is true, you must find it to be not true. [P] Include a special finding on that question, using a form that will be supplied to you." (Italics added)

Defendant argues that by omitting the word "designed" the jury did not have to determine whether he used a device that was *designed to* accelerate the fire, and could erroneously find the enhancement true based merely on his igniting of spilled gasoline, which according to him is not a device designed to accelerate a fire.

The thrust of defendant's argument is that as a result of the court's instruction, the jury could have improperly found the

enhancement true based on Davis's testimony, i.e., that a gasoline-filled bottle was thrown and broke after which the spilled gasoline was ignited. According to defendant, Davis's testimony does not establish that defendant used a device designed to accelerate the fire because the bottle served no purpose other than as a container for the gasoline, and gasoline per se is not a device designed to accelerate a fire but is instead a combustible substance designed for the purpose of propelling vehicles. Defendant goes so far as to suggest that the court had a sua sponte duty to apprise the jury that "the mere use of bottles as containers for gasoline" does not constitute use of a device designed to accelerate the fire under section 451.1, subdivision (a)(5).

Defendant acknowledges that a breakable gasoline-filled container with a lightable wick is a Molotov cocktail which he concedes *is* a "device designed to accelerate the fire" under section 451.1, subdivision (a)(5), and that Zacca's testimony that he used such a device does support a true finding on the enhancement. However, defendant argues that as a result of the erroneous instruction it is possible that the jury improperly found the enhancement true based on Davis's testimony which does not establish his use of a device designed to accelerate the fire and, therefore, the error is prejudicial.

***

Because the phrase "device designed to accelerate the fire" (§ 451.1, subd. (a)(5)) is capable of more than one meaning, statutory construction is necessary, and appears to be an issue of first impression.

Section 451.1 was enacted in 1994 as part of urgency legislation creating new arson-related offenses and enhancements and amending various statutes for the purpose of increasing the penalties for arson. (Stats. 1994, ch. 421, § 2, eff. Sept. 7, 1994 (hereafter Sen. Bill No. 1309).)

8

Section 7 of Senate Bill No. 1309 provides: "This act is an urgency statute necessary for the immediate preservation of the public peace, health, or safety within the meaning of Article IV of the Constitution and shall go into immediate effect. The facts constituting the necessity are: ¶ In order to establish a meaningful deterrent to the increase in the incidence of arson throughout the state and to reduce the devastation created therefrom, it is necessary that this act take effect immediately." In addition to adding the section 451.1 enhancement, Senate Bill No. 1309 added section 451.5 establishing the offense of aggravated arson punishable by a state prison term of 10 years to life, added section 452.1 establishing a sentence enhancement for persons convicted of unlawfully causing a fire (§ 452) if certain factual circumstances are found, and amended sections 451, 454 and 1203.06. (Stats. 1994, ch. 421, § § 1, 3, 4, 5, 6, eff. Sept. 7, 1994.) Supporters of Senate Bill No. 1309 argued, " 'This bill would increase the penalties for the worst arsonists who exhibit a specific intent to inflict damage or who in fact inflict serious damage or who commit a repeat offense and pose a continuing threat to society.' " (Sen. Floor Analysis of Sen. Bill No. 1309 (1993-1994 Reg. Sess.) Aug. 26, 1994, p. 4; quoting Com., Bill Analysis of Sen. Bill No. 1309 (1993-1994 Reg. Sess.) as introduced Apr. 4, 1994, p. 6 [the express purpose of the bill according to the sponsor].)

***

Clearly, then, the purpose of section 451.1 is to deter arson by increasing the penalties for arsonists who exhibit a specific intent to inflict damage by causing the arson by use of a device designed to accelerate the fire.

***

The issue is whether the jury could have reasonably concluded, based on Davis's testimony, that a gasoline-filled bottle, which after being thrown, broke and expelled and dispersed gasoline, a fire accelerant, which was then ignited, is a device *designed* to accelerate the fire under section 451.1, subdivision (a)(5). In view of the record, a rational jury could have concluded only that the gasoline-filled bottle was a device designed to accelerate the fire and that the Impostors arson was caused by defendant's use of such device.

The evidence was undisputed that defendant threw the gasoline-filled bottle. Based on that evidence the jury could properly have found that defendant intended the bottle containing the accelerant gasoline to serve as a missile or projectile, whose purpose was to disperse the accelerant at a distance farther away from him and/or over a greater surface area than could be otherwise achieved. Dispersal of a fire accelerant at a greater distance and/or over a greater area would serve to accelerate, i.e., hasten or increase, the fire's spread. No evidence was presented suggesting that the gasoline-filled bottle served any purpose other than as a device intended to accelerate the fire. In addition, the undisputed testimony of Ryan and Wright established that the Impostors fire was deliberately set, i.e., caused by use of an accelerant. No evidence was presented that the fire was caused by anything other than defendant's use of the device which accelerated it, or that the gasoline was expelled from the bottle accidentally. Further, the undisputed testimony that defendant was in possession of and used at least several gasoline-filled bottles to cause . . . [another] arson . . . the day after the Impostors arson underscores the lack of any possible explanation other than that the device consisting of the gasoline-filled bottle was designed to accelerate the fire, and that defendant caused the arson at Imposters by use of the device.

***

In finding the enhancement true, the jury necessarily found that defendant did more than use a match to ignite poured gasoline, that he used a device to accelerate the fire. Based on the record before us, we conclude that no rational juror could find that defendant used a device to accelerate the fire, but fail to find that the device was designed to accelerate the fire and that the Impostors arson was caused by defendant's use of such device.

The judgment is affirmed.

D. Question

♦ Is an enhancement to a sentence a question of fact or a question of law? If you have trouble in answering this question, look to see who makes the determination--is it the judge or the jury? What does this tell you about enhancements?

IV. Self-Assessment

1. California is in the minority of jurisdictions that do not authorize the death penalty.
   A. True   B. False

2. Enhancements are increased punishments for crimes committed in a more serious manner.
   A. True   B. False

3. Infractions are not punishable by confinement in a state prison.
   A. True   B. False

4. "Wobblers" are crimes that are punishable either as misdemeanors or infractions.
   A. True   B. False

5. A "serious felony" under California law does not include carjacking.
   A. True   B. False

CHAPTER TWO

Constitutional Limits on Criminal Law

Constitutional limitations on crimes include *ex post facto* laws (laws which make a defendant's act criminal after the act was committed), as well as the manner in which actions can be criminalized. For example, as you will soon study, the Constitution mandates that criminal laws must clearly state the prohibited conduct so that ordinary people can understand it. Finally, the Constitution prohibits the criminalization of protected conduct, such as Freedom of Speech and Freedom of Religion.

This chapter focuses on the California Constitution and the cases which interpret it. This chapter has two focal points. First, *when* does the Constitution place limits on California criminal laws? Second, *where* does the Constitution place limits on California criminal laws? Although our focus is on the California Constitution, in most instances constitutional analysis under either California or federal constitutional law reaches the same conclusion. The reason for the similar outcomes is simple: a state must provide criminal defendants with at least as much protection as the United States Constitution allows.

However, that does not mean that all constitutional issues will have the same outcome. The United States Constitution provides the *minimum protections*. However, a state may grant criminal defendants *greater protection* than the United States Constitution requires, if the state so desires.

On a final note, we want to advise you that this chapter contains the only non-California case in this book. The section on Freedom of Religion contains a United States Supreme Court decision as well as a California State Supreme Court decision. This will give you an opportunity to compare federal protections and limitations as opposed to state protections and limitations.

I. VAGUENESS

A. Comments

In this case, the defendant challenges his conviction on the grounds that the California "lynching" statute is unconstitutionally vague. The thrust of the defendant's argument is that the statutory definition of "lynching" runs contrary to the everyday meaning of the word and is therefore impermissibly vague.

B. Case

PEOPLE v. JONES
Court of Appeal, Fourth District, Division 2
18 Cal.App.3d 437 (1977)

KERRIGAN, Acting P. J.

About 9:30 p.m. on June 30, 1969, two Santa Ana police officers on routine car patrol observed Mercy Roaches Sandoval, age 18, throwing bottles in the street near a take-out restaurant establishment. The officers pulled into the restaurant, called for backup units, left their vehicle, and approached Sandoval. The defendant, Jones, was noted standing at the order window at that time. Sandoval, standing amidst broken glass, had slurred speech and was placed under arrest for being drunk in public. He staggered while being escorted to the patrol unit.

Defendant approached the arresting officer and asked him what he was doing. When told that Sandoval had been placed under arrest, defendant shouted, 'no, you're not. We talked to your Chief, and you pigs are supposed to stay off the lot (restaurant premises). We'll handle our own problems.' Defendant jumped on a bench located in the restaurant patio. With arms upraised and gesturing towards the patrol car, he yelled, 'Don't let them take him away'; 'Let's get 'em'; 'Don't let the fucking pigs take him away.' His exhortations and obscenities were directed to a gathering crowd of some 50 people. The officers and patrol car soon became the target of bottles and debris.

With Sandoval in the back seat, the officers attempted to leave, but were prevented from doing so by a car which blocked the driveway. As they attempted

to back away from the roadblock, defendant opened the rear door of the patrol car, partially entered, and pulled out Sandoval. Defendant was assisted by an unidentified male in a yellow jacket. Together they supported Sandoval and dragged him into the crowd.

There was no pursuit since by then the crowd had converged on the patrol car, and the officers were still under bombardment. They hurriedly left the scene.

Defendant testified in his own behalf to the effect that he witnessed the escape but did not participate in it; he remained at the order window throughout and did not harangue the crowd. Several witnesses corroborated his testimony, including Sandoval, who admitted being the escapee. Sandoval maintained that he was assisted out of the police vehicle by a fellow Mexican, not the defendant.

Defendant contends that [the lynching statute contained in section 405 of the Penal Code] is unconstitutionally vague and uncertain. Primarily, defendant relies on the difference between the statutory and dictionary definitions of the term 'lynching.'

Section 405a, entitled, 'Lynching: definition,' provides: 'The taking by means of a riot of any person from the lawful custody of any peace officer is a lynching.'

The primary thrust of defendant's attack on the statute is directed to the variance between the statutory and dictionary definitions of 'lynching.'

The origin of the term apparently was taken from the actions of one 'Lynch' who was a judicial officer in Pottsylvania, Virginia, during the Revolutionary War; felonies were to be tried in Williamsburg, some 200 miles away; due to the distance, the appearance of witnesses was uncertain, and there was great difficulty in transporting the accused; British presence in the area made court sessions erratic; consequently, Lynch began to administer justice from Pottsylvania; the change of forum was against the law, but justified. 'Lynching' came to mean the situation wherein a group of persons usurps ordinary government powers and exercises correctional authority over others. The word generally includes the infliction of summary punishment without benefit of trial or authority of law, and has also been popularly regarded as 'mob vengeance on persons suspected of crime.'

A statute which forbids or requires the doing of an act in terms so vague that men of common intelligence must necessarily guess at its meaning and differ as to its application violates the first essential of due process of law. A statute is fatally vague only when it exposes a potential actor to some risk or detriment without giving him fair warning of the proscribed conduct.

The case at bar presents no vagueness problem. Defendant's quarrel is that the Legislature chose to define a word in terms other than its traditional definition. Broadly speaking, crimes in the United States are what the laws of the individual states make them, subject to the prohibition against bills of attainder, *ex post facto* laws, and the restrictions imposed by the Thirteenth and Fourteenth Amendments. The statute is clear on its face, and defendant was placed on notice that the removal of a person from the lawful custody of a peace officer by means of riot was prohibited, no matter what consequences inured to the person so removed.

The judgment of conviction is affirmed.

C.   Questions

♦   Do you think the court reached the right decision in this case?

♦   Do you think the defendant should be convicted of "lynching" when the ordinary meaning of the word is so different?

♦   Did the defendant's conduct meet the statutory definition of "lynching?"

II.　RIGHT TO PRIVACY

A.　Comments

Unlike the United States Constitution, the California Constitution specifically sets forth a right to privacy clause. Although the United States Supreme Court has held that a right of privacy emanates from other constitutional provisions, California's constitution actually specifically states a right to privacy.

B.　Constitution

Art. I, section 1

All people are by nature free and independent and have inalienable rights. Among these are enjoying and defending life and liberty, acquiring and possessing and protecting property, and pursuing and obtaining safety, happiness and privacy.

C. Questions

- ◆ Why do you think the California Constitution specifically sets forth a right to privacy when the United States Constitution has no articulated right to privacy?

- ◆ Can you think of any advantages or disadvantages to specifically including a privacy provision in the California Constitution?

- ◆ Can you think of any particular privacy rights that might be affected by either having or not having a specific constitutional right to privacy?

III.　CRUEL OR UNUSUAL PUNISHMENT

A. Comments

The following California state constitutional provisions demonstrate that California prohibits cruel *or* unusual punishment. This is in contrast to the language of the federal constitutional provision contained in the Eighth Amendment, which prohibits cruel *and* unusual punishment.

B. Constitution

Section 6
Excessive bail shall not be required, nor excessive fines imposed, nor shall cruel or unusual punishments be inflicted, nor shall witnesses be unreasonably detained.

Section 17
Cruel or unusual punishment may not be inflicted or excessive fines imposed.

C. Questions

♦ Do you think that the slight difference in wording between the federal and state Constitutions is significant?

♦ If you think the difference in wording is significant, when do you think this difference could become important?

IV. FREEDOM OF RELIGION

A. Comments

The two cases below both deal with freedom of religion and the use of peyote (an hallucinogenic drug) in Native American religious practices. The first case is a California case from the 1960s decided by a very liberal California Supreme Court and authored by the well-known Justice Tobriner. The second case is a United States Supreme Court opinion from the 1990s decided by a more conservative court and authored by Justice Antonin Scalia. (Note: In 1996, six years after the United States Supreme Court opinion, Congress gave the Native

American Church an exemption for the religious use of peyote. However, the exemption does not apply to all religious groups who use hallucinogenic drugs for religious purposes.)

B. Case

PEOPLE v. WOODY
Supreme Court of California
61 Cal.2d 716 (1964)

TOBRINER, Justice.

On April 28, 1962, a group of Navajos met in an Indian hogan in the desert near Needles, California, to perform a religious ceremony which included the use of peyote. Police officers, who had observed part of the ceremony, arrested defendants, who were among the Indians present. Defendants were later convicted of violating section 11500 of the Health and Safety Code, which prohibits the unauthorized possession of peyote. When the police entered the hogan and charged the participants with the use of peyote, one of the Indians handed the officers a gold-colored portrait frame containing a photostatic copy of the articles of incorporation of the Native American Church of the State of California. The articles declared: 'That we as a people place explicit faith and hope and belief in the Almighty God and declare full, competent, and everlasting faith in our Church things which and by which we worship God. That we further pledge ourselves to work for unity with the sacramental use of peyote and its religious use.'

The state agreed at trial at the time of the arrest defendants and the other Indians were performing a religious ceremony which involved the use of peyote. Defendants pleaded not guilty to the crime of illegal possession of narcotics, contending that their possession of peyote was incident to the observance of their faith and that the state could not constitutionally invoke the statute against

them without abridging their right to the free exercise of their religion. The trial proceeded without a jury; the court held defendant's guilty and imposed suspended sentences.

Defendants' defense, if any, must lie in their constitutional objection. We do not doubt that even though technically peyote is an 'hallucinogen' rather than a narcotic, the state, pursuant to the police power, may proscribe its use. Only if the application of the proscription improperly infringes upon the immunity of the First Amendment can defendants prevail.

Although the prohibition against infringement of religious belief is absolute, the immunity afforded religious practices by the First Amendment is not so rigid. But the state may abridge religious practices only upon a demonstration that some compelling state interest outweighs the defendants' interests in religious freedom.

The first step requires an exploration into the particulars of this case to determine whether the Health and Safety Code imposes any burden upon the free exercise of defendants' religion. An examination of the record as to the nature of peyote and its role in the religion practiced by defendants as members of the Native American Church of California compels the conclusion that the statutory prohibition most seriously infringes upon the observance of the religion.

The plant *Lophophora williamsii*, a small, spineless cactus, found in the Rio Grande Valley of Texas and northern Mexico, produces peyote, which grows in small buttons on the top of the cactus. Peyote's principal constituent is mescaline. When taken internally by chewing the buttons or drinking a derivative tea, peyote produces several types of hallucinations, depending primarily upon the user. In most subjects it causes extraordinary vision marked by bright and kalcidoscopic colors, geometric patterns, or scenes involving humans or animals. In others it engenders hallucinatory symptoms similar to those produced in cases of schizophrenia, dementia praecox, or paranoia. Beyond its hallucinatory effect, peyote renders for most users a heightened sense of comprehension; it fosters a feeling of friendliness toward other persons.

Peyote, as we shall see, plays a central role in the ceremony and practice of the Native American Church, a religious organization of Indians. Although the church claims no official prerequisites to membership, no written membership rolls, and no recorded theology, estimates of its membership range from 30,000 to 250,000, the wide variance deriving from differing definitions of a 'member.' As the anthropologists have ascertained through conversations with members, the theology of the church combines certain Christian teachings with the belief that peyote embodies the Holy Spirit and that those who partake of peyote enter into direct contact with God.

Peyotism discloses a long history. A reference to the religious use of peyote in Mexico appears in Spanish historical sources as early as 1560. Peyotism spread from Mexico to the United States and Canada; American anthropologists describe it as well established in this country during the latter part of the

nineteenth century. Today, Indians of many tribes practice Peyotism. Despite the absence of recorded dogma, the several tribes follow surprisingly similar ritual and theology; the practices of Navajo members in Arizona practically parallel those of adherents in California, Montana, Oklahoma, Wisconsin, and Saskatchewan.

The 'meeting,' a ceremony marked by the sacramental use of peyote, composes the cornerstone of the peyote religion. The meeting convenes in an enclosure and continues from sundown Saturday to sunrise Sunday. To give thanks for the past good fortune or find guidance for future conduct, a member will 'sponsor' a meeting and supply to those who attend both the peyote and the next morning's breakfast. The 'sponsor,' usually but not always the 'leader,' takes charge of the meeting; he decides the order of events and the amount of peyote to be consumed. Although the individual leader exercises an absolute control of the meeting, anthropologists report a striking uniformity of its ritual.

A meeting connotes a solemn and special occasion. Whole families attend together, although children and young women participate only by their presence. Adherents don their finest clothing, usually suits for men and fancy dresses for the women, but sometimes ceremonial Indian costumes. At the meeting the members pray, sing, and make ritual use of drum, fan, eagle bone, whistle, rattle and prayer cigarette, the symbolic emblems of their faith. The central event, of course, consists of the use of peyote in quantities sufficient to produce an hallucinatory state.

At an early but fixed stage in the ritual the members pass around a ceremonial bag of peyote buttons. Each adult may take four, the customary number, or take none. The participants chew the buttons, usually with some difficulty because of extreme bitterness; later, at a set time in the ceremony any member may ask for more peyote; occasionally a member may take as many as four more buttons. At sunrise on Sunday the ritual ends; after a brief outdoor prayer, the host and his family serve breakfast. Then the members depart. By morning the effects of the peyote disappear; the users suffer no aftereffects.

Although peyote serves as a sacramental symbol similar to bread and wine in certain Christian churches, it is more than a sacrament. Peyote constitutes in itself an object of worship; prayers are directed to it much as prayers are devoted to the Holy Ghost. On the other hand, to use peyote for nonreligious purposes is sacrilegious. Members of the church regard peyote also as a 'teacher' because it induces a feeling of brotherhood with other members; indeed, it enables the participant to experience the Deity.

Finally, devotees treat peyote as a 'protector.' Much as a Catholic carries his medallion, an Indian G.I. often wears around his neck a beautifully beaded pouch containing one large peyote button.

The record thus establishes that the application of the statutory prohibition of the use of peyote results in a virtual inhibition of the practice of defendants' religion. To forbid the use of peyote is to remove the theological heart of Peyotism. Having reached this conclusion, we must undertake the second step in the analysis of the constitutional issue: a determination of whether the state has demonstrated that 'compelling state interest' which necessitates an abridgement of defendants' First Amendment right. The state asserts that the compelling reason for the prohibition of Peyotism lies in its deleterious effects upon the Indian community, and even more basically, in the infringement such practice would place upon the enforcement of the narcotic

laws because of the difficulty of detecting fraudulent claims of an asserted religious use of peyote. The prosecution further claims that the cases support these positions. We set forth the reasons why we believe the contentions to be unfounded.

The People urge that 'the use of peyote by Indians in place of medical care, the threat of indoctrination of small children,' and the 'possible correlation between the use of this drug and the possible propensity to use some other more harmful drug' justify the statutory prohibition. The record, however, does not support the state's chronicle of harmful consequences of the use of peyote.

The evidence indicates that the Indians do not in fact employ peyote in place of proper medical care; and, as the Attorney General with fair objectivity admits, 'there was no evidence to suggest that Indians who use peyote are more liable to become addicted to other narcotics than non-peyote using Indians.' Nor does the record substantiate the state's fear of the 'indoctrination of small children'; it shows that Indian children never, and Indian teenagers rarely, use peyote. Finally, as the Attorney General likewise admits, the opinion of scientists and other experts is 'that peyote…works no permanent deleterious injury to the Indian…. ' Indeed, as we have noted, these experts regard the moral standards of members of the Native American Church as higher than those of Indians outside the church.

The Attorney General also argues that since 'peyote could be regarded as a symbol, one that obstructs enlightenment and shackles the Indian to primitive conditions' the responsibility rests with the state to eliminate its use. We know of no doctrine that the state, in its asserted omniscience, should undertake to deny to defendants the observance of their religion in order to free them from the suppositious 'shackles' of their 'unenlightened' and 'primitive condition.'

Turning to the state's second contention, that the threat of fraudulent assertions of religious immunity will render impossible the effective enforcement of the narcotic laws.

That other states have excepted from the narcotic laws the use of peyote, and have not considered such exemption an impairment to enforcement, weakens the prosecution's forebodings. New Mexico in 1959, and Montana in 1957, amended their narcotics laws to provide that the prohibition against narcotics 'shall not apply to the possession, sale or gift of peyote for religious sacramental purposes by any bona fide religious organization incorporated under the laws of the state.' Arizona has reached a similar result by judicial decree.

We have weighed the competing values represented in this case on the symbolic scale of constitutionality. On the one side we have placed the weight of freedom of religion as protected by the First Amendment; on the other, the weight of the state's 'compelling interest.' Since the use of peyote incorporates the essence of the religious expression, the first weight is heavy. Yet the use of peyote presents only slight danger to the state and to the enforcement of its laws; the second weight is relatively light. The scale tips in favor of the constitutional protection.

We know that some will urge that it is more important to subserve the rigorous enforcement of the narcotic laws than to carve out of them an exception for a few believers in a strange faith. They will say that the exception may produce problems of enforcement and that the dictate of the state must overcome the beliefs of a minority of Indians. But the problems of enforcement here do not inherently differ from those of other situations which call for the detection of fraud. On the other hand, the right to free religious expression embodies a precious heritage of our history. In a mass society, which presses at every point toward conformity, the protection of a self-expression, however unique, of the individual and the group becomes ever more important. The varying currents of the subcultures that flow into the mainstream of our national life give it depth and beauty. We preserve a greater value than an ancient tradition when we protect the rights of the Indians who honestly practiced an old religion in using peyote one night at a meeting in a desert hogan near Needles, California.

The judgment is reversed.

C. Case

OREGON DEPARTMENT OF HUMAN RESOURCES v. SMITH
Supreme Court of the United States
494 U.S. 872 (1990)

SCALIA, J.

Oregon law prohibits the knowing or intentional possession of a "controlled substance" unless the substance has been prescribed by a medical practitioner.

Respondents Alfred Smith and Galen Black (hereinafter respondents) were fired from their jobs with a private drug rehabilitation organization because they ingested peyote for sacramental purposes at a ceremony of the Native American Church, of which both are members. When respondents applied to petitioner Employment Division (hereinafter petitioner) for unemployment compensation, they were determined to be ineligible for benefits because they had been discharged for work-related "misconduct." The Oregon Court of Appeals reversed that determination, holding that the denial of benefits violated respondents' free exercise rights under the First Amendment.

On appeal to the Oregon Supreme Court, petitioner argued that the denial of benefits was permissible because respondents' consumption of peyote was a crime under Oregon law. The Oregon Supreme Court reasoned, however, that the criminality of respondents' peyote use was irrelevant to resolution of their constitutional claim--since the purpose of the "misconduct" provision under which respondents had been disqualified was not to enforce the State's criminal laws but to preserve the financial integrity of the compensation fund, and since that purpose was inadequate to justify the burden that disqualification imposed on respondents' religious practice. [T]he court concluded that respondents were entitled to payment of unemployment benefits.

Before this Court in 1987, petitioner continued to maintain that the illegality of respondents' peyote consumption was relevant to their constitutional claim. We agreed, concluding that "if a State has prohibited through its criminal laws certain kinds of religiously motivated conduct without violating the First Amendment, it certainly follows that it may impose the lesser burden of denying unemployment compensation benefits to persons who engage in that conduct." We noted, however, that the Oregon Supreme Court had not decided whether respondents' sacramental use of peyote

was in fact proscribed by Oregon's controlled substance law, and that this issue was a matter of dispute between the parties. Being "uncertain about the legality of the religious use of peyote in Oregon," we determined that it would not be "appropriate for us to decide whether the practice is protected by the Federal Constitution."

The Free Exercise Clause of the First Amendment, which has been made applicable to the States by incorporation into the Fourteenth Amendment, provides that "Congress shall make no law respecting an establishment of religion, or prohibiting the free exercise thereof...." U.S. Const., Amdt. 1. The free exercise of religion means, first and foremost, the right to believe and profess whatever religious doctrine one desires. Thus, the First Amendment obviously excludes all "governmental regulation of religious beliefs as such." The government may not compel affirmation of religious belief, punish the expression of religious doctrines it believes to be false, impose special disabilities on the basis of religious views or religious status, or lend its power to one or the other side in controversies over religious authority or dogma.

But the "exercise of religion" often involves not only belief and profession but the performance of (or abstention from) physical acts: assembling with others for a worship service, participating in sacramental use of bread and wine, proselytizing, abstaining from certain foods or certain modes of transportation. It would be true, we think (though no case of ours has involved the point), that a State would be "prohibiting the free exercise [of religion]" if it sought to ban such acts or abstentions only when they are engaged in for religious reasons, or only because of the religious belief that they display. It would doubtless be unconstitutional, for example, to ban the casting of "statues that are to be used for worship purposes," or to prohibit bowing down before a golden calf.

Respondents in the present case, however, seek to carry the meaning of "prohibiting the free exercise [of religion]" one large step further. They contend that their religious motivation for using peyote places them beyond the reach of a criminal law that is not specifically directed at their religious practice, and that is concededly constitutional as applied to those who use the drug for other reasons. They assert, in other words, that "prohibiting the free exercise [of religion]" includes requiring any individual to observe a generally applicable law that requires (or forbids) the performance of an act that his religious belief forbids (or requires). As a textual matter, we do not think the words must be given that meaning. Our decisions reveal that the latter reading is the correct one. We have never held that an individual's religious beliefs excuse him from compliance with an otherwise valid law prohibiting conduct that the State is free to regulate.

Values that are protected against government interference through enshrinement in the Bill of Rights are not thereby banished from the political process. Just as a society that believes in the negative protection accorded to the press by the First Amendment is likely to enact laws that affirmatively foster the dissemination of the printed word, so also a society that believes in the negative protection accorded to religious belief can be expected to be solicitous of that value in its legislation as well. It is therefore not surprising that a number of States have made an exception to their drug laws for sacramental peyote use. See, e.g., Ariz.Rev.Stat.Ann. §§ 13-3402(B)(1)-(3) (1989); Colo.Rev.Stat. § 12-22-317(3) (1985); § N.M.Stat.Ann. S 30-31-6(D) (Supp.1989). But to say that a nondiscriminatory religious-practice exemption is permitted, or even that it is desirable, is not to say that it is constitutionally required, and that the appropriate occasions for its creation can be discerned by the courts. It may fairly be said that leaving accommodation to the political process will place at a relative disadvantage those religious practices that are not widely engaged in; but that unavoidable consequence of democratic government must be preferred to a system in which each conscience is a law unto itself or in which judges weigh the social importance of all laws against the centrality of all religious beliefs.

It is so ordered.

D. Questions

♦ Did you notice that these two cases arose in a slightly different procedural context? In the *Woody* case, the issue was a criminal conviction based on the use of peyote. The *Smith* case, on the other hand, involved a denial of unemployment benefits. Do you think that these factual differences were determinative in the different outcomes of the two cases? Why or why not?

♦ One interesting aspect of these cases is to note what each court emphasizes. Which case emphasized the law and which case emphasized cultural values? Do you think this has anything to do with the time frames in which these cases were decided?

♦ According to the United States Supreme Court, it is constitutionally permissible for a state to exempt sacramental peyote use from the operation of drug laws, although it is not constitutionally required to do so. Do you agree with this?

◆ Finally, did you notice that the *Woody* case provides an example of a state court granting greater constitutional protection than the federal constitution provided? In this case, California allowed the use of peyote for religious purposes. According to United States Supreme Court Justice Scalia, however, exemption was not required under the *federal* constitution. Thus, Oregon could ban peyote if it so desired. The final paragraph of the *Smith* case points out also that the less widely accepted a religious practice involved, the more likely that it can be restricted. Do you think this is just? Notice the contrast to the last paragraph of *Woody* in which the California Supreme Court opines that "the protection of a self-expression, however unique, of the individual and group becomes ever more important." Do you think *Smith* or *Woody* is the better result?

◆ Do you think there should be one national law regulating drug use? If so, how do you think *Woody* would have been decided?

V. DOUBLE JEOPARDY

A. Comments

The California Penal Code contains a specific prohibition against double jeopardy. The practical application of this statute becomes clearer when you read the case that interprets the law.

B. Statute

Penal Code section 654

(a) An act or omission that is punishable in different ways by different provisions of law shall be punished under the provision that provides for the longest potential term of imprisonment, but in no case shall the act or omission be punished under more than one provision. An acquittal or conviction and sentence under any one bars a prosecution for the same act or omission under any other.

C. Comments

You will probably need to read this case more than once. This case is a bit difficult to comprehend because the concept of double jeopardy is a complex one. "Double jeopardy" often baffles students because of the confusion between prosecution and punishment. In this case, the court distinguishes between multiple punishments as opposed to multiple prosecutions. Pay particular attention to the court's hypothetical fact pattern involving a defendant who "blows up an airplane." This hypothetical fact pattern is instructive in differentiating between multiple prosecutions and multiple punishments for purposes of double jeopardy.

D. Case

KELLETT V. SUPERIOR COURT OF SACRAMENTO COUNTY
Supreme Court of California, In Bank.
63 Cal.2d 822 (1966)

TRAYNOR, C. J.

On October 15, 1964, officers of the Sacramento Police Department, called to the scene of a disturbance, arrested petitioner who was standing on a public sidewalk with a pistol in his hand. On that day he was charged in the municipal court with committing a misdemeanor (exhibiting a firearm in a threatening manner). On November 17, 1964, after a preliminary hearing at which it appeared that petitioner had been convicted of a felony, he was charged by information in the superior court with committing a felony (possession of a concealable weapon by a person who has been convicted of a felony).

On January 20, 1965, petitioner pleaded guilty to the charge of exhibiting a firearm in a violent manner and was sentenced to 90 days in the county jail. On January 26, 1965, he moved in the superior court to dismiss the information charging a violation of possession of a concealable weapon by a convicted felon on the ground that it was barred by Penal Code section 654. The motion was denied.

Petitioner contends that exhibiting and possessing the pistol constituted a single act and that therefore his prosecution for the second offense is barred by his conviction of the first offense. The Attorney General contends that even if the evidence at petitioner's preliminary hearing did not show possession apart from that involved in first violation, it is reasonable to infer that petitioner

possessed the pistol for some time before exhibiting it and that at his trial a separate act of possession within the meaning of section 654 may be readily established.

If only a single act or an indivisible course of criminal conduct is charged as the basis for a conviction, the defendant can be punished only once although he may have violated more than one statute. Whether a course of criminal conduct is divisible and therefore gives rise to more than one act within the meaning of section 654 depends on the intent and objective of the actor. Penal Code section 954 provides for the joinder in a single accusatory pleading of two or more offenses connected in their commission or having a common element of substantial importance in their commission. Had both offenses been joined in a single prosecution, the People might have shown that the object and intent of the petitioner in brandishing the weapon and his object in possessing it were entirely unrelated. The People might also have shown that the petitioner's possession of the weapon extended to a time beyond that during which he was observed brandishing it.

The rule against multiple prosecutions is a procedural safeguard against harassment and is not necessarily related to the punishment to be imposed; double prosecution may be precluded even when double punishment is permissible.' Thus, the punishment clause of section 654 does not apply when a single act of violence causes injury to several persons. A defendant who blows up an airplane killing all on board or commits an act that injures many persons is properly subject to greater punishment than a defendant who kills or harms only a single person. It does not follow, however, that such a defendant should be liable to successive prosecutions. It would constitute wholly unreasonable harassment in such circumstances to permit trials *seriatim* until the prosecutor is satisfied with the punishment imposed.

We recognize that in many places felonies and misdemeanors are usually prosecuted by different public law offices and that there is a risk that those in charge of misdemeanor prosecutions may proceed without adequately assessing the seriousness of a defendant's conduct or considering whether a felony prosecution should be undertaken. When the responsibility for the prosecution for the higher offense lies with a different public law office there is also the risk that a well advised defendant may plead guilty to a misdemeanor to foreclose a subsequent felony prosecution the misdemeanor prosecutor may be unaware of or may choose to ignore.

Cases may also arise in which the district attorney is reasonably unaware of the felonies when the misdemeanors are prosecuted. In such situations the risk that there may be waste and harassment through both a misdemeanor and felony prosecution may be outweighed by the risk that a defendant guilty of a felony may escape proper punishment. Accordingly, in such cases section 654 does not bar a subsequent felony prosecution except to the extent that such prosecution is barred by that section's preclusion of multiple punishment.

It bears emphasis, however, that the risk that a defendant guilty of a felony may escape proper punishment as a result of a conviction of a lesser offense is inherent in the preclusion by section 654 of multiple punishment. Thus, if an act or course of criminal conduct can be punished only once under section 654, either an acquittal or conviction and sentence under one penal statute will preclude subsequent prosecution in a separate proceeding under any other penal statute. Accordingly, to avoid these risks it has always been necessary for prosecutors carefully to assess the seriousness of a defendant's criminal conduct before determining what charges should be prosecuted against him.

[Judgment reversed.]

E. Questions

♦ The court's discussion regarding double jeopardy places the burden on the prosecution to make certain that it charges the defendant appropriately the first time. If the defendant is not charged properly the first time, the state runs the risk that future prosecution will be barred by the prohibition against double jeopardy. Do you think that this interpretation of the prohibition against double jeopardy is consistent with the legal underpinnings of our criminal justice system?

♦ What societal goals do you feel are either fulfilled or frustrated by this application of the prohibition against double jeopardy?

VI. FREEDOM OF SPEECH

A. Comments

The Legislature sometimes enacts laws targeted for the protection of a particular industry. The following case illustrates this point. The defendant questions whether the statute which provides the protection is unconstitutional.

B. Case

PEOPLE V. ANDERSON
Court of Appeal of California, Second Appellate District
235 Cal. App. 3d 586 (1991)

COOPER, J

Defendant appeals from his conviction of violation of Penal Code section 653w. The conviction was based on evidence which established that he possessed for sale some 4,500 audiotapes, identified by an expert witness as "pirate recordings." By this appeal, he challenges the constitutionality of the statute, contending that it [violates] the First Amendment to the United States Constitution.

***

The Statute

Penal Code section 653w was enacted as part of a comprehensive statutory scheme designed to prevent and punish the misappropriation of recorded music for commercial advantage or private financial gain. [Citation.] On the date of appellant's arrest, Penal Code section 653w provided in pertinent part as follows: "(a) A person is guilty of failure to disclose the origin of a recording or audiovisual work when, for commercial advantage or private financial gain, he or she knowingly advertises or offers for sale or resale, or sells or resells, ... or possesses for these purposes, any recording or audiovisual work, the outside cover box or jacket of which does not clearly and conspicuously disclose the actual true name and address of the manufacturer thereof and the name of the actual author, artist, performer, producer, programmer, or group."

Although other provisions of the "anti-piracy" legislation have been evaluated and upheld by the courts of this state [citations] the question of the constitutionality of the disclosure requirements of Penal Code section 653w appears to be one of first impression.

***

First Amendment

Most of the cases which have analyzed statutes compelling the disclosure of information have done so in the context of political speech. While this category of speech may be said to be the most zealously guarded by our constitution, nonetheless narrowly drawn statutes designed to serve a particular public need have been upheld.

***

The state's interest in enacting Penal Code section 653w is the desire to protect the public in general, and the many employees of the vast entertainment industry in particular, from the hundreds of millions of dollars in losses suffered as a result of the "piracy and bootlegging" of the industry's products. (Testimony before the Assem. Crim. Law and Pub. Saf. Com., June 1984, Atty. Gen. Analysis, Assem. Bill No. 3619 (1983-1984 Reg. Sess.) Aug. 1984.) The statute is narrowly and specifically drawn to meet that objective.

Although it is certainly conceivable that the statute could, as appellant argues, deter someone from reducing to taped form and distributing his seditious or potentially unpopular views, this outcome is unlikely, inasmuch as the statute applies only to those who possess or distribute such material "for commercial advantage or private financial gain." (Pen. Code, § 653w.) A truly zealous and committed proselytizer may distribute his or her anonymous views, reproduced in any form, free of charge and free from the restraints imposed by this statute.

California has a compelling interest in protecting the public from being victimized by false and deceptive commercial practices. [Citations.] "Protection of unwary consumers from being duped by unscrupulous sellers is an exigency of the utmost priority in contemporary society." [Citations.]

The second infirmity in appellant's constitutional challenge lies in the fact that the statute proscribes only "commercial speech." Thus, we are not confronted with the difficult task of drawing a distinction between talk for profit, and talk for other purposes or of determining the degree of First Amendment protection which should be accorded speech embodying both qualities. [Citation.] ¶ [As the United States Supreme Court has held], "The right of a commercial speaker not to divulge accurate information regarding his services is not ... a fundamental right." [Citation.]

We find no constitutional infirmity in Penal Code section 653w, which requires conspicuous disclosure of the name and address of the manufacturer of any audiotape or videotape offered or possessed for purposes of sale.

[The judgment is affirmed.]

C. Questions

♦ Assume that you were to read this case without knowing the jurisdiction in which it was decided. Are there any clues in the opinion which would indicate that California is the likely jurisdiction? (Hint: Which states have a "vast entertainment industry" which would need legislative protection?)

♦ Do you think that the defendant's First Amendment freedoms were violated by this opinion? Or do you think it was a clever argument to circumvent unlawful pirating of audio recordings?

VII. Self-Assessment

1. Limitations on criminal liability include *ex post facto* laws and laws which are impermissibly vague, but never protects criminal conduct arising out of a defendant's religious principles.
   A. True   B. False

2. The California Constitution cannot give more protection to criminal defendants than that provided by the United States Constitution.
   A. True   B. False

3. Double jeopardy means that a defendant cannot be punished more than once for an indivisible course of criminal conduct even if he has violated more than one statute.
   A. True   B. False

4. California's requirement that the manufacturer of any audiotape or videotape conspicuously disclose its name violates the First Amendment's Free Speech protections.
   A. True   B. False

5. The California Constitution does not prohibit against cruel or unusual punishment; only the United States Constitution protects against cruel or unusual punishment.
   A. True   B. False

CHAPTER THREE

Actus Reus: Criminal Act

Thoughts alone, without action, cannot be the basis for a crime. Every crime consists of a criminal act (actus reus) and a criminal intent (mens rea. (The only exception to this rule is the very narrow class of offenses known as "strict liability" offenses.) The common law requirement that a person is not guilty of a crime unless there is misconduct has been carried over to the Model Penal Code. The Model Penal Code states that criminal liability is based on a person's conduct.

The actus reus, or criminal act, most often involves an act of commission. Acts of commission arise when a defendant's intentional conduct violates a statutory prohibition. When a person kills, steals, or rapes, he or she has performed a criminal act, and an act of commission.

Less frequently, the law imposes a duty on a defendant to act affirmatively. When the law imposes an affirmative duty to act, failure to act can constitute criminal behavior. Crimes of omission most often occur where a defendant violates a duty arising out of a relationship (for example, a parent's duty to care for a child) or arising out of public duty (for example, a lifeguard's contractual obligation with a municipality to watch swimmers).

Crimes based on acts of omission are often problematic for courts. The most common thorny problem for courts revolves around duty. Does the law impose a duty on this defendant under the specific circumstances of this case? Because acts of omission are more problematic, this chapter focuses on failure to act.

I. ELDER ABUSE

A. Acts of Omission

The defendant in *Heitzman* was charged with criminal elder abuse, a relatively new statute. Because this is a relatively new law, the statute has not had the benefit of extensive judicial interpretation. The court in *Heitzman* addressed two critical questions that courts have not previously addressed. First, when does the affirmative duty to act arise? Second, to whom does the duty to act apply? In *Heitzman*, the defendant's failure to act is clear: she did not come to the aid of her father. The more troubling question is whether her inaction should subject her to criminal liability under the specific facts of this case.

When reading this case, you will notice the court's discussion of the distinction between moral duty and legal duty. It is an important distinction in this case. Make certain that you understand the court's determination of the two classes of people to whom the statute applies. Pay close attention to the court's analysis of a legal duty to act. Only if there is a duty to act can the defendant be held criminally liable.

Finally, this case was a hotly-contested one. The decision was a 4-3 decision. (There are seven justices on the California Supreme Court as opposed to nine justices on the United States Supreme Court.) Obviously, the question of duty in this case was a difficult one for the Supreme Court to answer. When a mere 4-3 majority reaches a decision, it would take only one justice to have a change of viewpoint to change the court's holding.

B. Case

PEOPLE V. HEITZMAN
Supreme Court of California
9 Cal. 4th 189 (1994)

LUCAS, C. J.

Penal Code section 368, subdivision (a), is one component of a multifaceted legislative response to the problem of elder abuse. The statute imposes felony criminal liability on "[a]ny person who, under circumstances or conditions likely to produce great bodily harm or death, willfully causes or permits any elder or dependent adult, with knowledge that he or she is an elder or dependent adult, to suffer, or inflicts thereon unjustifiable physical pain or mental suffering, or having the care or custody of any elder or dependent adult, willfully causes or permits the person or health of the elder or dependent adult to be injured, or willfully causes or permits the elder or dependent adult to be placed in a situation such that his or her person or health is endangered .."

***

We conclude that the statute may properly be upheld by interpreting its imposition of criminal liability upon "[a]ny person who ... permits ... any elder or dependent adult ... to suffer ... unjustifiable pain or mental suffering" to apply only to a person who, under existing tort principles, has a duty to control the conduct of the individual who is directly causing or inflicting abuse on the elder or dependent adult. Because the evidence in this case does not indicate that defendant had the kind of "special relationship" with the individuals alleged to have directly abused the elder victim that would give rise to a duty on her part to control their conduct, she was improperly charged with a violation of section 368(a). We therefore reverse the judgment of the Court of Appeal.

I. FACTS

The egregious facts of this case paint a profoundly disturbing family portrait in which continued neglect of and apparent indifference to the basic needs of the family's most vulnerable member, an elderly dependent parent, led to a result of tragic proportion.

29

Sixty-seven-year-old Robert Heitzman resided in the Huntington Beach home of his grown son, Richard Heitzman, Sr., along with another grown son, Jerry Heitzman, and Richard's three sons. On December 3, 1990, police were summoned to the house, where they discovered Robert dead in his bedroom. His body lay on a mattress that was rotted through from constant wetness, exposing the metal springs. The stench of urine and feces filled not only decedent's bedroom, but the entire house as well. His bathroom was filthy, and the bathtub contained fetid, green-colored water that appeared to have been there for some time.

Police learned that Jerry Heitzman was primarily responsible for his father's care, rendering caretaking services in exchange for room and board. Jerry admitted that he had withheld all food and liquids from his father for the three days preceding his death on December 3. Jerry explained that he was expecting company for dinner on Sunday, December 2, and did not want his father, who no longer had control over his bowels and bladder, to defecate or urinate because it would further cause the house to smell.

At the time of his death, decedent had large, decubitus ulcers, more commonly referred to as bedsores, covering one-sixth of his body. An autopsy revealed the existence of a yeast infection in his mouth, and showed that he suffered from congestive heart failure, bronchial pneumonia, and hepatitis. The forensic pathologist who performed the autopsy attributed decedent's death to septic shock due to the sores which, he opined, were caused by malnutrition, dehydration, and neglect.

Twenty years earlier, decedent had suffered a series of strokes that paralyzed the left side of his body. Defendant, 31-year-old Susan Valerie Heitzman, another of decedent's children, had previously lived in the home and had been her father's primary caregiver at that time. In return, defendant's brother Richard paid for her room and board. Richard supported the household by working two full-time jobs, and supplemented this income with decedent's monthly Social Security and pension checks.

One year prior to her father's death, defendant decided to move away from the home. After she moved out, however, she continued to spend time at the house visiting her boyfriend/nephew Richard, Jr. Since leaving to live on her own, she noticed that the entire house had become filthy. She was aware that a social worker had discussed with Jerry the need to take their father to a doctor. When she spoke to Jerry about it, he told her he had lost the doctor's telephone number the social worker had given him. She suggested to Jerry that he recontact the social worker. She also discussed with Richard, Jr., the need for taking her father to the doctor, but she never made the necessary arrangements.

In the last six weekends before her father died, defendant had routinely visited the household. She was last in her father's bedroom five weeks prior to his death, at which time she noticed the hole in the mattress and feces-soiled clothing lying on the floor. Another of decedent's daughters, Lisa, also visited the house that same day.

Two weeks prior to her father's death, defendant spent the entire weekend at the house. On Sunday afternoon, she saw her father sitting in the living room, and noticed that he looked weak and appeared disoriented. A week later, during Thanksgiving weekend, and several days prior to decedent's death, defendant again stayed at the house. Decedent's bedroom door remained closed throughout the weekend, and defendant did not see her father. On the day decedent died, defendant awoke midmorning and left the house to return to her own apartment. Around one o'clock in the afternoon, Jerry discovered decedent dead in his bedroom.

In a two-count indictment, the Orange County District Attorney jointly charged Jerry and Richard, Sr., with involuntary manslaughter (§ 192), and Jerry, Richard, Sr., and defendant with violating section 368(a). At the preliminary examination, the magistrate determined that, although defendant did not have care or custody of decedent as did her brothers, there was probable cause to believe she owed a duty of care to her father and that she had been grossly negligent in failing to carry out that duty. She was therefore held to answer along with her brothers for willfully permitting an elder to suffer unjustifiable physical pain and mental suffering. [The prosecution of Jerry and Richard, Sr. was clearly proper and is not challenged on appeal.]

On November 4, 1994, an information was filed in superior court charging defendant with a violation of section 368(a). Thereafter, she moved to set aside the information pursuant to section 995 on the basis that the evidence presented at the preliminary hearing failed to establish probable cause she had committed a crime. In relevant part, defendant argued that the evidence that she knew of her father's deteriorating condition did not create a duty for her to act to prevent the harm suffered by him. In its opposition to her motion, the prosecution contended that defendant's duty of care was established by section 368(a) itself, which imposes a duty on every person to not permit any elderly or dependent adult to suffer unjustifiable pain.

II. DISCUSSION

***

Section 368(a) purportedly reaches two categories of offenders: (1) *any person* who willfully causes or permits an elder to suffer, or who directly inflicts, unjustifiable pain or mental suffering on any elder, and (2) the elder's *caretaker or custodian* who willfully causes or permits injury to his or her charge, or who willfully causes or permits the elder to be placed in a dangerous situation. The statute may be applied to a wide range of abusive situations, including within its scope active, assaultive conduct, as well as passive forms of abuse, such as extreme neglect. [Citation.]

Defendant here was charged under section 368(a) with willfully *permitting* her elder father to suffer the infliction of unjustifiable pain and mental suffering. It was thus her *failure to act*, i.e., her failure to prevent the infliction of abuse on her father, that created the potential for her criminal liability under the statute. . . Unlike the imposition of criminal penalties for certain positive acts, which is based on the statutory proscription of such conduct, when an individual's criminal liability is based on the *failure* to act, it is well established that he or she must first be under an existing legal duty to take positive action. ([Citations]. "The non-action of one who has no legal duty to act is nothing.".)

A legal duty to act is often imposed by the express provisions of a criminal statute itself. [Citation.] Welfare and Institutions Code section 15630 provides an example. That statute specifically requires care custodians, health practitioners, adult protective services employees, and local law enforcement agencies to report physical abuse of elders and dependent adults. Those subject to the statutory duty to report who fail to do so face criminal liability. (Welf. & Inst. Code, *§ 15634*, subd. (d).) Notably, the statutory scheme encourages any person who knows or suspects that an elder or dependent adult has been the victim of abuse to report the abuse, but does not appear to impose the *legal duty* to do so. (See Welf. & Inst. Code, § 15631, subd. (a) ["Any ... person ... *may* report ...." (Italics added.)].)

When a criminal statute does not set forth a legal duty to act by its express terms, liability for a failure to act must be premised on the existence of a duty found elsewhere. [Citations.] A criminal statute may thus incorporate a duty imposed by another criminal or civil statute. [Citations.]

A criminal statute may also embody a common law duty based on the legal relationship between the defendant and the victim, such as that imposed on parents to care for and protect their minor children. [Citations.] Similarly, other special relationships may give rise to a duty to act. [Citations]

***

Accordingly, in order for criminal liability to attach under section 368(a) for willfully permitting the infliction of physical pain or mental suffering on an elder, a defendant must first be under a legal duty to act.

***

The Court of Appeal acknowledged that because the information charged defendant with violating section 368(a) by her failure to act, she must first have been under a duty to act in order for criminal liability to attach. The court found the existence of such a duty based on defendant's filial relationship to the decedent. Specifically, the court incorporated the statutory duty imposed on adult children to provide financial support for needy parents set forth in [other provisions of the California codes.]

The duty of adult children to provide support for needy parents is deeply rooted in our statutory law, and it is well established that the purpose of such legislation is " 'to protect the public from the burden of supporting people who have children able to support them.' " [Citations.]. . . .¶¶ [However,] the financial support statutes cannot be relied on to clarify the scope of the felony elder abuse statute. We discern no reasonable basis on which to conclude that the probable intent of the Legislature was to equate the statutory duty of financial support with the duty to prevent physical harm triggering felony criminal liability under section 368(a).

Reliance on the financial support statutes as the basis of a duty to prevent the infliction of abuse on an elder would appear to exclude from statutory protection those who are not financially needy. The Court of Appeal's comment that infirm parents with means would presumably hire competent caretakers presupposes that only those unable to afford professional care are abused or neglected, an observation that is not supported by the evidence. . . ..¶ Nor can such a duty be found in the legal relationship between defendant and the abused elder. Although at common law parents have long had a duty to care for and protect their minor children [citations], there is no corresponding common law obligation on adult children to protect and care for their aging parents [citations].

Focusing on the defendant's legal relationship with the elder victim thus fails to yield a satisfactory construction of the statute. As we shall explain, however, a special relationship between the defendant and the person inflicting pain or suffering on the elder does provide the basis for a reasonable and practical interpretation of the statutory language at issue here. Under such a statutory construction, in order for criminal liability to arise for *permitting* an elder to suffer unjustifiable pain or suffering, a defendant must stand in a special relationship to the individual inflicting the abuse on the elder such that the defendant is under an existing duty to supervise and control that individual's conduct.

* * *

The reasonableness of our construction of the statutory language is further supported by the structure of the statute itself. We previously noted that section 368(a) imposes felony criminal liability on any person who affirmatively causes or inflicts unjustifiable pain or suffering on an elder, as well as on anyone who permits the infliction of such abuse on an elder. Under this statutory language, the class of potential defendants includes both those who directly inflict the abuse as well as those who passively fail to act. It is appropriate, therefore, that the duty imposed on an individual to prevent abuse be of sufficient stature and seriousness to warrant the same potential for felony liability as that faced by the individual who directly inflicts or causes an elder to suffer unjustifiable pain or mental suffering.

Moreover, as noted earlier, the statutory scheme also provides that a *caretaker* or *custodian* who causes or permits injury or physical endangerment will incur criminal liability with a lesser degree of harm or potential harm to the victim. By limiting potential criminal liability for the failure to prevent abuse of an elder to those under an existing legal duty to control the conduct of the person inflicting the abuse, the apparent relationship of culpability to harm inherent in the statutory structure is both recognized and maintained.

* * *

III. DISPOSITION

Based on their status as Robert Heitzman's caretakers, felony criminal liability was properly imposed on Richard, Sr., and Jerry pursuant to section 368(a) for the role they played in bringing about their father's demise. . . ¶[G]iven defendant's failure to intercede on her father's behalf under the egregious circumstances presented here, we can well understand the prosecution's decision to charge defendant under section 368(a). Because the People presented no evidence tending to show that defendant had a *legal duty* to control the conduct of either of her brothers, however, we reverse the judgment of the Court of Appeal with directions to reinstate the trial court's order dismissing the charges against defendant.

* * *

We emphasize that our disposition of this case in no way signifies our approval of defendant's failure to repel the threat to her father's well-being. The facts underlying this case are indeed troubling, and defendant's alleged indifference to the suffering of her father cannot be condoned. The desire to impose criminal liability on *this* defendant cannot be accomplished, however....

The judgment of the Court of Appeal is reversed.

BAXTER, J.

I respectfully dissent. The majority essentially holds that even though defendant knew her aged and disabled father was living in her brothers' home under conditions that were painful, degrading, and ultimately fatal, she cannot be criminally prosecuted for her failure to act because she did not stand in a "special relationship" with either her father or her brothers. . . . The majority suggests that its decision to engraft a special relationship requirement onto the elder abuse statute charged in this case is consistent with the underlying legislative intent. (Pen. Code, § 368.)

***

[A]s argued by the People in this case, the language and history of section 368 . . . indicate[s] that [the statute] appl[ies] to *any* person who is guilty of *criminal* negligence under the particular circumstances. The majority's special relationship requirement appears to dishonor this clear intent.

***

Distilled, the elder abuse statute imposes felony criminal liability for particular injurious acts or omissions by persons having *care or custody* of an elder, but it *also* punishes as a felon "[a]ny person" who "inflicts ... unjustifiable physical pain or mental suffering" upon an elder under circumstances "likely to produce great bodily harm or death," or who "willfully causes *or permits*" such suffering to occur "with knowledge" that the victim is an elder. (§ 368, subd. (a), italics added.) As noted by the majority, the case against defendant implicates the statute only insofar it applies to "any person" who "permits" an elder to suffer serious, unjustifiable pain or suffering

***

[The misconduct in this case is clear.] [T]he preliminary hearing record indicates that defendant--formerly her father's caretaker--knew he was paralyzed, incontinent, and completely dependent upon others to feed, clean, and move him. For a period of at least six weeks before her father died, defendant repeatedly visited and spent the night in the home where her brothers and father lived. Defendant had actual knowledge during this time that her father required, but did not receive, medical attention; that his person and physical surroundings had become filthy from human waste and debris; that the mattress from which he could not move without assistance was damp and rotted through; and that he was confined alone in his room for long stretches of time.

Nevertheless, defendant did not take *any* steps to assist her father during this period. She did not attempt to obtain professional help (e.g., telephoning the doctor, social worker, or paramedics); to care for him while present in the home (e.g., feeding or cleaning him); or to discuss with other family members the possibility of making different care arrangements (e.g., hospitalization or professional caretaking assistance). The evidence further discloses that defendant's father died as a result of the deplorable conditions of which defendant was actually or presumably aware (septic shock from bed sores, malnutrition, and dehydration).

In light of the foregoing, I would affirm the judgment of the Court of Appeal insofar as it reversed . . . dismissing the case.

Mosk, J., and Werdegar, J., concurred.

C. Questions

- ♦ In determining the issue of a legal duty to act, the Court looked to another statute that required an affirmative duty to act. What statute did the Court refer to and what affirmative duty did that statute impose?

♦ The majority and dissenting opinions agree on the underlying facts of the case. They do disagree, however, on the answer to the critical legal question. Did this defendant have a duty to act? Here, the two opinions reach opposite conclusions. With whom do you agree, the majority or the dissenting opinion? What is the reason for your conclusion?

♦ At the beginning of this case there was a note regarding the closeness of this opinion. (It was a 4 to 3 decision.) If the count were to revisit the same facts in the near future, do you think the case would turn out the

♦ In enacting Penal Code section 368, subdivision (a), is the Legislature attempting to legislate morality? Or is there another underlying purpose for this legislation?

♦ If you were a legislator considering this statute, would you change the language of the statute? If you decide that the statute should be changed, how would you rewrite it?

♦ Is this statute likely to be different 50 years from now? If so, how would it change?

II. Self Assessment

1. Acts of omission form the bases for the most common types of criminal acts.
    A. True   B. False

2. Legal duties always arise out of familial relationships; they are never mandated by statute.
    A. True   B. False

3. At common law, the most common duty toward a family member was a duty of a parent to a child.
    A. True   B. False

CHAPTER FOUR

Mens Rea: Criminal Intent

As mentioned at the beginning of the last chapter, a required mental state is necessary for the commission of a criminal offense. Except for a few strict liability offenses which base liability solely on conduct, criminal liability requires criminal intent at the time of the wrongdoing. Criminal intent, however, is not necessarily the intent to commit a *crime*; criminal intent may simply be the intent to do an *act*, an act prohibited by law.

Criminal intent is a complex topic for many reasons. First, the classification of criminal intent, or mens rea, differs from jurisdiction to jurisdiction. Some states, such as California, rely on common law concepts, and use terms such as "general intent" and "specific intent" to describe the defendant's mental state. Other states, such as Kentucky, have adopted the Model Penal Code classifications of intent classifying mental states in four categories: purposely, knowingly, recklessly, and negligently.

The topic of criminal intent is further complicated by the differing criminal intents that states adopt *for the same crime*. Different mental states for the same crime are most apparent with modern crimes that do not have a long-established common law history. An example of a modern statute with varying criminal intent is the crime of animal abuse, which you encountered in Chapter One. Animal abuse statutes in some states require that the defendant act "negligently." Other states, however, require a higher mental state and will not find a defendant criminally liable unless he acted "willfully." Although the underlying actus reus may be the same, the statutes do all not agree on the required mens rea.

In assessing a defendant's mental state, California law relies heavily on common law concepts. We will examine definitions of the terms as well as their applications. Finally, we will look at the impact of voluntary intoxication on a defendant's ability to form the necessary mental state.

As you study this chapter, it is important that you become familiar with the various intent definitions. This will help you later when you study specific criminal offenses. Also, note how courts establish a defendant's state of mind. Obviously, no one can get inside an accused's mind and search the memory vault to see what was going on at some distinct point in time when a crime was committed. As you read, observe how courts assess an individual defendant's mental state.

I. GENERAL INTENT

A. Comments

The *Reznick* case below sets forth the tests for determining a defendant's intent. The court carefully recounts the specific facts on which it relies to make its determination. From this detailed factual recitation, you can better understand how the court reached its decision regarding the defendant's intent. (Note: *Reznick's* holding, that a defendant's knowledge regarding the age of the victim was material to a charge of contributing to the delinquency of a minor, has been subsequently overruled.) However, the case's discussion of general and specific intent is still valid.

If you are a careful reader, you will also pick up the court's guidelines for determining when a crime is a general intent crime. As the court teaches, unless there is a specific intent set forth in the statute, a crime requires only a general intent to do an *act* (as opposed to intent to commit a *crime*). The law presumes that a person intends the natural and direct consequences of his or her act. Thus, a defendant need not intend to commit a crime in order to have the required mental state to satisfy a "general intent" crime.

Following the *Reznick* case is the *Rathert* case, which was decided 54 years after *Reznick*. *Rathert* demonstrates that the concept of "intent" under California is still a troublesome area of law, even 54 years later.

B. Case

PEOPLE V. REZNICK
District Court of Appeal, First District, Division 1
75 Cal.App. 2d 832 (1946)

SCHOTTKY, J. pro tem.

Appellant was charged in the information with contributing to the delinquency of a minor in violation ,it being alleged that appellant did willfully, unlawfully and knowingly allow one Anita Vasquez, 14 years of age, to be registered in a hotel as the wife of a sailor, they not then being married. Appellant appeals from the judgment of conviction.

There is little dispute as to the facts shown by the record. The complaining witness, Anita Vasquez, at the time of the alleged crime was 14 years of age. On November 13, 1945, accompanied by two other girls, two marines and one sailor, she went to the Uptown Hotel on Fillmore Street in San

Francisco where all six were registered by appellant, then on duty as clerk. The girls all stood at the desk while each of the boys registered. The appellant did not ask the ages of the girls but did ask the boys if the girls were their wives and was informed that they were. Each boy registered with one of the girls as Mr. and Mrs. The other two girls were aged 14 and 17 years, and the only baggage carried by these six persons, who were together at the time they registered, was one suitcase and one paper bag. The complaining witness, after being registered by appellant, was taken to a room where she remained all night with the sailor. The other two girls were likewise taken to rooms where each remained all night with one of the marines.

Appellant admitted that he was on duty at the hotel on the night in question and identified the registration of the complaining witness and her escort but testified that he had no recollection of having seen her before. He testified that he was very busy in performing his duties on the night in question and had registered 26 rooms and about 50 people. Upon objection made by the district attorney he was not permitted to testify as to what his usual practice was in handling registrations.

Appellant's next assignment of error is the following statement of the trial court: 'The Court: It wouldn't make any difference if he did a thousand well if he makes a mistake in one of the registrations; his ignorance of the actual age of the girl is no defense. ..Well, it is the duty of these people to know the ages of the girls they are registering there.' [The pertinent statute] provides in part as follows: 'Any person who commits any act or omits the performance of any duty, which act or omission causes or tends to cause or encourage any person under the age of twenty-one years to come within

the provisions of any of the subdivisions of section 700 or which act or omission contributes thereto .is guilty of a misdemeanor. ...' Among the persons under 21 years of age enumerated in [the law] as being within the jurisdiction of the juvenile court is one 'Who is leading, or from any cause is in danger of leading, an idle, dissolute, lewd, or immoral life.' There can be no doubt that if appellant committed the act it would be immaterial whether or not he knew the age of the minor.

[S]ection 20 of the Penal Code provides that 'In every crime or public offense there must exist a union, or joint operation of act and intent. ... But this does not mean that a positive, willful intent to violate the law is an essential ingredient of every offense. Sometimes an act is expressly prohibited by statute, in which case *the intentional doing of the act, regardless of good motive or ignorance of its criminal character*, constitutes the offense denounced by law. [Emphasis added.]

It appears from the record in this case that appellant, as clerk of the Uptown Hotel, permitted Anita Vasquez, a girl of 14, to be registered as the wife of a sailor and at the same time permitted two other girls, aged 14 and 17, to be registered as the wives of two marines. The six came into the hotel at the same time and had only one suit case and a paper bag. Appellant merely asked the men if the girls were their wives but made no other effort to ascertain the ages of the girls or whether they were in fact the wives of the men. Appellant was a hotel clerk of many years' experience and the circumstances shown by the record should have created in his mind a strong suspicion that Anita Vasquez was not the wife of the sailor, and a very slight inquiry would no doubt have convinced him that she was not. There can be no doubt as to the sufficiency of the evidence to sustain the judgment of conviction. As hereinbefore pointed out, no prejudicial error occurred in the trial of the case.

In view of the foregoing the judgment and order are affirmed.

C. Question

♦ Do you think the result in this case would be the same today? What are the reasons for your conclusion?

D. Comments

Although mens rea is an ancient doctrine and has been discussed in court cases for hundreds of years, it still creates problems for modern courts. The following case defines a specific intent crime and contrasts it with a general intent crime. As you can see, even the California Supreme Court acknowledges the difficulties in differentiating between general and specific intent. Note how the court resolves the dilemma of classifying general intent and specific intent crimes.

E. Case

PEOPLE V. RATHERT, JR.
Supreme Court of California
24 Cal. 4th 200 (2000)

WERDEGAR, J.

In this case we define the mental state necessary to violate Penal Code section 529, paragraph 3 (hereafter sometimes paragraph 3), prohibiting false personation. The Court of Appeal held the statute requires an intent to subject the impersonated individual to liability for suit or prosecution.

***

We conclude section 529, paragraph 3, by its terms, is violated when one intentionally falsely personates another and, in such assumed character, does *any* act that *might* cause the liability or benefit described in the statute. Paragraph 3, in other words, requires the existence of no state of mind or criminal intent beyond that plainly expressed on the face of the statute. Accordingly, we reverse the decision of the Court of Appeal.

FACTS

About 9:35 p.m. on March 22, 1996, defendant entered a Lucky supermarket in Rancho Palos Verdes. He approached store clerk Carlos Mariscal with a check and a driver's license, asking Mariscal "if it was okay to cash the check before [defendant] started getting groceries" and stating he wanted the check approved by the manager. The Talcro Financial Services check was made out to one Chris Laughrey and endorsed by Laughrey. Recognizing that Laughrey, the person pictured on the license, was obviously not defendant, Mariscal called the manager, Sergio Montez, who told defendant he would have to verify the check. Defendant acquiesced and said he would remain there and buy some groceries.

Montez recognized the check as similar to one he had refused several days earlier. Another Lucky supermarket had then cashed that check and later discovered it was invalid. Both checks had been drawn on a closed account.

Montez asked Michael Gutierrez, another employee, to keep an eye on defendant. Meanwhile, Montez telephoned the other Lucky store to verify that the earlier check was of the same kind as the one defendant was attempting to cash. He then called the police.

Defendant abruptly left the store for the parking lot when the police drove up. He entered an El Camino car on the passenger's side. Gutierrez waved down Deputy Sheriff Chris Knox, who had been patrolling the Lucky parking lot in his vehicle, and told Knox, "That's him." Knox followed the El Camino as it drove out of the parking lot, stopped it, and detained defendant and the driver. Defendant gave Knox two false names.

Defendant testified that, on the day he was arrested, he had met his friend, Cherise Hartley, at her house in San Pedro. Hartley asked him if he would cash a check for her, as she needed money to pay for food, diapers and rent. Chris Laughrey, the father of her child, had given her the check and permission to cash it, but was then in a rehabilitation center. She showed defendant a previously endorsed check and Laughrey's driver's license. Hartley told defendant, and he believed, the check was good. He agreed to help her, and they drove to the Lucky store. His account of what happened there generally accorded with the testimony of the store personnel, except he denied leaving the store because of the arrival of the police. Defendant testified he never said he was Chris Laughrey, but he admitted saying he had no other identification and that he intended to pass himself off as Laughrey in order to cash the check. When the manager took the check, saying he would have to verify it, defendant felt something was not quite right, so he went outside to ask Hartley if there was a problem with the check. She told him to get into the car and "forget it." When arrested, defendant gave a false name because he was then on parole and would have been "assumed guilty of anything."

***

At issue here is whether, as defendant urges, paragraph 3 of section 529 requires, for conviction, that defendant impersonated Chris Laughrey, specifically intending to cause Laughrey to become liable to any suit or prosecution or to pay any sum of money, or specifically intending to benefit himself or another.

***

"Specific and general intent," we have cautioned, "have been notoriously difficult terms to define and apply ...." [Citation.] The standard formulation of the two concepts appears i[s] "When the definition of a crime consists of only the description of a particular act, without reference to intent to do a further act or achieve a future consequence, we ask whether the defendant intended to do the proscribed act. This intention is deemed to be a general criminal intent. When the definition refers to defendant's intent to do some further act or achieve some additional consequence, the crime is deemed to be one of specific intent." [Citation.]

Resolution of this case does not require us to fit the offense of false personation into either the specific or the general intent category. Such classification of offenses is necessary "only when the court must determine whether a defense of voluntary intoxication or mental disease, defect, or disorder is available; whether evidence thereon is admissible; or whether appropriate jury instructions are thereby required. [Citation.]" . . . This case aptly illustrates the general principle that--other than circumstances involving a mental state defense--'the characterization of a crime as one of specific intent [or general intent] has little meaningful significance in instructing a jury. The critical issue is the accurate description of the state of mind required for the particular crime.' [Citations].

***

Section 529, paragraph 3 does not explicitly require that a defendant who impersonates another specifically intend to cause the latter to become liable to any suit or prosecution or to pay any sum of money, or specifically intend to benefit defendant himself or another person. The Legislature included in paragraph 3 none of the language typically denoting specific intent, such as "with the intent that" or "for the purpose of." [Citation.] To the contrary, paragraph 3 is framed in language reasonably susceptible of only one interpretation: that the Legislature sought to deter and to punish all acts by an impersonator that might result in a liability or a benefit,

Defendant [further] argues that, when section 529, paragraph 3 is considered in the context of its surrounding statutes [citation], the section obviously contains a requirement of a specific intent to cause another person harm or wrongfully to benefit someone. This is because virtually all other impersonation statutes, according to defendant, include an element of specific intent to defraud, or some similar mens rea, or some wrongful conduct in addition to the impersonation. (E.g., § § 528 [marriage under false personation], 530 [receiving money or property under false personation]; see also § 146a, subd. (b) [impersonating a state public officer, investigator or inspector]; Veh. Code, § 27 [impersonating a California Highway Patrol officer].) We find defendant's argument unpersuasive. . . . To the extent, moreover, that other statutes include a specific intent element, the omission of such an element in section 529 weighs in favor of our interpretation.

DISPOSITION

The judgment of the Court of Appeal is reversed.

F. Questions

- What did the court hold? Is this a general intent or specific intent crime? Do you agree with the Court's holding?

- The court observes that it is often unnecessary to classify crimes. The court gives, however, two particular instances in which determinations of general and specific intent crimes are necessary. What are those two instances?

- What is the test that the court set forth for determining the defendant's intent?

- For a general intent crime, does the defendant have to *intend* to commit a crime?

- For a general intent crime, does the defendant have to *know* that his conduct is criminal?

- What facts does the court rely on in making its determination that the defendant had the necessary general intent for him to be guilty of contributing to the delinquency of a minor?

II. SPECIFIC INTENT

A. Comment

Unlike general intent crimes, specific intent crimes require that a defendant commit a criminal act with a specific state of mind. Usually, the criminal statutes will describe the necessary specific intent (for example, "with the intent to defraud").

The case below is a pre-*Roe v. Wade* decision. It deals with abortion and a criminal prosecution based on old anti-abortion laws. As you probably already know from everyday experience, abortion is legal in California these days (subject to certain restrictions, of course). It is, however, still a good case for review for two reasons.

First, the case gives you a good factual context on which to base the court's discussion of specific intent. Look closely at the trial court's instruction. What specific intent is contained in that instruction?

Second, this case demonstrates the importance of careful reading. If you were to simply glance at the case and assume that the case is no longer good law because abortion is legal in California, you would have missed some important aspects of the case. For example, you would not have noticed that the defendant performing the operation was not even a medical doctor. Certainly that would be as relevant today as it was back in 1953 when the case was decided. Even though modern law permits abortion, qualified medical personnel must perform an abortion. Furthermore, if you had immediately dismissed this case, you would have missed the court's instruction regarding the meaning of specific intent and how to determine specific intent, which is still valid today.

B. Case

PEOPLE V. GALLARDO
Supreme Court of California
41 Cal.2d 57 (1953)

GIBSON, C. J.

Glynn, who is not a doctor, owned and operated an establishment, consisting of a hospital and medical offices, which was under surveillance by the police during the month of March, 1950. On the last day of the month the police entered the premises while Gallardo, a licensed osteopathic physician and surgeon, was attending a woman patient in an operating room. Upon hearing the noise made by the officers, Gallardo removed an instrument from the woman's body, threw the instrument into a washroom, and ran out into the backyard where he was arrested. Glynn was arrested shortly thereafter in an alley at the rear of the property. He then had in his possession over $2,000 in cash and a piece of paper which contained the names of three of the twelve women upon whom abortions were assertedly performed. The police also obtained from the hospital and from Glynn records containing the names of all but two of the twelve women.

The twelve women named in the abortion counts testified, and it can be inferred from their testimony that each of them was pregnant and desired to terminate her pregnancy, that she went to Glynn's establishment for the purpose of obtaining an abortion and that someone there used instruments on her in order to accomplish that purpose. Eleven of the women who visited the hospital were relieved of their pregnancies, and Gallardo was using an instrument on the twelfth one when the police entered.

Gallardo, testifying in his own behalf, admitted that he made a physical examination of the reproductive organs of eleven of the women and that in some instances he performed operations which required incisions in the lower portion of the abdomen. He denied, however, that anything he did was for the purpose of procuring a miscarriage. Gallardo testified that he did not examine or treat the other woman, but she identified him as the person who performed an abortion upon her.

Defendants contend that the evidence is insufficient to support convictions on the counts charging abortions in that the prosecution failed to establish that the operations were not necessary to preserve life within the meaning of the [stated] exceptions.

It is contended that the court misdirected the jury by giving the following instruction: 'You are instructed that every person who uses or employs any instrument or other means whatever upon a woman with intent thereby to procure the miscarriage of such woman, unless the same is necessary to preserve her life, is guilty of a criminal offense. In that connection, I instruct you further that to constitute the crime of abortion it is immaterial whether the woman is pregnant or not.' It is settled that the prosecution need not establish that the woman was actually pregnant, and a defendant may have the necessary intent to procure a miscarriage where he merely believes that the woman upon whom he performs an abortion is pregnant. The defendants argue, however, that the last sentence of the instruction is too broad and may have led the jury to believe that the prosecution was not required to show an intent to procure a miscarriage. Although belief that the woman was pregnant has some bearing on intent and therefore is not wholly immaterial, when the two sentences of the instruction are read together it does not appear how the jury could have been misled.

[The judgment is affirmed.]

43

III. Transferred Intent

A. Comments

The doctrine of transferred intent imposes criminal liability where the defendant's conduct harms an unintended victim. The typical transferred intent situation occurs when a person's criminal intent is transferred (by chance or misfortune) to a person other than the intended victim. Transferred intent can also include situations where an unintended victim is the target of criminal activity *as well as* the intended victim. Transferred intent is also known as "constructive intent."

B. Case

PEOPLE V. SCOTT
Supreme Court of California
14 Cal. 4th 544 (1996)

BROWN, J.

A jury convicted defendants Damien Scott and Derrick Brown of various crimes for their part in a drive-by shooting which resulted in the death of one person and injury to several others. We must decide in this case whether the doctrine of transferred intent may be used to assign criminal liability to a defendant who kills an unintended victim when the defendant is also prosecuted for the attempted murder of an intended victim.

Under the classic formulation of California's common law doctrine of transferred intent, a defendant who shoots with the intent to kill a certain person and hits a bystander instead is subject to the same criminal liability that would have been imposed had " 'the fatal blow reached the person for whom intended.' " [Citation.] In such a factual setting, the defendant is deemed as culpable as if he had accomplished what he set out to do.

Here, it was established at trial that defendants fired an automatic weapon into a public park in an attempt to kill a certain individual, and fatally shot a bystander instead. The case presents the type of factual setting in which courts have uniformly approved reliance on the transferred intent doctrine as the basis of determining a defendant's criminal liability for the death of an unintended victim. Consistent with a line of decisions beginning with *Suesser* nearly a century ago, we conclude that the jury in this case was properly instructed on a transferred intent theory of liability for first degree murder.

Moreover, defendants' exposure to a murder conviction based on a transferred intent theory of liability was proper regardless of the fact they were also charged with attempted murder of the intended victim. Contrary to what its name implies, the transferred intent doctrine does not refer to any actual intent that is "used up" once it has been employed to convict a defendant of a specific intent crime against an intended victim. Rather, the doctrine of transferred intent connotes a policy. *As applied here, the transferred intent doctrine is but another way of saying that a defendant who shoots with an intent to kill but misses and hits a bystander instead should be punished for a crime of the same seriousness as the one he tried to commit against his intended victim.* (Emphasis added.)

In this case, defendants shot at an intended victim, missed him, and killed another person instead. In doing so, defendants committed crimes against two persons. Defendants' criminal liability for causing the death of the unintended victim may be determined on a theory of transferred intent in accordance with the classic formulation of the doctrine under California common law. Their criminal liability for shooting at the intended victim with an intent to kill is that which the law assigns.

The Court of Appeal correctly concluded that the trial court's instruction to the jury on transferred intent as it related to the charge of murder was proper.

We affirm the judgment of the Court of Appeal.

C. Questions

♦ Do you think the defendant should have been punished for both crimes?

♦ Do you think punishing him for both crimes was inherently "unfair"?

♦ Applying the double jeopardy concept that you learned earlier, why does this "double" punishment not violate the principles of double jeopardy?

IV. Self-Assessment

1. Strict liability offenses require no criminal intent at the time of wrongdoing.
   A. True   B. False

2. California law adopts the same classifications of mental states as does the Model Penal Code.
   A. True   B. False

3. The Model Penal Code adopts the "specific intent" and "general intent" categories of mens rea, consistent with the common law.
   A. True   B. False

4. The doctrine of transferred intent imposes criminal liability on a defendant for the intentional infliction of harm on an unintended victim.
   A. True   B. False

5. The Model Penal Code does not contain a specific "vicarious liability" category of criminal responsibility.
   A. True   B. False

CHAPTER FIVE

Parties to Crimes and Vicarious Liability

Party liability has also been called "accessory liability." Party liability imposes criminal responsibility on persons who help another to commit a crime. Under the common law, there were four categories of party liability: principals in the first degree (those who actually committed the offense), principals in the second degree (those who were either actually or constructively present), accessories before the fact (those who aided another to commit a crime but were not actually or constructively present), and accessories after the fact (those who knew a felony had been committed and helped the felon to escape arrest, trial or punishment.)

As you will soon learn from the statutes below, California departs from the old common law in its classification of parties to crimes. Although some of the old terminology still exists, many of the distinctions do not. The relevant California party liability definitions to know are: principals, accessories, and accomplices. The Model Penal Code also abandons the traditional common law classifications, focusing on concepts of legal liability.

Vicarious liability is a slightly different concept from the party liability. Party liability laws impose criminal liability for *sharing in an activity* by criminal defendants. Vicarious liability, on the other hand, imposes criminal liability for the *acts of third parties* and involves no complicity among wrongdoers. Vicarious liability often arises in an employment context where a supervisor is held criminally liable for the criminal acts of an employee who is acting within the scope of his employment. (The Model Penal Code does not specifically discuss "vicarious" liability.)

I.   PARTY LIABILITY

A. Comments

The several statutes below contain California definitions for principles, accessories, and accomplices. Pay special attention to the accessory liability statute. (California law (consistent with modern trends) permits conviction for accessories where the principal is neither convicted nor prosecuted, which is contrary to the common law.) When you read Penal Code section 972, consider why you think the Legislature enacted that provision, which changed the common law rule.

B. Statutes

Principles: Penal Code section 31

WHO ARE PRINCIPALS. All persons concerned in the commission of a crime, whether it be felony or misdemeanor, and whether they directly commit the act constituting the offense, or aid and abet in its commission, or, not being present, have advised and encouraged its commission, and all persons counseling, advising, or encouraging children under the age of fourteen years, lunatics or idiots, to commit any crime, or who, by fraud, contrivance, or force, occasion the drunkenness of another for the purpose of causing him to commit any crime, or who, by threats, menaces, command, or coercion, compel another to commit any crime, are principals in any crime so committed.

Accessories: Penal Code section 32

Every person who, after a felony has been committed, harbors, conceals or aids a principal in such felony, with the intent that said principal may avoid or escape from arrest, trial, conviction or punishment, having knowledge that said principal has committed such felony or has been charged with such felony or convicted thereof, is an accessory to such felony.

Abrogation of common-law distinctions: Penal Code section 971

The distinction between an accessory before the fact and a principal, and between principals in the first and second degree is abrogated; and all persons concerned in the commission of a crime, who by the operation of other provisions of this code are principals therein, shall hereafter be prosecuted, tried and punished as principals and no other facts need be alleged in any accusatory pleading against any such person than are required in an accusatory pleading against a principal.

Accomplices: Penal Code section 1111

A conviction cannot be had upon the testimony of an accomplice unless it be corroborated by such other evidence as shall tend to connect the defendant with the commission of the offense; and the corroboration is not sufficient if it merely shows the commission of the offense or the circumstances thereof. An accomplice is hereby defined as one who is liable to prosecution for the identical offense charged against the defendant on trial in the cause in which the testimony of the accomplice is given.

Accessory liability: Penal Code section 972

An accessory to the commission of a felony may be prosecuted, tried, and punished, though the principal may be neither prosecuted nor tried, and though the principal may have been acquitted.

II. AIDING AND ABETTING

A. Comments

The first aiding and abetting case you will read is *People v. Beeman,* a very famous California case that is well known to both prosecutors and defense attorneys. This case is rather long both in its recitation of the facts and in its legal reasoning. However, the case is important for three reasons.

First, the case discusses the required mental state to support an aiding and abetting conviction.

Second, *Beeman* provides an example of the California Supreme Court resolving a conflict in the lower appellate courts. (Conflicting viewpoints in the lower appellate courts are one reason why the California Supreme Court grants review to decide a case.) You will read the Supreme Court's discussion of the conflicting holdings from the district courts of appeal and how the court resolves the conflict.

Third, the case gives you the opportunity to see how a court resolves questions about proper jury instructions. Standard jury instructions are often taken from case law. This case gives you an example of how courts review jury instructions and fashion new instructions either by a revision of the language to make it more precise or by the correction of erroneous language.

B. Cases

PEOPLE V. BEEMAN
Supreme Court of California.
35 Cal.3d 547 (1984)

REYNOSO, J.

James Gray and Michael Burk drove from Oakland to Redding for the purpose of robbing appellant's sister-in-law, Mrs. Marjorie Beeman, of valuable jewelry, including a 3.5-carat diamond ring. They telephoned the residence to determine that she was home. Soon thereafter Burk knocked at the door of the victim's house, presented himself as a poll taker, and asked to be let in. When Mrs. Beeman asked for identification, he forced her into the hallway and entered. Gray, disguised in a ski mask, followed. The two subdued the victim, placed tape over her mouth and eyes and tied her to a bathroom fixture. Then they ransacked the house, taking numerous pieces of jewelry and a set of silverware. The jewelry included a 3.5-carat, heart-shaped diamond ring and a blue sapphire ring. The total value of these two rings was over $100,000. In the course of the robbery, telephone wires inside the house were cut.

Appellant was arrested six days later in Emeryville. He had in his possession several of the less valuable of the stolen rings. He supplied the police with information that led to the arrests of Burk and Gray. With Gray's cooperation appellant assisted police in recovering most of the stolen property.

Burk, Gray and appellant were jointly charged. After the trial court severed the trials, Burk and Gray pled guilty to robbery.

At appellant's trial they testified that he had been extensively involved in planning the crime. Burk testified that he had known appellant for two and one-half years. He had lived in appellant's apartment several times. Appellant had talked to him about rich relatives in Redding and had described a diamond ring worth $50,000. According to Burk the feasibility of robbing appellant's relatives was first mentioned two and one-half months before the incident occurred. About one week before the robbery, the discussions became more specific. Appellant gave Burk the address and discussed the ruse of posing as a poll taker. It was decided that Gray and Burk would go to Redding because appellant wanted nothing to do with the actual robbery and because he feared being recognized. On the night before the offense appellant drew a floor plan of the victim's house and told Burk where the diamond ring was likely to be found. Appellant agreed to sell the jewelry for 20 percent of the proceeds.

After the robbery was completed, Burk telephoned appellant to report success. Appellant said that he would call the friend who might buy the jewelry. Burk and Gray drove to appellant's house and showed him the 'loot.' Appellant was angry that the others had taken so much jewelry, and demanded that his cut be increased from 20 percent to one-third.

Gray's testimony painted a similar picture. Gray also had known appellant for approximately two years prior to the incident. Gray said Burk had initially approached him about the robbery, supplied the victim's address, and described the diamond ring. Appellant had at some time described the layout of the house to Gray and Burk and had described to them the cars driven by various members of the victim's family. Gray and Burk, but not appellant, had discussed how to divide the proceeds. Both Gray and Burk owed money to appellant. In addition, Burk owed Gray $3,200.

According to Gray appellant had been present at a discussion three days before the robbery when it was mentioned that appellant could not go because his 6 foot 5 inch, 310-pound frame could be too easily recognized. Two days before the offense, however, appellant told Gray that he wanted nothing to do with the robbery of his relatives. On the day preceding the incident appellant and Gray spoke on the telephone. At that time appellant repeated he wanted nothing to do with the robbery, but confirmed that he had told Burk that he would not say anything if the others went ahead.

Gray confirmed that appellant was upset when he saw that his friends had gone through with the robbery and had taken all of the victim's jewelry. He was angered further when he discovered that Burk might easily be recognized because he had not disguised himself. Appellant then asked them to give him all of the stolen goods. Instead Burk and Gray gave appellant only a watch and some rings which they believed he could sell. Gray and Burk then traveled to San Jose where they sold the silverware for $900. Burk used this money to flee to Los Angeles. Sometime later appellant asked for Gray's cooperation in recovering and returning the property to the victim. On several occasions when Burk called them for more money, appellant stalled and avoided questions about the sale of the jewelry.

Appellant Beeman's testimony contradicted that of Burk and Gray as to nearly every material element of his own involvement. Appellant testified that he did not participate in the robbery or its planning. He confirmed that Burk had lived with him on several occasions, and that he had told Burk about Mrs. Beeman's jewelry, the valuable diamond ring, and the Beeman ranch, in the course of day-to-day conversations. He claimed that he had sketched a floor plan of the house some nine months prior to the robbery, only for the purpose of comparing it with the layout of a house belonging to another brother. He at first denied and then admitted describing the Beeman family cars, but insisted this never occurred in the context of planning a robbery.

Appellant stated that Burk first suggested that robbing Mrs. Beeman would be easy some five months before the incident. At that time, and on the five or six subsequent occasions when Burk raised the subject, appellant told Burk that his friends could do what they wanted but that he wanted no part of such a scheme.

Beeman admitted Burk had told him of the poll taker ruse within a week before the robbery, and that Burk told him they had bought a cap gun and handcuffs. He further admitted that he had allowed Burk to take some old clothes left at the apartment by a former roommate. At that time Beeman told Burk: 'If you're going to do a robbery, you can't look like a bum.' Nevertheless, appellant explained that he did not know Burk was then planning to commit this robbery. Further, although he knew there was a possibility Burk and Gray would try to rob Mrs. Beeman, appellant thought it very unlikely they would go through with it. He judged Burk capable of committing the crime but knew he had no car and no money to get to Redding. Appellant did not think Gray would cooperate.

Appellant agreed that he had talked with Gray on the phone two days before the robbery, and said he had then repeated he did not want to be involved. He claimed that Burk called him on the way back from Redding because he feared appellant would report him to the police, but knew appellant would want to protect Gray, who was his closer friend.

Appellant claimed he told the others to come to his house after the robbery and offered to sell the jewelry in order to buy time in which to figure out a way to collect and return the property. He took the most valuable piece to make sure it was not sold. Since Burk had a key to his apartment, appellant gave the diamond ring and a bracelet to a friend, Martinez, for safekeeping. After Burk fled to Los Angeles, appellant showed some of the jewelry to mutual acquaintances in order to lull Burk into believing he was attempting to sell it. During this time Burk called him on the phone several times asking for money and, when appellant told him of plans to return the property, threatened to have him killed.

When confronted with his prior statement to the police that he had given one of the rings to someone in exchange for a $50 loan, appellant admitted making the statement but denied that it was true. He also claimed that his statement on direct examination that 'his [Burk's] face was seen. He didn't wear a mask. Didn't do anything he was supposed to do. ...' referred only to the reason Gray had given for wanting to return the victim's property.

Appellant requested that the jury be instructed that aiding and abetting liability requires proof of intent to aid. The request was denied. After three hours of deliberation, the jury submitted two written questions to the court: 'We would like to hear again how one is determined to be an accessory and by what actions can he absolve himself'; and 'Does inaction mean the party is guilty?' The jury was reinstructed in accord with the standard instructions. The court denied appellant's renewed request that the instructions be modified explaining that giving another, slightly different instruction at this point would further complicate matters. The jury returned its verdicts of guilty on all counts two hours later.

Penal Code section 31 provides in pertinent part: 'All persons concerned in the commission of a crime, ... whether they directly commit the act constituting the offense, or aid and abet in its commission, or, not being present, have advised and encouraged its commission, ... are principals in any crime so committed.' Thus, those persons who at common law would have been termed accessories before the fact and principals in the second degree as well as those who actually perpetrate the offense, are to be prosecuted, tried and punished as principals in California. (See , Pen. Code, § 971.) The term 'aider and abettor' is now often used to refer to principals other than the perpetrator, whether or not they are present at the commission of the offense.

The jury instruction defines principals to a crime to include ''Those who, with knowledge of the unlawful purpose of the one who does directly and actively commit or attempt to commit the crime, aid and abet in its commission ..., or ... Those who, whether present or not at the commission or attempted commission of the crime, advise and encourage its commission. ... ' The jury instructions further define aiding and abetting as follows: 'A person aids and abets the commission of a crime if, with knowledge of the unlawful purpose of the perpetrator of the crime, he aids, promotes, encourages or instigates by act or advice the commission of such crime.'

Appellant asserts that the current instructions, substitute an element of knowledge of the perpetrator's intent for the element of criminal intent of the accomplice, in contravention of common law principles and California case law. He argues that the instruction given permitted the jury to convict him of the same offenses as the perpetrators without finding that he harbored either the same criminal intent as they, or the specific intent to assist them, thus depriving him of his constitutional rights to due process and equal protection of the law.

The People argue that the standard instruction properly reflects California law, which requires no more than that the aider and abettor have knowledge of the perpetrator's criminal purpose and do a voluntary act which in fact aids the perpetrator. The People further contend that defendants are adequately protected from conviction for acts committed under duress or which inadvertently aid a perpetrator by the limitation of the liability of an aider and abettor to those acts knowingly aided and their natural and reasonable consequences. Finally, the People argue that the modification proposed by appellant is unnecessary because proof of intentional aiding in most cases can be inferred from aid with knowledge of the perpetrator's purpose.

There is no question that an aider and abettor must have criminal intent in order to be convicted of a criminal offense. Decisions of this court dating back to 1898 hold that 'the word 'abet' includes knowledge of the wrongful purpose of the perpetrator and counsel and encouragement in the crime' and that it is therefore error to instruct a jury that one may be found guilty as a principal if one aided or abetted. The act of encouraging or counseling itself implies a purpose or goal of furthering the encouraged result. 'An aider and abettor's fundamental purpose, motive and intent is to aid and assist the perpetrator in the latter's commission of the crime.' The essential conflict in current appellate opinions is between those cases which state that an aider and abettor must have an intent or purpose to commit or assist in the commission of the criminal offenses.

We agree that the facts from which a mental state may be inferred must not be confused with the mental state that the prosecution is required to prove. Direct evidence of the mental state of the accused is rarely available except through his or her testimony. The trier of fact is and must be free to disbelieve the testimony and to infer that the truth is otherwise when such an inference is supported by circumstantial evidence regarding the actions of the accused.

The weight of authority and sound law require proof that an aider and abettor act with knowledge of the criminal purpose of the perpetrator and with an intent or purpose either of committing, or of encouraging or facilitating commission of, the offense. When the definition of the offense includes the intent to do some act or achieve some consequence beyond the actus reus of the crime, the aider and abettor must share the specific intent of the perpetrator. By 'share' we mean neither that the aider and abettor must be prepared to commit the offense by his or her own act should the perpetrator fail to do so, nor that the aider and abettor must seek to share the fruits of the crime. Rather, an aider and abettor will 'share' the perpetrator's specific intent when he or she knows the full extent of the perpetrator's criminal purpose and gives aid or encouragement with the intent or purpose of facilitating the perpetrator's commission of the crime. The liability of an aider and abettor extends also to the natural and reasonable consequences of the acts he knowingly and intentionally aids and encourages.

The California jury instructions inadequately defines aiding and abetting because it fails to insure that an aider and abettor will be found to have the required mental state with regard to his or her own act. While the instruction does include the word 'abet,' which encompasses the intent required by law, the word is arcane and its full import unlikely to be recognized by modern jurors. Moreover, even if jurors were made aware that 'abet' means to encourage or facilitate, and implicitly to harbor an intent to further the crime encouraged, the instruction does not require them to find that intent because it defines an aider and abettor as one who 'aids, promotes, encourages or instigates.' Thus, as one appellate court recently recognized, the instruction would 'technically allow a conviction if the defendant knowing of the perpetrator's unlawful purpose, negligently or accidentally aided the commission of the crime.'

We suggest that an appropriate instruction should inform the jury that a person aids and abets the commission of a crime when he or she, acting with (1) knowledge of the unlawful purpose of the perpetrator; and (2) the intent or purpose of committing, encouraging, or facilitating the commission of the offense, (3) by act or advice aids, promotes, encourages or instigates, the commission of the crime.

The convictions are reversed.

C. Questions

♦ Under the *Beeman* decision, does an aider and abettor have to have criminal intent in order to be convicted of a criminal offense?

♦ What is the necessary *mens rea* that the prosecution must prove in order for a defendant to be properly convicted under an aiding and abetting theory?

♦ Why did the court formulate the specific test that it did in this case?

♦ Do you agree with the court's decision based on the facts presented in this case?

D. Comments

The following case, *Hopkins,* analyzes the actus reus of aiding and abetting. The procedure at the beginning of the case is a bit convoluted. In a nutshell, the defendant had been charged by a grand jury indictment. He entered a guilty plea to the charges against him. He later made a motion to withdraw his guilty plea, which the court granted. After the court allowed him to withdraw his plea, the defendant challenged the indictment itself, claiming that there was no probable cause to support the grand jury's indictment. When the defendant was successful and the indictment was set aside, the prosecution appealed the decision. It is at this point that the appellate court enters the conflict to determine if the dismissal of the indictment was proper.

E. Case

PEOPLE V. HOPKINS
Court of Appeal, First District, Division 2
101 Cal.App.2d 704 (1951)

SCHOTTKY, J. pro tem.

By an indictment respondent was accused of manslaughter in that he "did willfully, unlawfully, feloniously and without malice kill one Herbert Caro." After pleading not guilty respondent was permitted to withdraw his plea, whereupon he moved to set aside the indictment on the ground that it was returned without reasonable or probable cause. His motion was granted, and this appeal was taken by the People. (Pen. Code, § 1238.)

The transcript of the grand jury hearing which was before the court on the motion shows that six witnesses testified.

The cause of death appears from the testimony of the doctor on duty at the Park Emergency Hospital in San Francisco early Sunday morning, September 18, 1949, when decedent was brought in by respondent in his car. He diagnosed the case as one of narcotic poisoning, and learned from respondent that decedent had taken heroin. After emergency treatment decedent was taken to the San Francisco Hospital where he died that day.

An inspector of the San Francisco Police Department on the homicide detail was the principal witness before the grand jury. He testified that he investigated the case on the day of decedent's death and took a statement from respondent. The substance of it, according to the officer's testimony, was that on September 17 respondent left his ship in the early afternoon and after going over to Marin County returned to San Francisco about 11:30 p. m. About an hour later he visited a tavern where he saw decedent whom he had known for approximately three years. They engaged in conversation and after respondent had told decedent about his voyage decedent asked him "if he would like to get high to-night" to which he assented and they left the place in respondent's car. Respondent gave decedent $13 and about 15 minutes later decedent returned to the car, having purchased some heroin. They then drove out to Funston Avenue where they stopped, opened the package, and decedent produced an eye-dropper which he filled with water at a service station. They drove around a few blocks and then parked on 14th Avenue beside the Park-Presidio Boulevard "where they took a cap of heroin and mixed it in a spoon, heated it, and after they had it mixed, Hopkins said he took a shot in the arm, and then he said Caro took a shot, he held his arm with a handkerchief. Q. Hopkins said he held Caro's arm? A. Yes. He had wrapped a handkerchief around it to force the veins out. And that Hopkins took a shot. He said he took another one, and that Hopkins took another one. The first one he thought he took in the arm, and the second one somewhere down around the wrist. After Caro took the second shot, he said he felt sick, so he got out of the car and attempted to heave. He wasn't able to. And Hopkins said, he got out, walked around the front of the car, and that Caro was practically unconscious then, he had to drag him back into the car, put him in the back seat, and from there he drove him to the Park Emergency Hospital, where he was admitted and treated by doctors."

When respondent manipulated the handkerchief- tourniquet around decedent's arm he assisted him in the commission of an unlawful act not amounting to a felony. As a result of these acts decedent died.

Section 31, Penal Code, provides that "All persons concerned in the commission of a crime, whether it be felony or misdemeanor, and whether they directly commit the act constituting the offense, or aid and abet in its commission ... are principals."

The help which respondent gave decedent brings respondent within the provisions of section 31. That he aided is clear; that he abetted is equally clear, since he and decedent had deliberately set out together with the purpose of doing that which [the law] denounced.

In order to charge respondent with manslaughter it was not necessary for the testimony before the grand jury to show that he injected the heroin, since section 31 draws no line between persons who "directly commit the act constituting the offense" and those who "aid and abet in its commission." Both are principals. If respondent had not touched decedent's arm or otherwise physically aided him, but had merely stood by and kept a lookout for passers-by he could still be charged as a principal under section 31, Penal Code. The trial court erred in granting the motion to dismiss the indictment.

The order dismissing the indictment is reversed.

F. Questions

♦ In the *Hopkins* case, what specific act (application of tourniquet, drive to the hospital, etc.) did the defendant perform to trigger an aiding and abetting theory?

♦ Do you agree with the court's remarks that even if Hopkins had only been a lookout, he could still be charged as a principal? Do you think the defendant's liability should be the same if he was merely acting as a lookout? If not, what should his liability be, if any?

III. Vicarious Liability

A. Comments

One of the most frequently cited vicarious liability cases is *United States v. Park*, a United States Supreme Court opinion. *Park* is very similar to the California case, *In re Marley*. The *Park* case involved a supervisor's criminal liability for an employee's violation of health and safety laws relating to foods. Similarly, in *Marley* the defendant (a proprietor of a meat market) was held accountable for an employee's violation of weights and measures laws. Although this is an old case, it is very instructive on the point of vicarious liability and the public policy considerations behind vicarious liability offenses.

B. Case

IN RE CLAY MARLEY, ON HABEAS CORPUS
Supreme Court of California
29 Cal. 2d 525 (1946)

SCHAUER

Petitioner, the proprietor of a meat market, was convicted of a violation of *section 12023* of the Business and Professions Code, and sentenced to ninety days in the county jail. The mentioned section provides as follows: "Every person who by himself or his employee or agent, or as the employee or agent of another, sells any commodity, at, by, or according to gross weight or measure, or at, by, as, of, or according to any weight, measure or count which is greater than the true net weight, ... is guilty of a misdemeanor." Petitioner seeks release through habeas corpus on the ground that the quoted statute is unconstitutional as it is sought to be applied to the facts here shown. With this position we are compelled to disagree.

The record discloses that on or about March 22, 1945, an employee of the Office of Price Administration, named Mrs. Punteney, accompanied openly by one other woman (named Mrs. Sampson) and surreptitiously by two men (one of them named Delaney), all of the same calling, appeared at the counter of petitioner's meat market in Los Angeles County and requested of petitioner's clerk and employee, one Dennis, that the latter sell her one veal steak and four or five lamb chops. Dennis weighed the selections, told Mrs. Punteney and Mrs. Sampson the respective prices, and wrapped the meat. Mrs. Punteney then showed Dennis her "identification" and summoned Delaney "who was waiting outside the door," and together they checked the weight of the meat, which was found to be less than that which would correspond, according to Office of Price Administration price charts posted in the market, to the prices charged. About two weeks later Delaney signed the complaint upon which petitioner's conviction is based. Dennis was also named as a defendant, was convicted, and was penalized by a $ 100 fine. It is undisputed that petitioner did not participate personally in the transaction here involved, was absent from the premises at the time it occurred, and had at no time instructed Dennis to give short weight.

The general rule of law as repeatedly enunciated and emphasized by the courts of California and of other jurisdictions is that a master or principal before he can be held criminally responsible for the act of an employee or agent must be proved to have "knowingly and intentionally aided, advised, or encouraged the criminal act." [Citations.] [In a prior case the court] declared that "Before one can be convicted of a crime by reason of the acts of his agent a clear case must be shown. The civil doctrine that a principal is bound by the acts of his agent within the scope of the agent's authority has no application to criminal law. [Citations.]"

In limited qualification of the general rule, however, legislative bodies in California as well as in other jurisdictions have adopted various statutes positively forbidding certain acts and imposing criminal liability upon the master if the act is knowingly performed by his servant within the scope of the latter's authority. Such statutes have dealt with the sale of intoxicating liquor; of pure foods and drugs and with the operating of gaming establishments and of saloons, and have been upheld by the courts. [Citations.]

Such exceptions are also recognized . . . by the observation that "under statutes positively forbidding certain acts irrespective of the motive or intent of the actor, a principal or master may be criminally liable for his agent's or employee's act done within the scope of his employment. ..." [Citation.]

And in the field of weights and measures, the rule is that where, as here, the statute provides that "whoever, himself or by a servant or agent, is guilty of giving false or insufficient weight or measure shall be punishable, evidence of giving short weight by defendant's servant in his absence warrants a conviction of defendant." [Citation.] In these cases it is the duty of the defendant to know what the facts are that are involved or result from his acts or conduct. Statutes punishing the sale of adulterated foods or prohibiting the sale of intoxicating liquor to minors are most frequently found in this class of cases. The use of false weights could well come within this field of the law.

Inasmuch as the Legislature of this state has seen fit, in the exercise of its power, to impose upon petitioner criminal liability for the offense which was committed by his e, we cannot, in the light of the authorities above cited, hold that the statute as written, or as applied here, invades a constitutional right of the petitioner. The seemingly (upon the record before us) disproportionate severity of the penalty assessed by the trial judge against this petitioner, as compared to that meted out against his codefendant, who was the primary actor, does not constitute a legal basis for intervention by habeas corpus. The writ of habeas corpus heretofore issued is discharged and petitioner is remanded to custody.

CARTER, J. I dissent.

Broadly speaking this case brings into sharp focus the clash between conflicting social philosophies which are reflected in the interpretation of constitutional and statutory provisions. That is, should the burden be placed upon an innocent and blameless employer, engaged in a business not in itself harmful to the public, of risking conviction of a crime and service of a jail sentence because of the mistake, intentional or not, of his employee? The majority opinion answers this question in the affirmative. With this conclusion I cannot agree. In my opinion there are no considerations of public policy or general welfare which warrant such a departure from the long established rule that criminal intent is a necessary element of a crime. Various situations can be imagined which render intolerable, and shocking to one's sense of justice, the construction placed by the majority opinion on the statute here involved. Similar statutes could be passed relating to the sale of railroad tickets or the cashing of checks which would make criminally liable the officers of a railway or banking corporation for an error made by an employee in overcharging a customer for a ticket or short changing a customer in the cashing of a check. Upon the occurrence of such an event in a remote section of the state where the railroad or bank was operating, the president and other officers of the railroad or bank who might reside in a metropolitan area hundreds of miles from the place where the crime was committed could be arrested and sent to jail for an alleged violation committed by a ticket clerk or bank teller. Likewise a merchant, who had been inducted into military service and who left his business in charge of a manager, could be sent to jail for violation of such a statute committed during his absence in military service when he had no knowledge whatever of what was taking place in his place of business. In such a case there is nothing an employer can do to protect himself, as the act of the employee is one which depends entirely upon use of his own faculties and senses and it is impossible for the employer to determine with any degree of accuracy whether the faculties and senses of the employee are functioning properly and accurately during all his working hours. These considerations, in my opinion, outweigh any benefit or advantage which may be gained to the public by an interpretation of a statute which places upon an innocent and blameless employer criminal responsibility for an act of his employee.

C. Questions

♦ Do you feel that the defendant in this case should be held responsible when he did not personally participate in the wrongdoing and was not even present at the time it occurred?

♦ What you think is the Legislature's purpose behind making those in a supervisorial capacity responsible for the wrongdoings of employees?

♦ Is the majority or dissenting opinion the better-reasoned opinion? Explain your choice.

IV. Self-Assessment

1. The concept of "aiding and abetting" requires an act or advice which promotes, encourages, or instigates the commission of a crime.
   A. True   B. False

2. Consistent with modern law, California consolidates several of the common law party liability categories.
   A. True   B. False

3. "Vicarious liability" often arises in an employer-employee setting.
   A. True   B. False

4. Under both modern California law and common law, perpetrators are classified as principals.
   A. True   B. False

5. Under California law, accomplices are only those persons who are liable for the identical offense as charged against the defendant.
   A. True   B. False

CHAPTER SIX

UNCOMPLETED CRIMES: ATTEMPT, CONSPIRACY, AND SOLICITATION

The old term for uncompleted crimes is "inchoate offenses." "Inchoate" means an imperfectly or not completely performed crime. That is, inchoate offenses are those which have begun, but which have not yet been completed. In California, there are three classifications of inchoate offenses: 1) solicitation, 2) conspiracy, and 3) attempt. Consistent with general principles of American law, the criminalization of these activities fulfills useful societal goals. First, it protects society from the greater harm that results from the completed crimes. Second, it punishes the criminally minded so that they do not escape justice because either mere chance or circumstance prevented them from completing their criminal objective.

We will take these crimes in order from the act least likely to result in completed crime to the act most likely to result in a completed crime. Thus, we will proceed from solicitation (the crime farthest removed from the completed crime), to conspiracy, and finally to attempt (the crime closest to the completed crime). By taking these crimes in this sequence, you can see the difference among the actus rea of these uncompleted offenses.

I. SOLICITATION

A. Comments

There are two interesting points to glean from the following statute. First, note that the Legislature has set forth very specific conduct which triggers Penal Code section 653f. (Note: Most of the statutory language regarding punishment has been edited from the statute. As you would expect, solicitation of more serious offenses is punished more seriously.)

Second, observe that the Legislature has defined the standard of proof within the statute itself. Usually, evidentiary matters are not contained within the statute that defines the crime. This statute is an exception. When you read the statute, consider why the Legislature included questions of proof within the definition of the crime itself.

B. Statute

Penal Code section 653f

Every person who, with the intent that the crime be committed, solicits another to offer, accept, or join in the offer or acceptance of a bribe, or to commit or join in the commission of carjacking, robbery, burglary, grand theft, receiving stolen property, extortion, perjury, forgery, kidnapping, arson or assault with a deadly weapon or every person who, with the intent that the crime be committed, solicits another to commit rape, sodomy, oral copulation.

***

(f) An offense charged in violation of Penal Code section 653(f) must be proven by the testimony of two witnesses or by one witness and corroborating circumstances.

C. Question

♦ Now that you have read the statute, why do you think the Legislature specifically provided a section on proof when defining the crime of solicitation and its punishment?

D. Comments

The following case discusses the issue of proof regarding the crime of solicitation. When reading this case, consider whether or not the defendant's conduct was sufficient to meet the statutory elements. Also consider whether or not solicitation (as interpreted by this court) requires *agreement* as an element of the offense.

E. Case

PEOPLE V. BURT
Supreme Court of California
45 Cal.2d 311 (1955)

TRAYNOR, J.

The evidence presented at the trial established that defendant solicited the prosecutrix in Los Angeles to get acquainted with men at hotels in the Los Angeles area and to persuade them to accompany her to Tijuana, Mexico, to engage in [illegal] sexual intercourse. The prosecutrix reported the solicitations to the police and the scheme was never carried out.

***

[Defendant challenges his conviction on two grounds. First, he contends] that it is significant that no acts were done in furtherance of the commission of the crime. However, defendant's argument cannot withstand analysis.] Legislative concern with the proscribed soliciting is demonstrated not only by the gravity of the crimes specified but the fact that the crime, unlike conspiracy, does not require the commission of any overt act. It is complete when the solicitation is made, and it is immaterial that the object of the solicitation is never consummated, or that no steps are taken towards its commission.]

[Second], defendant contends that a reversal is required because his solicitations were not proved by the testimony of two witnesses or by that of one witness and corroborating circumstances, as required by section 653f of the Penal Code. Defendant's solicitations were proved by the testimony of the prosecutrix and by that of a police officer who overheard them by means of a listening device installed, with her permission, in the prosecutrix's home.

Furthermore, a tape recording of the conversation overheard by the police officer was introduced in evidence, and defendant admitted in his own testimony that he had participated in the conversation that the officer had recorded and had solicited the prosecutrix in the manner described above. Defendant explained, however, that he had made the solicitations without any intent to carry out the extortion scheme but merely as an excuse to become acquainted with the prosecutrix whom he wished to know

'socially.'

The slight variation between the testimony of the prosecutrix and the police officer as to the details of carrying out the proposed extortion is of no significance, for the tape recording shows that the two variations were in fact suggested by defendant as alternative means by which the extortion could be effected. Thus, in the light of the well-established rule that the corroborative evidence need not be strong nor sufficient in itself, without the aid of other evidence, to establish the fact in issue, we must conclude that the testimony of the prosecutrix and of the police officer and the recording of defendant's conversation with the prosecutrix are more than adequate to satisfy the requirements of section 653f. Moreover, the admissions in defendant's own testimony supply sufficient corroborative evidence.

[Judgment affirmed.]

F. Questions

♦ Assume that instead of the "slight variation" between the testimony of the victim and the police officer, there had been a large discrepancy between their testimonies. Do you think that the court would have ruled the same way? Why or why not?

♦ In this case, the crime that was solicited was to be completed outside the defendant's own state. Do you think that is a significant fact? Why or why not?

♦ Does the proposed place of completion of a crime in any way change the legislative goal of punishing the criminally minded?

II. CONSPIRACY

A. Comments

When reading the short statute below, note that the crime of conspiracy in California does require some overt act. In California, agreement alone is insufficient to constitute conspiracy. Also observe the Legislature's inclusion of a clause regarding place of trial for defendants charged with conspiracy. B

B. Statute

Penal Code section 184

No defined agreement amounts to a conspiracy, unless some act, beside such agreement, be done within this state to effect the object thereof, by one or more of the parties to such agreement and the trial of cases of conspiracy may be had in any county in which any such act be done.

C. Questions

- As you have read in the statute, the Legislature allows a defendant to be tried in any county. Assume, for example, that a defendant who lives in Santa Cruz (Santa Cruz County) plans to blow up the state capitol building in Sacramento. In order to accomplish this, he needs the help of several of his criminal companions. These former partners in crime, however, are located throughout the state. One is in Fresno (Fresno County), one is in San José (Santa Clara County), and another is in Redwood City (San Mateo County). The defendant travels to each location to speak with each partner in crime. After he has spoken with each one of his "friends" in the various locations, has his conduct gone far enough to fulfill the elements of conspiracy? If so, where could he properly be tried?

- Assume now that the defendant has (in addition to speaking with all of his friends) given them a set of plans for building the explosive device. Has the defendant's conduct gone far enough to fulfill the elements of conspiracy? If so, where could he legally be tried under the statute?

D. Comments

In this case, the court discusses whether or not a defendant can be convicted of conspiracy of a "simulated" crime. Look carefully at court's reasoning in resolving this issue. Also observe the distinction that the court makes between aiding and abetting and conspiracy.

E. Case

PEOPLE V. MARRONE
District Court of Appeal, Fourth District
210 Cal.App. 2d 299 (1962)

[Appellant Frank Marrone and six other defendants were charged with kidnapping and conspiracy to commit kidnapping. Seven overt acts were charged. Appellant argued that the victim (in exchange for a share of the ransom) agreed to simulate a kidnapping. Appellant argues that he cannot be guilty of a "simulated" kidnapping. In this excerpt of the opinion, the court discusses the impact of a "simulated" kidnapping on the conspiracy charge.]

GRIFFIN, P. J.

The gist of the offense of conspiracy is the formation of a combination with others to do some unlawful act or some lawful act by unlawful means. Conspiracy is a separate and distinct offense from the crime which is a substantive object of the conspiracy. Conspiracy is not synonymous with aiding or abetting or participating; it implies an agreement to commit a crime, while to aid and abet requires actual participation in the act constituting the offense. A conspirator does not have to participate in the crime conspired. In a previous case, this court held that common design is the essence of conspiracy, and the crime can be committed whether or not the parties comprehend its entire scope, whether they act in separate groups or together, or whether they act by the same or different means known or unknown to some of them, if their actions consistently lead to the same unlawful result. That case was a prosecution for conspiracy to violate narcotics laws. In one count, the defendant was charged with conspiring to encourage another to violate a law, which had been declared to be unconstitutional. This court held that, that section being unconstitutional, there can be no criminal conspiracy to violate a statute which does not state a crime or public offense.

In another case, the court said that as a general proposition larceny is not committed when the property is taken with the consent of its owner. In the instant case, the trial court instructed the jury that if the victim and the defendant Marrone consented to and simulated the crime of kidnapping, the defendant Marrone could not be convicted of the crime of kidnapping. This is no doubt the accepted rule.

[One legal writer] recites as a recognized rule that: 'When the charge is for criminal conspiracy, it is said to be essential that the purpose of the conspiracy be alleged and that the averment show that that purpose was one for which it is criminal to agree.'

[The court in an Illinois case] declared that: 'It is not sufficient to sustain a conviction on a particular charge to prove that the defendant is guilty of some other charge or of generally bad and criminal conduct, but the proof must establish his guilt of the particular charge in the indictment.'

The prosecution must show that the accused intended to do an unlawful act. It therefore appears that if Frank Marrone and the victim, Antonio Alessio, entered into an agreement to simulate the kidnapping of the victim for the purpose of ransom, it not being an offense, the agreement and acts of the defendant Marrone would not amount to a conspiracy to commit the act charged.

[Judgment is affirmed on other grounds.]

F. Question

♦ If there had been no question regarding the "victim's" cooperation, would there have been any doubt regarding the defendant's guilt? Why or why not?

III. ATTEMPT

A. Comments

As the following statute makes clear, attempt goes farthest towards completion of the underlying offense. Observe how the Legislature has determined the punishment for attempt. The Legislature has linked punishment for attempt crimes to the underlying completed offense. When you read the following statutes, make a special note of the mental elements required to support an attempt conviction.

B. Statute

Penal Code section 664

Every person who attempts to commit any crime, but fails, or is prevented or intercepted in its perpetration, shall be punished where no provision is made by law for the punishment of those attempts, as follows:

(a) If the crime attempted is punishable by imprisonment in the state prison, the person guilty of the attempt shall be punished by imprisonment in the state one-half the term of imprisonment prescribed upon a conviction of the offense

prison for one-half the term of imprisonment prescribed upon a conviction of the offense attempted.

(b) If the crime attempted is punishable by imprisonment in a county jail, the person guilty of the attempt shall be punished by imprisonment in a county jail for a term not exceeding one-half the term of imprisonment prescribed upon a conviction of the offense attempted

Penal Code section 21a

An attempt to commit a crime consists of two elements: a specific intent to commit the crime, and a direct but ineffectual act done toward its commission.

C. Comments

The following case discusses the relationship between the crime of attempt and the defendant's inability to complete the offense. When reading the case, pay special attention to the facts that prevented the defendants from completing the crime. Was this a case of legal impossibility or is it a case of factual impossibility? (Note: Legal impossibility exists when the defendant cannot complete a crime because of a legal technicality. On the other hand, factual impossibility exists when it appears impossible from the facts that the crime can be completed.)

D. Case

People v. Figelman
District Court of Appeal, Fourth District
33 Cal.App.2d 100 (1939)

Griffin, J.

The defendants and appellants were charged with attempted grand theft from the person of one A. F. Hitchcock.

Appellants contend that the evidence was insufficient to sustain the verdict and judgement [because there was] only an ineffectual effort to pick or take property from an empty pocket on the person of one Hitchcock, It is argued that by reason of the fact that the evidence established that there was no money in the particular pocket at the time, it would be an absurdity to hold that a person could attempt to steal that which is not there to be stolen.

The case cited by appellants sets forth the elements of attempt, i. e., (1) a specific intent to commit the crime and (2) a direct ineffectual act done towards its commission. It is there stated also that a mere intention to commit a specified crime does not amount to an attempt, nor is mere preparation alone sufficient, but there must be something more than mere menaces, preparation or planning.

The overt act need not be the last proximate act to the consummation of the offense attempted to be perpetrated, but it must approach sufficiently near it to stand either as the first or some subsequent step in a direct movement towards the commission of the offense after the preparations constitutes an act done toward the commission of a crime.

It would be useless to attempt to lay down any rule by which an act might be characterized as overt or otherwise in a particular case. General principles must be applied in each case as nearly as can be, with a view to working out substantial justice. The question of what overt act is sufficient to constitute an attempt to commit a crime has been the subject of much discussion by both text writers and courts, and there is some conflict in the decisions. In the early English cases the view seems to have been adopted that to constitute an attempt the overt act must be the final one towards the completion of the offense, and of such a character that unless it had been interrupted, the offense itself would have been committed.

This extreme doctrine has not been accepted in this country and certainly not in this state. But assuming that mere preparation is not in all cases an attempt to commit the crime, it is well settled in this country that it is not necessary to constitute an attempt that the act done should be the last proximate one for the completion of the offense.

It is the condition of appellants' minds and their conduct in the attempted consummation of their design which determines whether there was an actual attempt to commit the crime. Here appellants did their utmost to effect the consummation of the crime intended by them. They failed only by reason of a cause or causes not previously apparent to them.

'It is a well-settled principle of criminal law in this country,' says our Supreme Court 'that where the are made. Whenever the design of a person to commit a crime is clearly shown, slight acts done in furtherance of that design will constitute an attempt, and the courts should not destroy the practical and common-sense administration of the law with subtleties as to what constitutes preparation and what criminal result of an attempt is not accomplished simply because of an obstruction in the way of the thing to be operated upon, and these facts are unknown to the aggressor at the time, the criminal attempt is committed. Thus an attempt to pick one's pocket or to steal from his person, when he has nothing in his pocket or on his person, completes the offense to the same degree as if he had money or other personal property which could be the subject of larceny.'

We cannot conclude that the evidence is insufficient because the victim's money was in his front pocket. We are thoroughly convinced that appellants' argument must be rejected as untenable and that the evidence in the instant case establishes the inescapable corollary and the conclusion is irresistible that the attempt to commit the offense has been sufficiently charged and that the offense as pleaded has been sufficiently established.

The judgments and orders appealed from are affirmed

E. Questions

◆ Do you think the court reach the right result in this case? Why or why not?

◆ Apply the court's reasoning to the following situations:

The defendant attempts to kill a homeless man, not knowing at the time he stabbed him that he was already dead. Should he be found guilty of attempted murder?

The defendant attempts to steal a Monet painting on exhibit at the DeYoung Museum. Defendant breaks into the museum, not knowing that the Monet had traveled south to San Diego the week before. Is an attempted theft conviction warranted in this case?

IV. Self-Assessment

1. Of the three inchoate offenses, conspiracy is the crime closest to the completed offense.
    A. True   B. False

2. Unlike most other California statutes, the statute defining solicitation contains within its provisions the evidentiary requirements for proof.
    A. True   B. False

3. The crime of conspiracy in California requires no overt act for the crime of conspiracy.
    A. True   B. False

4. "Impossibility" is always an available defense to an attempt crime.
    A. True   B. False

5. Under California law, the crime of attempt is a general intent crime.
    A. True   B. False

CHAPTER SEVEN

Defenses To Criminal Liability: Justifications

Under the common law, there were two types of defenses: justifications (where the defendant has committed an act that the law does not want to prohibit) and excuses (where the law does not consider the defendant's actions blameworthy.) In this chapter you will look at statutes and cases discussing defenses to criminal liability. Specifically, you will get an opportunity to look at justifications that absolve the criminal defendant from liability under California law. Some of these concepts will be familiar to you from general principles of common law. Some, however, will be more modern twists on well-established principles.

I. SELF-DEFENSE

A. Comments

Penal Code sections 197 and 198 set forth California's law of self-defense and define "reasonable fear" which permits a defendant to invoke the law of self-defense. When reading Penal Code section 197, focus on the four categories of justifiable self-defense. As for the reasonable fear requirement of Penal Code section 198, note that the law states that the reasonable person standard is the proper test to determine if the fear was sufficient to constitute justifiable homicide.

B. Statutes

Self-defense: Penal Code section 197

Homicide is justifiable when committed by any person in any of the following cases:

1. When resisting any attempt to murder any person, or to commit a felony, or to do some great bodily injury upon any person; or,

2. When committed in defense of habitation, property, or person, against one who manifestly intends or endeavors, by violence or surprise, to commit a felony, or against one who manifestly intends and endeavors, in a violent, riotous or tumultuous manner, to enter the habitation of another for the purpose of offering violence to any person therein; or,

3. When committed in the lawful defense of such person, or of a wife or husband, parent, child, master, mistress, or servant of such person, when there is reasonable ground to apprehend a design to commit a felony or to do some great bodily injury, and imminent danger of such design being accomplished; but such person, or the person in whose behalf the defense was made, if he was the assailant or engaged in mutual combat, must really and in good faith have endeavored to decline any further

struggle before the homicide was committed; or,

4. When necessarily committed in attempting, by lawful ways and means, to apprehend any person for any felony committed, or in lawfully suppressing any riot, or in lawfully keeping and preserving the peace.

Reasonable fear: Penal Code section 198

Justifiable homicide; sufficiency of fear:

A bare fear of the commission of any of the offenses mentioned in subdivisions 2 and 3 of Section 197, to prevent which homicide may be lawfully committed, is not sufficient to justify it. But the circumstances must be sufficient to excite the fears of a reasonable person, and the party killing must have acted under the influence of such fears alone.

C. Comments

The following case discusses reasonable fear. Obviously, in order to make a determination whether or not a defendant's fear was "reasonable" the court must focus on detailed, specific facts. To make a determination whether a not killings were committed with complete justification, the court relies on the record as a whole to reach its decision. Also note, the case discusses the doctrine off transferred intent which you have already in studied in Chapter Three.

D. Case

PEOPLE V. LEAVITT
Court of Appeal, Second District, Division 4, California.
156 Cal.App.3d 500 (1984)

KINGSLEY, J.

Defendant and Lusko were business partners, sharing a suite of offices in Torrance. Defendant's wife, Grace, worked in the business and had daily contact with Lusko, while defendant largely occupied his working days elsewhere in connection with his other, independent, business interests. Defendant, Lusko and Grace socialized together as a threesome.

In March 1981, Grace left defendant, without warning and without telling him where she was going, and moved into a condominium rented for her by Lusko. At the time, Grace was considering divorcing defendant and accepting Lusko's proposal of marriage. Subsequently, defendant called the Torrance suite several times, attempting to locate Grace; pursuant to Grace's instructions, he was falsely told that she had stopped coming into work and that no one knew where she was. Defendant also hired a private detective to follow Lusko, but Lusko appeared to notice that he was being tailed, and failed to lead the detective to Grace.

On April 26, defendant bought a gun under a false name. The next day he went to the door of the Torrance suite, parking his car somewhere other than in the suite lot, but did not go in. The day after, on April 28, he again went to the suite and again parked his car elsewhere. This time he entered. According to prosecution witnesses, a brief series of shots was heard along with a woman's screams, within seconds after defendant's entry. A short time later, defendant approached two employees and asked them where Grace was; he pointed a gun, while pulling the trigger, at each of them, but the gun clicked without firing.

Defendant drove away, stopping to throw the gun in a trash can, and eventually arrived at a hospital, where he was examined and admitted. He was found to be dazed and confused, suffering from acute high blood pressure, and displaying a bruise on his head. Police arrested him at the hospital.

The shots that defendant had fired in the suite killed Lusko and Robert Richards, a customer of Lusko's who had entered the suite to pick up a receipt just before he was shot. The bodies lay in adjoining offices, Richards' with a gunshot wound in the back of his head fired from a distance of 20 inches or more, and Lusko's with two gunshot wounds in the body (one a defensive-type wound), a third to the back of the head and a fourth in the right ear. The latter two wounds were both mortal and both inflicted from a distance of one to two inches.

The only eyewitnesses to the killings were defendant, and Grace, who testified on his behalf. According to Grace, she greeted defendant when he entered her office, but became frightened and screamed for Lusko when defendant approached her; Lusko then ran in, followed by Richards. Grace heard shots and ran away. This testimony was somewhat contrary to what Grace had told the police on the day of the killings. At that time, she had stated that she witnessed no confrontation and had not seen defendant at all; rather, she only heard some shots and saw a bloodied Lusko running while she was coming out of the bathroom.

Defendant testified that when Grace screamed for Lusko, Lusko and Richards ran up and attacked him, Richards hitting him with fists and Lusko with a club, while telling him he was about to die. Defendant hit back at both men, then shot at Lusko and

next at Richards, after which Richards was 'out of the picture.' The fight with Lusko continued until defendant, in a dazed state, shot at him several more times.

Regarding the events leading up to the killings, defendant testified that he suspected Lusko not only of knowing where Grace was (though not of any romantic involvement with her), but also of stealing from the partnership. When defendant told Lusko of the latter suspicion, Lusko threatened to 'sic' a hired killer on him. Defendant took the threat seriously, but nonetheless made an April 28 appointment to see Lusko because of pressing business matters. He bought the gun to protect himself in the event Lusko used the appointment as an opportunity to have him killed, and went to the suite a day early in order to avoid a possible ambush. Since Lusko was not there on the 27th, defendant returned on the 28th.

Defendant denied pulling the trigger on the two employees he approached after the killings. He had no explanation for why he had given a false name when buying the gun, other than that he did not want anyone to know of the purchase.

The jury was instructed that a defendant who kills in self-defense is guilty of no crime and that a defendant who kills out of the honest but unreasonable belief in the necessity to act in self-defense is guilty only of manslaughter. Defendant requested that the jury also be instructed on how the doctrine of 'transferred intent' applies to each of these defenses. His proposed instructions stated that (1) if defendant killed Richards inadvertently while exercising self-defense as to Lusko, then he should be acquitted of the Richards homicide; and (2) if he killed Richards inadvertently while exercising an honest but unreasonable belief in the necessity to act in self-defense as to Lusko, then he could be found guilty of manslaughter for the Richards homicide. Defendant now contends that the trial court erred in refusing these instructions.

We agree that the doctrine of transferred intent is available as a defense in California. Under this doctrine, just as 'one's criminal intent follows the corresponding criminal act to its unintended consequences,' so too one's lack of criminal intent follows the corresponding non-criminal act to its unintended consequences. Thus, a defendant is guilty of no crime if his legitimate act in self-defense results in the inadvertent death of an innocent bystander.

Here, however, there was no substantial evidence to support a theory of transferred intent as to the Richards homicide, because the evidence showed that Richards' death could not have been the inadvertent result of defendant's attempt to defend himself from Lusko. Defendant testified that he first took a 'potshot' at Lusko in office number 3, Richards subsequently circled around him, he then shot 'at' Richards after which Richards was 'out of the picture,' and that no more shots were fired until his struggle with Lusko moved into office number 4. The coroner testified that the shot which killed Richards resulted in instantaneous death; Richards' body was found in office number 3, and Lusko's in number 4. This evidence shows that the only shot which could have killed Richards was the one defendant fired 'at' him. Had Richards been hit by the initial 'potshot,' he would not have been alive to subsequently circle around defendant; had he been hit by any of the shots fired in number 4, he would not have been alive to move back to number 3, nor would he have been 'out of the picture' before these shots were fired. As such, the evidence is irreconcilable with the theory that Richards was inadvertently felled by a shot meant for Lusko.

Defendant next contends that there was insufficient evidence of manslaughter in that the record establishes complete self-defense as a matter of law. We disagree.

'[W]here the evidence is uncontroverted and establishes all of the elements for a finding of self-defense it may be held as a matter of law that the killing was justified; however, where some of the evidence tends to show a situation in which a killing may not be justified then the issue is a question of fact for the jury to determine. [Citation.] Where the evidence is uncontroverted, but reasonable persons could differ on whether the resort to force was justified or whether the force resorted to was excessive, then the issue is a question of fact for the trier of fact. [Citations.]'

Here, assuming-as defendant does-that we must accept the jury's implied finding that defendant was justified in using some degree of force, reasonable persons could certainly differ on whether the force resorted to was excessive. Both victims were shot in the back of the head and at least one of Lusko's wounds was administered while he was incapacitated and dying if not already dead. Lusko may have been armed with a club, but Richards was weaponless. Defendant's subsequent action in pulling the trigger on two employees was highly probative of a willingness to attempt unjustified violence.

Moreover, if the degree of force used was influenced by any motivations aside from a belief in the necessity to act in self-defense, then manslaughter was an appropriate verdict on that ground alone. In order for homicide to be completely justified in self-defense, 'the circumstances must be sufficient to excite the fears of a reasonable person, and the party killing must have acted under the influence of such fears alone.' (Pen. Code, Section 198), Here, in light of the evidence of a rather classic motive and of defendant's clandestine gun purchase, a reasonable trier could have found that, even assuming defendant had the right to use some force in self-defense, he was less than candid regarding the degree of danger he actually faced, and his response was attributable more to a preconceived intent to kill than to the actual danger.

Our task is not so complex as was the jury's. We need only determine whether the record as a whole could support a finding of two intentional killings committed with less than complete justification. The record is more than sufficient in this respect.

[Judgment affirmed.]

E. Questions

♦ Do you think the defendant was justified in using some degree of force?

♦ Do you think that the defendant exceeded the degree of force that a reasonable person would have used under the circumstances? If so, what level of force do you think would have been appropriate under these circumstances?

II. MISCELLANEOUS STATUTORY PROVISIONS

A. Comments

The following three statutes contain examples of the use of justifiable force. Note the particularity with which the Legislature permits the use of justifiable force.

B. Statutes

Defense of Home: Penal Code section 198.5

Any person using force intended or likely to cause death or great bodily injury within his or her residence shall be presumed to have held a reasonable fear of imminent peril of death or great bodily injury to self, family, or a member of the household when that force is used against another person, not a member of the family or household, who unlawfully and forcibly enters or has unlawfully and forcibly entered the residence and the person using the force knew or had reason to believe that an unlawful and forcible entry occurred.

As used in this section, great bodily injury means a significant or substantial physical injury.

Execution of Public Duties: Penal Code section 196

JUSTIFIABLE HOMICIDE BY PUBLIC OFFICERS. Homicide is justifiable when committed by public officers and those acting by their command in their aid and assistance, either--

1. In obedience to any judgment of a competent Court; or,

2. When necessarily committed in overcoming actual resistance to the execution of some legal process, or in the discharge of any other legal duty; or,

3. When necessarily committed in retaking felons who have been rescued or

have escaped, or when necessarily committed in arresting persons charged with felony, and who are fleeing from justice or resisting such arrest.

c. Resisting Unlawful Arrests: Penal Code section 692

LAWFUL RESISTANCE, BY WHOM MADE.
Lawful resistance to the commission of a public offense may be made:
1. By the party about to be injured;
2. By other parties.

C.   Question

♦ Although many statutes are couched in more general language, these statutes are quite specific. Why do you think the Legislature drafted these statutes with particularity?

III. Self-Assessment

1.   Excuse defenses were used at common law for purposes of relieving the defendant of all criminal responsibility.
      A. True   B. False

2.   A person who kills another at the direction of a public officer is not guilty of homicide, even if the victim was not posing a threat to the perpetrator.
      A. True   B. False

3.   Under California law, a person is entitled to resist an unlawful arrest.
      A. True   B. False

4.   "Reasonable fear" is based on a subjective standard.
      A. True   B. False

CHAPTER EIGHT

Defenses To Criminal Liability: Excuses

At common law, excuse defenses are based on the concept that defendants are not morally responsible for their conduct, when their conduct occurs under certain circumstances, such as insanity. Most of these California specific materials are similar to general principles of American law. However, both the language of the statutes and particularly the court opinions which follow them bear the stamp of California.

I. AGE

A. Comments

California Penal Code section 26 statutorily defines presumptions regarding persons who are capable of committing crimes. The language of the statutes often sounds archaic, reflecting their common law heritage.

B. Statute

Penal Code section 26

Persons capable of committing crime; exceptions

All persons are capable of committing crimes except those belonging to the following classes:

One--Children under the age of 14, in the absence of clear proof that at the time of committing the act charged against them, they knew its wrongfulness.

Two--Idiots.

Three--Persons who committed the act or made the omission charged under an ignorance or mistake of fact, which disproves any criminal intent.

Four--Persons who committed the act charged without being conscious thereof.

Five--Persons who committed the act or made the omission charged through misfortune or by accident, when it appears that there was no evil design, intention, or culpable negligence.

Six--Persons (unless the crime be punishable with death) who committed the act or made the omission charged under threats or menaces sufficient to show that they had reasonable cause to and did believe their lives would be endangered if they refused.

74

II. INSANITY

A. Comments

"Insanity" is a legal concept not a clinical or psychological concept. As a legal defense, insanity is well accepted. However, the definition of insanity varies among different states. Some states are more generous in defying insanity, while others are more restrictive.

In the following statutes, the California Legislature makes clear that personality disorders alone do not constitute insanity. Furthermore, the statutes plainly state that expert witnesses are not to make determinations of insanity. Rather, the determination of insanity is one that is be made by the trier of fact. Thus, in California, it is not proper for an expert witness to testify whether or not a defendant was "insane." (You will note that Penal Code section 29 makes reference to the "guilt phase" of a trial. Under California law, where a defendant's sanity is at issue, the trial is bifurcated, with the guilt phase and sanity phase tried separately.)

B. Statutes

Penal Code section 25.5

Basis of defense; plea of not guilty by reason of insanity:

In any criminal proceeding in which a plea of not guilty by reason of insanity is entered, this defense shall not be found by the trier of fact solely on the basis of a personality or adjustment disorder, a seizure disorder, or an addiction to, or abuse of, intoxicating substances.

Penal Code section 29

Mental state; restriction on expert testimony; determination by trier of fact:

In the guilt phase of a criminal action, any expert testifying about a defendant's mental illness, mental disorder, or mental defect shall not testify as to whether the defendant had or did not have required mental states which include, but are not limited to, purpose, intent, knowledge, or malice aforethought, for the crimes charged. The question as to whether the defendant had or did not have the required mental states shall be decided by the trier of fact.

III. DIMINISHED CAPACITY

A. Comments

In reading the following statute, observe that the Legislature has decreed that the statute abolishing diminished capacity applies to both adult proceedings as well as juvenile court proceedings.

B. Statute

Penal Code section 25a

The defense of diminished capacity is hereby abolished. In a criminal action, as well as any juvenile court proceeding, evidence concerning an accused person's intoxication, trauma, mental illness, disease, or defect shall not be admissible to show or negate capacity to form the particular purpose, intent, motive, malice aforethought, knowledge, or other mental state required for the commission of the crime charged.

IV. MENTAL DISEASE OR DEFECT

A. Comments

Penal Code section 28 contains two important points. First, mental disease or defect is not synonymous with insanity. Second, the statute specifically rejects any reliance on diminished capacity, diminished responsibility, or irresistible impulse as excuses for criminal conduct. Also, as you read, you will notice that a "mental disease or defect" is not defined. The issue is one that must be decided on a case-by-case basis with individual defendants.

B. Statute

Penal Code section 28

Evidence of mental disease, mental defect or mental disorder:

(a) Evidence of mental disease, mental defect, or mental disorder shall not be admitted to show or negate the capacity to form any mental state, including, but not limited to, purpose, intent, knowledge, premeditation, deliberation, or malice aforethought, with which the accused committed the act. Evidence of mental disease, mental defect, or mental disorder is admissible solely on the issue of whether or not the accused actually formed a required specific intent, premeditated, deliberated, or harbored malice aforethought, when a specific intent crime is charged.

(b) As a matter of public policy there shall be no defense of diminished capacity, diminished responsibility, or irresistible impulse in a criminal action or juvenile adjudication hearing

C. Question

♦ Penal Code section 28 specifically bars the use of mental disease or defect as an excuses for criminal conduct. However, the statute does provide that mental disease or defect is admissible in certain circumstances. Make certain that you understand when a mental disease or defect is admissible. When can mental disease or defect be used to a defendant's benefit (even if it cannot be relied on to excuse criminal conduct)? [Hint: Consider the defendant's required state of mind to commit a specific intent crime.]

V. "SYNDROME" DEFENSES

A. Comments

In recent years, there has been an increase in defenses that have been dubbed "syndrome defenses." These new defenses have multiplied in recent years. These syndrome defenses have included such varied defenses as rape trauma syndrome, the battered women syndrome, and the cultural defense. (The *Wu* case, below, relies on one of the most difficult "syndrome" defenses, the cultural defenses).

Some legal commentators have used the phrase, the "abuse excuse" to characterize a defendant's use of personal hardships (especially child abuse in his or her own adolescence) to try to minimize the culpability of his or her misconduct. These 'abuse excuses" or other syndrome defenses differ from traditional excuse defenses in that they are more commonly used to mitigate the seriousness of the offense (that is, the sentence that is imposed) rather than to exonerate the defendant from all criminal liability.

The *Wu* case is not citable as authority. The subsequent history at the beginning of the case states that the case was ordered not published. However, the case is included for your studies because of the interesting problem that it presents: the impact that culture may have on a person's mental state. Even though this case is depublished does not mean that this is a moot issue. There are other cases involving the use of the cultural defense across the United State. In many of these cases, defendants have relied on culture to mitigate either their crime or their punishment.

This case is particularly important because it, along with a few other unpublished California cases and a New York case, sparked a controversy among legal scholars about the use of culture as a valid defense. As you read the case, consider how this defendant raises the issue of culture in her defense.

B. Cases

PEOPLE V. WU
Court of Appeal of California, Fourth Appellate District
Formerly published at 235 Cal. App. 3d 614 (1991)

NOTICE:

NOT CITABLE - ORDERED NOT PUBLISHED

TIMLIN, Acting P. J.

I

INTRODUCTION

Helen Wu, also known as Helen Hamg Ieng Chau (defendant), was convicted of the second-degree murder of her son, Sidney Wu (Sidney), following trial by jury. Her motion for a new trial was denied and she was sentenced to a prison term of 15 years to life. She filed timely notice of appeal, and contends that the court committed reversible error by (1) refusing to instruct the jury on the defense of unconsciousness, and (2) refusing to instruct the jury on her theory of the case.

Initially, we note that the facts presented at trial, while not in conflict as to certain specific events, did vary considerably as to whether defendant had "motherly" feelings toward the victim, her son, whether she was a "traditional" Chinese woman, and, based on the above noted factors, whether the motive for his death was a desire for revenge against Sidney's father or guilt over having not taken good care of the child and fear that he would be ill-treated in the future.

The prosecution's theory seems to have been that defendant killed Sidney because of anger at Sidney's father, and to get revenge. The defense's theory was that defendant believed that Sidney, who lived with his father in the United States, was looked down upon and was ill-treated by everyone except his paternal grandmother because he had been borne out of wedlock, and that when she learned that the grandmother was dying of cancer, she felt trapped and, in an intense emotional upheaval, strangled Sidney and then attempted to kill herself so that she could take care of Sidney in the afterlife.

The only issues on appeal are whether the trial court committed prejudicial error by refusing to give two instructions requested by defendant, one related to the defense of unconsciousness, and one related to the effect her cultural background might have had on her state of mind when she killed Sidney.

***

II

FACTS

Defendant was born in 1943 in Saigon, China. At the age of 19, in about 1962 or 1963, she moved to Macau. She married and had a daughter, who was 25 years old at the time of the trial of this matter in February 1990. In 1963, she met Gary Wu (Wu), the son of one of her friends. That same year Wu went to the United States, and married Susanna Ku. He opened several restaurants in the Palm Springs area.

After eight years of marriage, defendant was divorced, and became employed, writing statistics for greyhound races. She was apparently betrothed to remarry in the mid-1970's, but her fiancé developed lung cancer and died. His sister, Nancy Chung (Chung), became defendant's close friend and confidante. According to Chung, Chung's brother made her promise to help defendant because defendant was a kind, moral person, not greedy, but too trusting.

In 1978 or 1979, defendant was contacted by Wu, who had heard that she was divorced and had a daughter. Wu told her his marriage was unsatisfactory because his wife could not have children. According to defendant, Wu told her he planned to divorce his wife. They discussed the possibility that defendant could come to the United States and conceive a child for Wu. Defendant believed Wu would marry her after he divorced his wife. Defendant was in love with Wu, and Wu gave defendant money to deposit in a joint bank account and sent her $20,000 so she could apply for a visa to the United States.

In November 1979, defendant came to the United States. When defendant arrived, he hugged and kissed her, told her his divorce proceedings would be completed soon and he definitely would marry her. Defendant lived with Wu's mother. Wu's wife believed she was a family friend. At Wu's request defendant had brought $15,000 of the money he had sent her and they opened a joint account together.

In December 1979 or January 1980, Wu and his wife Susanna were divorced; however, Wu did not tell defendant that he had obtained a divorce. Defendant conceived a child by Wu in the early part of 1980, and then moved into an apartment, where she was visited by Wu. After the child, Sidney, was born in November 1980, Wu apparently made no overtures regarding marriage. Depressed, defendant, who could not speak English, could not drive, and who had no support system in the United States, told Wu she intended to return to Macau, apparently expecting that this information would cause him to try to persuade her to stay.

Wu did not try to persuade defendant to stay, so in February 1981, she returned home but left Sidney with Wu. She could not take the baby because no one knew she had a baby and she and Sidney would have been humiliated in China. She told only her closest friend, Chung, who had already learned of defendant's pregnancy from Chung's daughters who were going to college in the United States, that she had borne a child out of wedlock; such a thing was apparently considered to be particularly shameful among people of defendant's culture.

From 1981 to 1988 defendant regularly asked Wu to bring Sidney to visit her, but to no avail. In 1981, Wu said he could only come for the summer and defendant told him she wanted Sidney to stay and if he could not, then she did not want to see him because it would be harder after he left. In 1984, Wu asked defendant to visit him but she did not want to come until she was married, then she and her son would have dignity and status.

In September 1987, Wu told defendant he needed money for his restaurant business. She finally told him that if he would bring Sidney to visit her, she would loan him money for his restaurants.

In January 1988, Wu brought Sidney, who was then seven years old, to visit defendant in Hong Kong. Defendant showed him $100,000 cash and a receipt for a certificate of deposit of a million Hong Kong dollars. Both the cash and the deposited funds had been loaned to defendant by Chung, after defendant admitted to Chung that she had lured Wu into bringing Sidney to see her with the promise of a loan. On that visit, Wu proposed marriage, but defendant declined, depressed over the fact that the marriage proposal seemed to be because of "her" money, and because she did not know if Wu were still married or not. Defendant was so discouraged by these beliefs that she attempted to throw herself out of the window of Chung's apartment, but was restrained by Chung, Chung's daughter, and a servant.

According to Chung, Wu, while in Hong Kong, suggested that if Chung invested money in his restaurant business, he could be her sponsor for American citizenship, because the communists would be taking over control of Hong Kong in a few years. Chung declined, saying she did not know anything about the restaurant business. Wu then said there was another way to help her, and when she asked how, he said he could marry her. Chung asked, "What about Helen?" Wu replied by indicating that there was enough time for him to first marry Chung and to later marry defendant. Wu later wrote Chung a letter suggesting the marriage, which he followed up with a telephone call asking if Chung had received his letter. Chung politely cooled these advances by denying she had received the letter, which, however, she saved, and which was produced at trial. Chung did not tell defendant of Wu's advances.

During the next year defendant worked and traveled with Chung. She wanted to see Sidney but she did not know if Wu was still married and did not want to upset her son's life. In August 1989, defendant, who was on a vacation trip to Las Vegas and San Francisco with Chung, as Chung's guest, apparently heard that Wu's mother, Sidney's paternal grandmother, was terminally ill, so she came to Palm Springs to visit. While there, she was told by the grandmother that when the grandmother died, she, defendant, should take Sidney because Wu would not take good care of him. She was given similar advice by Sandy, Wu's cousin.

Toward the end of August, Wu told defendant that they were going to Las Vegas. Defendant stated she did not want to go. Wu told her it was important that she go, as "she was the main character" because they were going to be married. Defendant and Wu were married on September 1. On September 5, they went to Los Angeles to consult an attorney about immigration law. Defendant, following the marriage and consultation, was still of the opinion that Wu had married her because of his belief that she had a lot of money. During the drive home from Los Angeles, this belief was reinforced by Wu's comments. When she asked if he had married her for her money, he responded that until she produced the money, she had no right to speak. Defendant asked Wu whether the marriage was not worthwhile simply for the purpose of legitimizing Sidney, and Wu replied that many people could give him children. Defendant told Wu he would be sorry. She later explained that remark meant that she was thinking about returning to Macau and killing herself.

After the trip to the lawyer, defendant told Wu to get her a plane ticket for September 16 so that she could return to Macau. She asked him not to let Sidney know that she was leaving, because she wished to have 10 days of happiness with her son. Wu wanted to know if defendant was going to get the money, which made her very angry. Defendant gave Wu $6,300, her own money, and told him he liked money too much.

On September 9, the evening of the killing, defendant was playing with Sidney. Earlier that day defendant had interceded on Sidney's behalf when Wu hit Sidney when Sidney would not get out of the family car. Wu had gone to the restaurant to put on two birthday parties, apparently for his friend Rosemary. Defendant and Sidney played and talked, and defendant told Sidney that she knew what he liked because of the mother-child bond between them.

Sidney told defendant that Wu said she was "psychotic" and "very troublesome." He then told defendant that

Rosemary was Wu's girlfriend, and that the house they lived in belonged to Rosemary. He also told her that Wu made him get up early so Wu could take Rosemary's daughters to school in the morning and if he did not get up, Wu would scold and beat him. He said Wu loved Rosemary more than him. Defendant began to think about what she had been told by Sidney's grandmother and Sandy concerning her taking care of Sidney. She began to experience heart palpitations and to have trouble breathing. She told Sidney she wanted to die, and asked him if he would go too. He clung to her neck and cried. She then left the bedroom, and obtained a rope by cutting the cord off a window blind. She returned to the bedroom and strangled Sidney. According to defendant, she did not remember the strangling itself. She stopped breathing, and when she started breathing again, she was surprised at how quickly Sidney had died. She then wrote a note to Wu to the effect that he had bullied her too much and "now this air is vented. I can die with no regret," but did not mention Sidney's killing in the note. She then attempted to strangle herself, failed, went to the kitchen and slashed her left wrist with a knife, and then returned to the bedroom and lay down next to Sidney on the bed, having first placed a waste-paper basket under her bleeding wrist to catch the blood so that the floor would not be dirtied.

Wu returned home several hours later, and discovered defendant and Sidney. He called the police, and the paramedics were also summoned. The police determined that Sidney was dead. The paramedics tested defendant's vital signs, and determined that although her pulse and blood pressure were normal, she exhibited a decreased level of consciousness.

Dr. Michael Mostyn, the doctor who saw defendant when she was taken to the emergency room, testified that she had cut the veins in her wrist, but not the arteries, which are normally deeper beneath the surface than the veins, and that venous bleeding, if not irritated or prevented from clotting with the use of hot water, would stop, and that in his opinion a person who had simply slashed their veins, rather than their arteries, would not die. He also testified that this fact was not common knowledge to the "man on the street."

Dr. Saul Faerstein, a physician specializing in psychiatry, testified, after reviewing pictures of the wounds on defendant's wrists, that they did not appear to have been inflicted by a "malingerer," that they were the type of wound which a layperson, particularly one who was agitated, severely depressed, or confused, might make in a serious attempt to commit suicide. He also testified, as to the decreased state of consciousness in which defendant was found, that defendant might have fainted and then remained in a reduced level of consciousness, but that "we're talking about something more than fainting here," and "there are many, people may disassociate, people may have emotional reactions which are acute and severe, where suddenly they become confused, as a result of shock, as a result of some acute shock. Clearly the circumstances of what was going on with her son were overwhelming kinds of trauma that she was experiencing, and I believe that the shock she was experiencing were [sic] traumatic but psychological in or[i]gin."

Chung testified that two days after Sidney's death, she received a telephone call from Wu, who was fishing for information about how defendant had accumulated the money he believed she possessed. Chung evaded his questions, and then Wu told her that defendant had strangled Sidney and "committed" suicide, but that defendant had been saved. Chung then hired an attorney in Hong Kong to help defendant.

Defendant was charged with murder (Pen. Code, § 187) and, following a trial by jury, was convicted of second degree murder.

III

DISCUSSION

A. The Trial Court Committed Reversible Error by Refusing to Instruct the Jury on the Defense of Unconsciousness

[In the first part of the discussion, the Court discusses the defendant's contention that the trial court erred in failing to give an unconsciousness instruction to the jury. The Court agreed and remanded [sent the case back] to the trial court for retrial. In the second part of the discussion, the Court dealt with the defendant's assertion that the trial court erred in failing to instruct on the impact that the defendant's culture had on her state of mind.]

B. Upon Retrial, the Trial Court Should, if so Requested, Instruct the Jury on How Evidence of Defendant's Cultural Background Relates to Defendant's Theory of the Case

Defendant contends that the trial court erred by refusing to give an instruction which pinpointed a significant aspect of her theory of the case, i.e., an instruction which told the jury it could choose to consider the evidence of defendant's cultural background in determining the presence or absence of the various mental states which were elements of the crimes with which she was charged. we have already determined that the judgment must be reversed because of the failure to give an instruction on unconsciousness, we will address the issue of the propriety of an instruction pinpointing the cultural background theory of defendant's case for purposes of guiding the trial court on retrial.

Defendant requested the following instruction:

"You have received evidence of defendant's cultural background and the relationship of her culture to her mental state. You may, but are not required to, consider that the [sic] evidence in determining the presence or absence of the essential mental states of the crimes defined in these instructions, or in determining any other issue in this case."

At trial, the prosecutor objected to this instruction on the ground that "it's real touchy, in a major case, to be messing around with non-pattern jury instructions, ... People smarter than myself have put together all the pattern jury instructions. I think they have covered every conceivable type of crime, certainly in this case they have, and I don't think that we need to be giving the jury extra instructions."

In addition, the People stated the concern that there was no appellate law on the subject of instructions "cultural defenses," and that "the problem, apparently, to me, is that the jury has heard evidence about that, and whether we called it cultural defense, I don't know, but they certainly have heard the word 'culture' probably a thousand times in this trial; maybe not a thousand, but hundreds.

"So from that perspective, I assume counsel can argue, well, hey, you know, now that we've talked about it, we've got to give them some guidance of what to do with it. But I still oppose it, doesn't it [sic] make any sense. I just think we are making law that we simply are not in a position to make. There is no guidance in the appellate courts as far as I know on the issue of cultural jury instructions or cultural defense. I think the two pattern mental state instructions . . . cover that as best as they can be covered."

The trial court expressed the concern that the instruction would be "telling [the jury] that is the law." Although defendant's attorney specifically pointed out that the instruction merely told the jury that it could either consider or not consider the evidence of cultural background in determining defendant's mental state at the time of the crime, the trial court disagreed that that was the instruction's effect.

Ultimately, the court refused to give the instruction, commenting that it did not want to put the "stamp of approval on [defendant's] actions in the United States, which would have been acceptable in China."

***

The issue then is whether it was a correct statement of the law that the jury may consider evidence of defendant's cultural background in determining the presence or absence of the "essential mental states of the crimes defined in these instructions, or in determining any other issue in this case."

The essential mental states at issue here were (1) premeditation and deliberation, (2) malice aforethought, and (3) specific intent to kill. Generally speaking, all relevant evidence is admissible (Evid. Code, § 351), and the trier of fact may consider any admitted evidence. Here, the admission of evidence of defendant's cultural background was never objected to by the People; there is no argument that the evidence was relevant. The question then is, on what issues was such evidence relevant? As discussed below, this evidence clearly related to certain mental states, which are elements of the charged offense.

First, the evidence of defendant's cultural background was clearly relevant on the issue of premeditation and deliberation. The prosecution's theory was that defendant's statements on days before the killing to Wu and other family members indicated that she had planned to take revenge on Wu by killing Sidney in a Medea-like gesture. The evidence of defendant's cultural background offered an alternative explanation for the

statements (that defendant intended to kill herself) and also for motive behind the killing, that explanation being that the killing of Sidney (as opposed to defendant's own planned suicide) was not deliberate and premeditated, but instead occurred immediately after defendant learned from Sidney himself facts conclusively confirming, in defendant's mind, the statements by Gramma and Sandy, and her own observations, that Sidney was not loved by Wu and was badly treated.

Second, the evidence of defendant's cultural background was also relevant on the issue of malice aforethought and the existence of heat of passion at the time of the killing, which eliminates malice and reduces an intentional killing to voluntary manslaughter. (Pen. Code, § 192.) The court recognized that "heat of passion" was an issue in this case because it instructed the jury regarding heat of passion negating malice and further instructed the jury regarding the lesser-included offense of manslaughter.

***

Here, there was evidence that defendant had experienced a series of events for a 10-year period before and during her stay in late August and early September 1989 with Wu in California, from which the jury could have concluded that defendant was suffering from "pre-existing stress" at the time that Sidney told her things which confirmed her fear that Sidney, because he was not legitimate and because he had no mother to care for him, was not well-treated, and that things were going to get worse for him upon the death of his Gramma. The testimony related to defendant's cultural background was relevant to explain the source of such stress, as well to explain how Sidney's statements could have constituted "sufficient provocation" to cause defendant to kill Sidney in a "heat of passion."

The experts on transcultural psychology specifically testified that, in their opinion, defendant was acting while in an emotional crisis n5 during the time that she obtained the knife and cord, strangled Sidney and then slashed her own wrist, and that her emotional state was intertwined with, and explainable by reference to, her cultural background. processes" on her decision to strangle Sidney . . . .

***

Because the requested instruction was, for the most part, a correct statement of the law, n6 and because it was applicable to the evidence and one of defendant's two basic defenses in this case, upon retrial defendant is entitled to have the jury instructed that it may consider evidence of defendant's cultural background in determining the existence or nonexistence of the relevant mental states.

***

Because we have already decided that the judgment must be reversed because of the court's failure to give an instruction on unconsciousness, and because we only considered defendant's assertion that it was error not to give the cultural background instruction for purposes of guiding the trial court on retrial, we need not consider whether defendant was prejudiced by the failure to give the cultural background instruction.

***

The judgment is reversed.

C. Questions

♦ Do you agree with the court that evidence of the defendant's culture should have been admitted at trial? Why or why not?

♦ Does the admission of the defendant's culture (either to acquit the defendant or mitigate the offense) downplay the harm to the real victims in this case, the children?

♦ Does the admission of evidence of a defendant's culture individualize justice? Or does it give unequal protection to a handful of defendants?

♦ Do you think that the use of culture may work to a defendant's detriment? If so, how could you see the use of culture operating to a defendant's disadvantage? [Hint: Consider juror bias.]

D. Comments

As you can see from the order below, the respondent (the Attorney General's office) unsuccessfully petitioned the California Supreme Court to review the Court of Appeal's decision. In California, review by the California Supreme Court is discretionary and is similar (but not identical) to the review process in the United States Supreme Court.

The California Supreme Court did not grant the petition for review but did order the opinion "depublished." A depublished is not citable as authority. Some of the legal reporters will continue to print the case, but for reference only and not as precedent. Because the lower appellate courts initially make their own determinations regarding which of their cases they will publish, the lower appellate courts order cases published before the California Supreme Court can review the them.).

California's depublication process is fairly unique among state courts. California statutory and constitutional authority does allow the Supreme Court to depublish lower court opinions. The California Supreme Court has the power to depublish under Article VI of the California Constitution and under Rule 976 of the California Rules of Court.

Importantly, the Rules of Court do not require the California Supreme Court to state any reason for its action. Because there is no standard for depublication, the Supreme Court could depublish a case for a variety of reasons. For example, the decision might conflict with another Court of Appeal decision. By depublishing a conflicting case, the conflict between the two lower appellate courts is resolved. Also, if the Supreme Court does not approve of the result in the lower appellate court, the Supreme Court could order the opinion depublished. Alternatively, if the Supreme Court regards the decision as correctly decided, but disagrees with the lower court's legal reasoning it could order the case depublished. These are only three possible reasons for depublishing a lower appellate court opinion. Because the Supreme Court does not state its reason for depublishing a case, attorneys and legal scholars can only surmise what troubled the Supreme Court.

D. Case

PEOPLE V. WU
Supreme Court of California
No. S024083 (1991)

Respondent's petition for review DENIED.

The Reporter of Decisions is directed not to publish in the Official Appellate Reports the opinion in the above-entitled appeal, filed October 24, 1991, which appears at *235 Cal.App.3d 614*. (Cal. Const., Art. VI, Section 14; Rule 976, Cal. Rules of Court.)

E. Questions

♦ Although the California Supreme Court gives no reasons for its depublication orders, scholars and attorneys often speculate as to the real reasons that the California Supreme Court depublishes an opinion. Why do you think the Court depublished the *Wu* opinion?

♦ If you were sitting as a Justice of the California Supreme Court, would you have voted to depublish this case? Why or why not?

VI. DURESS

A. Comments

At common law, defendants were excused from responsibility for their actions where the acts were the result of necessity of duress. The defense of necessity applies where the forces of nature compel a person to act, even though illegally to prevent a greater harm from occurring. Duress, on the other hand, applies to coercion by another person which threatens imminent death, a great bodily harm to the defendant or another person, and where the defendant was not at fault in creating the underlying situation.

In the following case, the court must decide whether or not the defendant's driving under the influence was excusable based on the defense of duress. According to the defendant, he drove in an inebriated fashion because he feared for his girlfriend's safety. The defendant claimed that police officer's questionable conduct during a search made him apprehensive for her safety. The court must decide whether or not a reasonable person would have acted under duress under those circumstances.

As you may have already noticed, the appellate cases you have read so far have been either California Supreme Court opinions or opinions from one of California's six Court of Appeal districts. When you look at the heading of this case, however, you will notice something different. This case was decided in the appellate department of the superior court. Although felony appeals are heard in the intermediate appellate courts (in California, the "Courts of Appeal"), misdemeanor appeals are heard in the appellate department of the superior court. The difference between these two courts is more than merely one of semantics: appellate *court* opinions have the force of precedent whereas appellate *department* cases are persuasive only and not binding as authority. In short, California Supreme Court and Court of Appeal decisions have the force of precedence; appellate department cases do not.

B. Case

PEOPLE V. PENA
Appellate Department, Superior Court, Los Angeles County
197 Cal. Rptr. (1983)

BERNSTEIN, Judge

Appellant, Russell David Pena, appeals his conviction for violation of driving under the influence of intoxicating liquor. Appellant contends the trial court erred in refusing his proffered jury instruction, regarding appellant's theory of his defense. That theory was predicated on the presumed availability of what is generally termed the defense of duress. We hold that the defense was indeed available to appellant, and that the evidence at trial mandated a jury instruction on the subject. Accordingly, we reverse the judgment of conviction.

The evidence presented at appellant's trial was essentially undisputed. Los Angeles County Sheriff's Deputy Frank Webb testified that he first encountered appellant at approximately 4 a.m. on November 1, 1981. Webb, on patrol in Pico Rivera, observed appellant and Sara Marrufo, appellant's girlfriend, asleep in a parked car. Webb stated that "due to the late hour," he decided to investigate the situation. He exited his patrol vehicle and approached the parked car, at which time he stated that he smelled alcohol. Webb then ordered the occupants, appellant and Sara, to exit their vehicle and demanded to see written identification. Both parties complied. Following this, Webb undertook a search of the "suspects" assertedly to ascertain if either of them were in possession of "weapons." Sara, at the time she was subjected to Deputy Webb's "weapons search," was dressed in a somewhat unusual manner. She was wearing a long fur coat and, according to the engrossed statement, "was semi-nude thereunder, wearing only a very brief see-through teddy nightgown" (Sara testified that she and appellant had attended a Halloween costume party earlier in the evening, and that her costume was supposed to be that of a "flasher"). Webb ordered Sara to open her coat, which she did very briefly. Webb thereupon ordered her to again open her coat and to keep it open. Deputy Webb then examined Sara's body with his flashlight. Following this examination, the deputy turned Sara around and pulled her coat up from the rear and continued his examination with the flashlight.

During his interrogation and search of appellant and Sara Marrufo, Deputy Webb ascertained the following:

1. The vehicle in which appellant and his girlfriend had been sleeping was registered to Sara's sister;
2. Appellant lived "about one block" from the location of the events above described;
3. Sara lived about three miles from the location;
4. Sara's identification showed her to be 20 years of age.

Deputy Webb concluded the encounter by ordering Sara to enter his vehicle inasmuch as the deputy had decided to take Sara home. Webb's only asserted reason for this action was that it was for Sara's "protection." Webb drove from the scene with Sara in tow, leaving appellant in possession of Sara's sister's vehicle.

Appellant testified that he followed Webb and Sara in the sister's car. His reason for doing so was his fear for the physical safety of his girlfriend. Appellant had observed Webb's earlier weapons search of Sara; it is at this point the only conflict in the evidence develops. Deputy Webb testified that he drove Sara directly home and only after this, while "exiting Sara Marrufo's doorway," did he observe "an unusual black shadow" which proved to be appellant. Appellant was sitting in the vehicle earlier described, with the motor running. Recalling the alcohol odor at the scene of his original encounter with appellant and Sara, Webb felt that appellant had driven to his current location while under the influence of alcohol. He ordered appellant out of the vehicle and, according to Webb, thereupon administered field sobriety tests which appellant failed. Webb then arrested appellant. Subsequently, appellant took an "intoxilyzer" (breath) test which showed appellant's blood alcohol level to be approximately .15.

However, according to Sara, Webb stopped his car "by some railroad tracks"; at that point, Webb observed appellant to be following them. Webb stated to Sara that appellant "would be made sorry" for

88

following them. Webb then started his vehicle up again and drove to Sara's residence.

Appellant testified concerning his arrest by Webb as follows: After he was ordered out of the car in which he had followed Webb and Sara, appellant was immediately arrested and handcuffed by Webb. Appellant asserted that no field sobriety tests were administered to him by Webb, although he admitted to Webb that he had consumed several beers at the Halloween party he had earlier attended with Sara.

At both trials, appellant requested that the following instruction be given to the jury:

"Evidence has been received to the effect that the reason defendant, Russell Pena, drove the car was because he believed that Sara Marrufo was in physical danger."

"You are hereby instructed that if you find that it has been established by a preponderance of the evidence that the defendant had a good faith belief that Sara Marrufo might be in physical danger, and drove the car for her protection or to render possible aid, then you may acquit him based on this defense."

The trial court not only refused appellant's tendered instruction, but further instructed the jury, upon the panel's inquiry during its deliberations, that the defense of "justification" was in fact no defense to the charge.

The sole question on appeal is whether the trial court committed reversible error in refusing to instruct the jury, either by way of appellant's tendered instruction or a similar, court fashioned charge, regarding the applicability of the defense of duress.

The United States Supreme Court has had occasion to discuss the defenses of duress and necessity in the context of a prosecution for escape from lawful confinement. The high court observed as follows:

"Common law historically distinguished between the defenses of duress and necessity. Duress was said to excuse criminal conduct where the actor was under an unlawful threat of imminent death or serious bodily injury, which threat caused the actor to engage in conduct violating the literal terms of the criminal law. While the defense of duress covered the situation where coercion had its source in the actions of other human beings, the defense of necessity, or choice of evils, traditionally covered the situation where physical forces beyond the actor's control rendered illegal conduct the lesser of two evils. Thus, where A destroyed a dike because B threatened to kill him if he did not, A would argue that he acted under duress, whereas if A destroyed the dike in order to protect more valuable property from flooding, A could claim the defense of necessity.

Although California law regarding the "justification" defenses (i.e., "duress," "necessity," "compulsion," etc.) appears sparse in comparison to that of most American jurisdictions, there nonetheless exist several Court of Appeal decisions which provide some guidance as to the parameters of those defenses The most recent case noted that: "Although the exact confines of the necessity defense remain clouded, a well- established central element involves the emergency nature of the situation, i.e., the imminence of the greater harm which the illegal act seeks to prevent. The commission of a crime cannot be countenanced where there exists the possibility of some alternate means to alleviate the threatened greater harm." In Lovercamp, the leading California case regarding the applicability of the duress defense to a charge of prison escape, the court fashioned a five part judicial test for determining the availability of the defense. In such cases, the Lovercamp court observed that it was not formulating a new rule of law, but rather was applying "rules long ago established in a manner which effects fundamental justice In [another prior case] it was held that the burden of proof in cases in which duress was asserted by a defendant, required only that the defendant "raise a reasonable doubt that he had acted in the exercise of his free will."

Two issues of apparent first impression in this jurisdiction must be addressed before disposition of the instant appeal can be effected:

(1) Is the duress/necessity defense available to a defendant charged with misdemeanor driving under the influence?

(2) Is the duress/necessity defense available to a defendant who commits an unlawful act in an effort to prevent imminent harm to a third party?

With respect to the first question, it appears settled that the duress defense is available to a defendant charged with any crime except one which involves the taking of the life of an innocent person.

Thus, we hold that the defense of duress, is available, presuming other requisites of such a defense are satisfied, where a defendant is charged with the violation of driving under the influence.

It appears that no California case has directly addressed the question of whether the duress defense is available in situations wherein the coercive circumstances arise from threatened harm not to the defendant personally, but to some party other than the accused. The classic example is that of a bank teller whose child has been kidnapped. The kidnappers order the teller to use his position of trust at the bank to embezzle money for the kidnapers. The teller is informed that his child will be killed if he does not comply with the demands. The teller himself is not threatened with bodily harm. Would an embezzlement under such circumstances constitute a crime? It appears that virtually every jurisdiction in which the issue has been settled permits threats to third parties to satisfy the requisite coercive circumstance requirement so as to bring the duress defense into play. Perhaps the best articulation of the rationale for permitting threats to persons other than the defendant to allow invocation of these defenses, appears in a Massachusetts case: "Whatever the precise precedents, it is hardly conceivable that the law of the commonwealth, or, indeed, of any jurisdiction should mark as criminal those who intervene forcibly to protect others; for the law to do so would aggravate the fears which lead to the alienation of people from one another. To the fear of "involvement" and of injury to oneself if one answered a call for help would be added the fear of possible criminal prosecution.

The court also observed that some European countries have passed laws making it a criminal offense not to render aid in certain circumstances:

"It is instructive that the laws of some countries in Continental Europe denounce as a crime the failure to render help in given circumstances. Thus the West German Criminal Code, provides: 'Whoever does not render help in cases of accident, common danger or necessity although help is required and under the circumstances is exactable, and in particular is possible without danger of serious injury to himself and without violation of other important duties, will be punished by imprisonment up to one year or by fine.

In the case at bench, the People contend that California law restricts the application of duress type defenses to cases in which the defendant's person is the object of coercive threats of bodily harm. The People's argument cannot withstand scrutiny. To begin, nothing in the language of California statutes can be construed as limiting the applicability of the duress-necessity defenses to the circumstances therein described.

We hold that a defense of duress may properly be predicated upon threats of harm to persons other than the accused.

The following requirements have traditionally been held to be prerequisites to the establishment of the defense of justification/duress:

1. The act charged as criminal must have been done to prevent a significant evil;

2. There must have been no adequate alternative to the commission of the act;

3. The harm caused by the act must not be disproportionate to the harm avoided

4. The accused must entertain a good-faith belief that his act was necessary to prevent the greater harm;

5. Such belief must be objectively reasonable under all the circumstances; and

6. The accused must not have substantially contributed to the creation of the emergency.

We recognize that, under the requirements listed above there is no suggestion that the harm sought to be avoided be that of death or great bodily injury. As we have pointed out, the defense of duress is not limited to situations wherein the accused acted in reasonable fear of his life. Other sections of the Penal Code explicitly permit the commission of acts otherwise criminal, under circumstances where the actor need not be in fear of his life to be able to avail himself of the duress defense. Under the "disproportionate harms" requirement, it is plain that as the harm sought to be avoided decreases in seriousness the duress defense will excuse fewer and fewer acts undertaken to avoid that harm.

Lastly, with respect to the oft-cited "imminence" requirement of the defense, it is apparent that this requirement is included within the more general "no alternative" requirement. Obviously, the more imminent the peril, the less likely the existence of an alternative course of action.

We now evaluate the merits of the instant appeal in light of the foregoing legal principles. Appellant would be entitled to an acquittal of the charge against him, notwithstanding the fact of his operation of a motor vehicle while legally intoxicated, if he could convince the jury of the truth of the following:

(1) That he held a genuine belief that Sara Marrufo was in danger of assault by or through Deputy Webb;

(2) That appellant's good faith belief was objectively reasonable under the totality of the circumstances;

(3) That appellant operated his vehicle in obedience to his fear for Sara's safety and not for any other purpose;

(4) That appellant had no opportunity to engage alternative legal means of protecting Sara from the danger he believed she faced;

(5) That appellant was not substantially at fault in the creation of the emergency situation which he claims justifies his action in driving while intoxicated.

We observe that the requirement that appellant's fear be an objectively reasonable one does not require that appellant be in fact correct in his assessment of the situation. Rather, as in any situation where a defendant claims as his defense that the charged acts were justified as having been undertaken in response to some emergency circumstance (i.e., self- defense), the defendant may rely on what he reasonably believes to be true.

Whether appellant, in the instant case, had a reasonable belief that Sara was in danger from Deputy Webb is a question of fact. That Webb seemed clearly to be an on-duty police officer may be a factor to consider in assessing the reasonableness of defendant's fear, but it is certainly not the only such factor. Other considerations which the jury could properly weigh include the credibility of Deputy Webb's asserted reason for taking Sara from the scene against her apparent wishes, the reasonableness or unreasonableness of Webb's detention and search of appellant and Sara and the character of his search of Sara in particular.

We hold that the defense of justification was available to the appellant herein and the failure to so instruct the jury constituted prejudicial error. Accordingly, the judgment is reversed.

C. Questions

♦ Do you think that the defendant's "good faith belief" was objectively reasonable under the totality of the circumstances? What specific facts did you rely on to reach your conclusion?

♦ Based on your conclusion above, do you think the court reached the right decision when it held that it was error not to instruct the jury on the defense of duress?

VIII. VOLUNTARY INTOXICATION

A. Comment

Voluntary intoxication, refers to the defendant's intended introduction of any intoxicating substance (drugs, alcohol, etc.) Which either the defendant knows or knew is likely to produce an intoxicating condition. Involuntary intoxication, on the other hand, results from the ingestion of an intoxicating substance or from the unforeseeable reaction to an ingested substance.

The *Kelly* case states the rule regarding the impact of voluntary intoxication on a defendant's criminal intent. The court sets forth the rule for both general intent and specific intent crimes. Make certain that you understand when voluntary intoxication can and cannot impact a defendant's ability to form the necessary intent for a particular crime. The distinction is an important one.

B. Case

PEOPLE V. KELLY
Supreme Court of California
10 Cal.3d 565 (1973)

SULLIVAN, J.

Defendant has used drugs ever since she was 15 years old. In the fall of 1970, when she was 18 years old, she began taking mescaline and LSD, using those drugs 50 to 100 times in the months leading up to the offense. On December 6, 1970, her parents received a telephone call that defendant was being held at the police substation located at the Los Angeles International Airport after being found wandering about the airport under the influence of drugs. In response to the all, her parents picked up defendant at the airport and drove her back to their home in San Diego. Although they recognized that she was not acting normally, at defendant's request they drove her to her own apartment where she spent the night.

On the next morning, December 7, defendant telephoned her mother and asked to be driven to her parents' home. Mrs. Kelly did so but noticed that defendant "wasn't there"; she seemed to be "[j]ust wandering" and told her mother that she heard "a lot of noises, and a lot of people talking ...." Mrs. Kelly made defendant change into pajamas and lie down, and then went into the kitchen to prepare defendant's breakfast. Shortly thereafter, defendant entered the kitchen and, while Mrs. Kelly was turned toward the stove, repeatedly stabbed her mother with an array of kitchen knives. The police were called, defendant was arrested, and eventually charged.

Much of the evidence presented at the trial consisted of the reports and testimony of seven psychiatrists. Since there was substantial agreement among them, we briefly summarize their testimony, referring to illustrative examples of it in the footnotes. Defendant suffered from personality problems - according to one witness an underlying schizophrenia - but was normally a sane person. However, her voluntary and repeated ingestion of drugs over a two-month period had triggered a legitimate psychosis so that on the day of the attack, defendant was unable to distinguish right from wrong. Nevertheless, defendant was conscious in that she could perceive the events that were taking place.

The trial court heard considerable testimony that defendant was not acting simply as a person who, after ingesting drugs or alcohol is unable to perceive reality and reason properly. Rather, the drug abuse was deemed the indirect cause of a legitimate, temporary psychosis.

[T]he court found that while defendant was indeed psychotic both before and after the attack, [the defendant's mental state] was produced by the voluntary ingestion of hallucinatory drugs.

As Penal Code Section 22 provides: "No act committed by a person while in a state of voluntary intoxication is less criminal by reason of his having been in such condition. But whenever the actual existence of any particular purpose, motive, or intent is a necessary element to constitute any particular species or degree of crime, the jury may take into consideration the fact that the accused w   as intoxicated at the time, in determining the purpose, motive, or intent with which he committed the act."

[V]oluntary intoxication is only a partial defense to a criminal charge - that is, it may serve to negate the specific intent or state of mind requisite to the offense. It follows, therefore, that unconsciousness caused by voluntary intoxication is no defense to a general intent crime - by definition a crime in which no specific intent is required. Assault with a deadly weapon is such a crime, and we have held that the requisite general intent therefor may not be negated through a showing of voluntary intoxication.

[Judgment affirmed.]

C. Questions

♦ Do you think it was significant that the defendant was psychotic? Why or why not?

♦ Do you think the case would have turned out differently if the psychotic state was not self-induced?

♦ As a matter of policy, should the means by which the mental state originated have any impact on the outcome? State reasons to support your conclusion.

VIII. Self-Assessment

1. The doctrine of "transferred intent" cannot be applied to the self-defense doctrine.
   A. True   B. False

2. California has abolished that diminished capacity defense.
   A. True   B. False

3. "Syndrome defenses" are usually raised as issues in mitigation rather than exculpation.
   A. True   B. False

4. The duress defense is applicable only to homicides.
   A. True   B. False

5. Claims of involuntary and voluntary intoxication are treated identically as defenses.
   A. True   B. False

CHAPTER NINE

Crimes Against Persons:
Criminal Homicide

rimes involving the loss of human life are the most serious crimes in our criminal justice system. In our legal system (unlike many foreign legal systems), a crime involving the death of a human may be punished by a sentence of death.

You will soon be reading cases interpreting the different California homicide statutes. Although the language of the statutes themselves is fairly clear, applying the statutes to individual cases may be less clear. In this chapter we will observe the courts wrestling with some unusual circumstances that eventually led to a person's death. The courts have the difficult task of interpreting the laws to determine, which (if any) homicide laws the defendant has violated.

I.   MURDER

A. Comments

At common law, causing the death of another human being without justification or excuse constituted criminal homicide. However, for the homicide to rise to the level of murder, there had to be "malice aforethought." "Malice aforethought" should not be interpreted in an everyday sense; it has specific legal meaning. "Malice aforethought" can be any one of four mental states: intent to kill, intent to inflict great bodily harm, depraved heart (extreme recklessness) and felony murder. Any one of these four mental states is sufficient to constitute malice aforethought. First and second degree (which both require malice aforethought) murder are separated by the addition of the requirement of "premeditation and deliberation" for first-degree murder.

The California statute below defines murder, retaining the common law language of malice aforethought. Observe that the California crime of murder includes the death of a fetus. (California statutory law preceded the Federal passage of the bill for the protection of an unborn fetus during the commission of a crime, in March 2004.) You may wonder at this point about abortion and whether or not it is considered "murder" under California law. You will see the specific exception made for abortion under the definition of murder. However, the abortion exception does have limitations. Consider what circumstances an abortion might still be considered "murder" under the law.

When analyzing the actus reus of murder, keep in mind the factual situations in which a killing can occur. As for the mens rea of murder, consider whether California requires that a defendant have an intent to kill.

Also included in the statutes below is the statute that defines degrees of murder specific to California law. When reading this statute, note how many degrees of murder there are in California. Not all states have the same classifications of degrees of murder.

Finally, take a look at the factual situations that trigger the first-degree murder category. Again, not all states have identical situations that trigger first-degree murder convictions. The specific provisions in the law reflect value judgments on the part of the California legislature. Do you agree with those that are included? Do you think there are specific situations that should have been included and were not? Consider also the "carjacking" provision. When do you think this statute was added to the Penal Code?

B. Statutes

Definition of Murder: Penal Code section 187

(a) Murder is the unlawful killing of a human being, or a fetus, with malice aforethought.

(b) This section shall not apply to any person who commits an act that results in the death of a fetus if any of the following apply:

(1) The act complied with the Therapeutic Abortion Act

(2) The act was committed by a holder of a physician's and surgeon's certificate, as defined in the Business and Professions Code, in a case where, to a medical certainty, the result of childbirth would be death of the mother of the fetus or where her death from childbirth, although not medically certain, would be substantially certain or more likely than not.

(3) The act was solicited, aided, abetted, or consented to by the mother of the fetus.

(c) Subdivision (b) shall not be construed to prohibit the prosecution of any person under any other provision of law.

Degrees of Murder: Penal Code section 189

Murder which is perpetrated by means of a destructive device or explosive, knowing use of ammunition designed primarily to penetrate metal or armor, poison, lying in wait, torture, or by any other kind of willful, deliberate, and premeditated killing, or which is committed in the perpetration of, or attempt to perpetrate, arson, rape, carjacking, robbery, burglary, mayhem, kidnapping, train wrecking, or any murder which is perpetrated by means of discharging a firearm from a motor vehicle, intentionally at another person outside of the vehicle with the intent to inflict death, is murder of the first degree. All other kinds of murders are of the second degree.

To prove the killing was "deliberate and premeditated," it shall not be necessary to prove the defendant maturely and meaningfully reflected upon the gravity of his or her act.

C. Comments

The two cases in this section both deal with first degree murder convictions. However, the issues before the appellate courts are not the same. The first case struggles with the issue of transferred intent to kill; the second case reviews evidence sufficient to affirm a first-degree murder conviction.

The *McAuliffe* case gives you an example of transferred intent (which you have already studied) and applies the doctrine to murder. We have edited little from this case and have included the very detailed factual recitation set forth by the court regarding the circumstances surrounding the killing. When you read this case, consider why you think the court included so much factual detail.

D. Cases

PEOPLE V. MCAULIFFE
District Court of Appeal, Second District, Division 3
154 Cal.App.2d 332 (1957)

VALLEE, J.

The principal characters were John Thomas 'Jack' McAuliffe, the deceased; defendant Richard Gilbert McAuliffe; John Charles McAuliffe, defendant's brother; Virginia McAuliffe, wife of the deceased; and Susan McAuliffe, daughter of Virginia.

On August 8, 1956 defendant and his brother John drove from San Diego to Cayucos in San Luis Obispo County in John's pickup truck to visit with their uncle, Jack, at the latter's ranch during deer season. Defendant lived in El Cajon near San Diego. During the days following, they assisted Jack around the ranch and hunted with him. Their relations were amicable.

On August 13 defendant and Virginia went to San Luis Obispo. On the return trip they stopped at several bars, consumed beer, and Virginia bought a jug of wine. When they arrived at the ranch Virginia drank some of the wine, 'she was really putting it down.' Jack raised 'the devil about it,' 'jumped' on defendant and accused him of buying the wine for her. Defendant told Jack all he bought her was a couple of bottles of beer, that she got the wine herself; Jack 'just snorted,' and walked away. John

took Jack's side in the argument. That night defendant slept in the same room with his brother, John.

The next morning, August 14, 1956, Jack left early to go to Minetti's ranch to help with the harvesting. Later defendant and his brother, John, went to Cayucos. They spent the afternoon playing pool and drinking beer, wagering a drink of beer on the outcome of each game of pool. A dispute arose between them-John claimed defendant owed him a glass of beer; defendant claimed he did not. Defendant bought a glass of beer for himself, took one sip, and left for the restroom. While he was gone John drank defendant's glass of beer, left the saloon, and concealed himself in an adjoining building. When defendant returned from the restroom he asked who had drunk his beer. He was told his brother had. Defendant then became 'pretty ornery,' said 'I'm going to get that dirty so- and-so,' and left the saloon. Defendant looked for John but did not find him. He then got a piece of 2-inch pipe about 18 inches long, went to John's pickup truck, said, 'Well, I'll fix him. I'll bust his ignition switch, where he'll have to walk,' and hit the ignition switch with the pipe.

John saw what was going on, shouted to defendant to stop or he would have him arrested. As John approached, defendant swung the pipe at his head. A scuffle took place. John testified that during the scuffle defendant told him 'he was going to get both of us; he said we thought we were pretty smart S-B's, that he was going to get both of us before 12 o'clock.' A bystander testified he heard defendant say 'he'd have him [John] under the sod, before the night was over.' A peacemaker quieted the brothers and offered to buy each a beer. They went to a saloon and had a beer. The bystander suggested the brothers shake hands. John was willing but defendant refused. About 5:30 p.m. John said to defendant, 'If you're not ready to go back to the ranch by 6 o'clock, I'm going to go off without you.' John then left the saloon.

John left Cayucos alone in his pickup truck about 6 p.m. Defendant stayed in the saloon and when the bartender refused to serve him more beer he left and went to another. On John's return to the ranch he, Virginia, and Susan drove to the ranch where Jack was working. There John remarked to Minetti, 'Richard threatened to kill him in El Cajon. He threatened me today. The third time he'll probably get me.' The women returned to the McAuliffe ranch and hid two rifles belonging to the brothers. Another rifle belonging to Jack was in a corner of the kitchen. The women did not hide Jack's rifle. Jack and John returned to the ranch about 8:30 p.m. After supper they went upstairs to work on a new cartridge reloading machine. The machine was in an unused bedroom on the second floor.

Defendant left Cayucos about 7 p. m. and walked 7 miles to the ranch. On the way he was 'pretty ornery' and 'cussed his brother out.' When he arrived at the ranch he stopped at John's pickup truck and slammed the door. John heard the door slam; Jack said, 'See who that is'; John opened the window, saw it was defendant, and said in a loud voice, 'Get the hell away from the truck.' As defendant approached the house he called out, 'You S-B's have had it.'

Virginia and Susan were in the living room. It was about 10:30. On hearing defendant approach the house, Susan went upstairs and told Jack and John defendant had arrived. Defendant entered the house through the kitchen and walked into the living room. As he did so he said to Virginia, 'you dirty so- and-so's, what did you take the pick-up and make me walk seven miles home?' John testified he heard defendant say this. In the living room, the defendant looked toward the place where his rifle was usually kept. Not finding it, he walked back to the kitchen. After wandering around several minutes he picked up Jack's rifle, pumped it, forcing a shell into firing position. Virginia told him he had better put the gun down. He told her to mind her own business. Defendant walked out the back door and started up the stairs to the second floor, followed by the two women. As he started up the stairs Virginia shouted to Jack and John to watch out, that he was coming up with a gun. Defendant told her to shut up or he would shoot. As he neared the top of the stairs defendant said, 'you wise S-B's think you're pretty smart. You stole my pick-up and my rifle, and you let me walk seven miles from the town.'

Jack and John were in the loading room with the door closed. They heard what defendant said. Jack was 6 feet 2 inches tall and weighed 263 pounds. Jack told John to step back of the door, said 'I'm going to ask him to leave,' that he didn't want any drinking there and was going to ask him to take his gear and leave, 'head off down the road.' John said, 'Well, let me talk to him.' Jack replied in a loud voice, 'No, if he gets smart, I want first swing at him.' Susan testified she heard Jack say, 'Let me have the first swing at him.' John went behind the door. Jack went out of the door at a quick pace into a hallway leading to the stairs, with his hand raised. He was not armed. It was 11 feet 6 inches from the door to the top of the stairs. As Jack approached the stairs defendant fired. The shot was fatal. The bullet entered the mid-portion of the chest, hit the breast bone, went through the base of the heart just below the breast bone, went through the vertebrae, and wound up underneath the skin in the upper lumbar area of the back. After the shooting Jack was lying in the hall with his head near the top of the stairs. Virginia testified she did not hear any voices upstairs before the sound of the shot. Defendant went down the stairs and said to Virginia, 'Call the sheriff. I shot the S-B. Tell him to come and get me.' Defendant was arrested a short distance down the road from the house about 11:25 p. m. He was sober.

Defendant's version of the events prior to his return to the ranch on the night of the shooting conformed generally to the evidence of the People. He testified that after the dispute in the saloon at Cayucos he was 'pretty mad,' 'got pretty ornery,' and went looking for John; John pulled a knife in the scuffle at the pickup truck; he said to John, 'You cut me with that knife, you won't live to tell about it.' He denied otherwise threatening Jack or John. He thought the rifle he picked up in the kitchen was his and he was going up to bed. He clicked the loading mechanism to assure himself a shell was not in the chamber. As he was going up the stairs, Virginia yelled, 'Look out! Dick's coming upstairs, and he's got a gun.' He said, 'Shut up! I'm not going to shoot anybody. I'm just going up and go to bed.' He walked on up the stairs, heard a shuffling of feet, heard a door open, turned around, and there was his uncle coming out the door with his hands behind him. His uncle closed the door and yelled, 'I'll kill you, you lousy bastard.' He levered a shell into the chamber of the rifle. His uncle came charging at him with his right hand swinging. He knew his uncle was very violent, and thought he saw a knife in his left hand and that he was going to kill him; he levered a shell into the chamber; aimed the gun at his uncle's legs; yelled, 'Halt! Stop!' Jack kept coming; he jumped back and pulled the trigger.

Defendant contends that he is not guilty of murder because the victim was not the person he intended to kill. The crime may be murder although the person killed was not the one whom the accused intended to kill. One of the first cases in this state applying the so-called doctrine of transferred intent appears to have been People v. Suesser, 142 Cal. 354, in which the first paragraph of the criticized instruction was given and expressly approved. The court stated:

'In determining the criminality of the act of killing it will be immaterial whether the intent was to kill the person killed or whether the death of such person was the accidental or otherwise unintended result of the intent to kill some one else-the criminality of the act will be deemed the same.' ...

***

'The court therefore did not err in refusing defendant's instruction on this subject. We see nothing in the contention that the instruction on this subject, given at the request of the people, invaded the province of the jury. No other objection that demands notice is made thereto, and, so far as we can see, it correctly stated the law upon the subject under discussion.'

The malice was express, also the intent to take life, and because the defendant, in carrying out his threats and his felonious intent, took the life of his friend rather than the life of his supposed enemy, cannot excuse his act or reduce the degree of his crime.'

If one willfully, premeditatedly and of his malice aforethought commits or attempts to commit an assault upon a certain person with the intention of killing him, but in the execution of his design unintentionally kills another instead, it is nevertheless murder. The intent in such case is transferred by law from his intended victim to the person killed. In other words, the crime is exactly what it would have been if the person against whom the intent to kill was directed had been in fact killed.'

'Whether the three killings were the result of the victims obtruding themselves between the defendant and the object of his vengeance or were the result of 'mistake' in defendant's effort to kill the girl, they would, nevertheless, be murders of the first degree.' ''Where a person purposely and of his deliberate and premeditated malice attempts to kill one person but by mistake or inadvertence kills another instead, the law transfers the felonious intent from the object of his assault and the homicide so committed is murder in the first degree.'

It is argued there was no evidence that defendant fired the shot in the mistaken belief he was shooting at John, or that the shooting was inadvertent or accidental, or that Jack obtruded or placed himself between defendant and John. We think there was evidence from which the jury could have concluded that Jack obtruded or placed himself between defendant and John. There had been no difficulty of moment between defendant and Jack; there had been between defendant and John. Defendant testified he had no trouble with Jack before the offense in question, 'just little arguments.' The jury reasonably could have inferred that defendant started up the stairs to kill John; that Jack suspected it or knew it; that Jack, to protect John, had him stay in the room; and that Jack went out of the room and obtruded or placed himself between defendant and John.

[The judgment is affirmed.]

E. Questions

♦ Before you began reading the *McAuliffe* case, we asked you to consider why the court recited so much factual detail before discussing the applicability of the transferred intent doctrine to this case. What conclusion have you reached?

♦ Assume that before discussion of the transferred intent doctrine, the *McAuliffe* court had simply stated that the defendant and the intended victim had been quarreling prior to the defendant's mistakenly shooting Jack. (In essence, such a factual description is accurate, if quite abbreviated.) Would you have thought that the court reached the right decision regarding the transferred intent (of an intent to kill) without a detailed recitation of the facts leading up to the killing?

♦ With the *McAuliffe* court's finding of an intent to kill, which statutory classification(s) of homicide can this killing fall under?

F. Comments

The following case, *Helwinkel*, focuses on evidentiary matters. Specifically, *Helwinkel* discusses use of circumstantial evidence. As the court points out below, where the evidence relied on is largely circumstantial, the facts must be presented in great detail in order to support the affirmance of a conviction.

The case focuses on evidentiary issues rather than substantive issues. The case has been reported for a specific reason. The case has been included to counteract the media's portrayal of circumstantial evidence as inadmissible in a murder trial. Television and movies often portray zealous defense attorneys objecting to evidence being inadmissible in murder trials because it is "merely circumstantial evidence." This case demonstrates that the entertainment industry is wrong. In the *Helwinkel* case, the prosecutors relied on circumstantial evidence to "get their man" (or in this case, "their woman"). The conviction was no less valid because it relied largely on circumstantial evidence.

G. Case

PEOPLE V. HELWINKEL
Court of Appeal, Fifth District, California.
199 Cal.App.2d 207 (1962)

STONE, J.

Esther May Helwinkel was indicted for the murder of her husband, Lawrence R. Helwinkel. A jury trial resulted in a conviction of murder in the first degree..... She appeals from the judgment.

The facts must be stated at some length because defendant's conviction rested largely on circumstantial evidence, and the numerous events relating to her husband's death by poison cover a period of several months. On January 12, 1959, Lawrence R. Helwinkel was unmarried and a foreman of the Armour poultry plant at Turlock, California. He applied for membership in the World-Wide Group, a lonely hearts correspondence club, representing that his income was $3,000 a year, that he owned his own home and an automobile, that he had never been married, and that he never used intoxicating liquor. In describing the type of person of the opposite sex in whom he was interested, he stated, 'I would like to meet a woman who doesn't drink, but one who wants a good home and would make a pleasant companion.'

In February 1959, defendant met the deceased through the lonely hearts club. After corresponding for a while, defendant telephoned Helwinkel and asked if she could visit him. When he agreed, she drove to his home in Turlock; they were married May 6, 1959. Soon after the marriage Helwinkel became aware of defendant's drinking habit and that sometimes she indulged to excess. It was necessary upon one occasion to place her in the Livermore Sanitarium for treatment as an alcoholic, and on several occasions a doctor was called to treat her at her home. At the request of defendant, neighbors also called a doctor to treat her for intoxication. One of her neighbors testified that 'she always got so bad that she was lying down.'

The deceased told a doctor who was called to treat defendant for intoxication that he was concerned about her condition, that he did not know how to cope with the problem, and that prior to the marriage he knew nothing about her drinking. The husband told neighbors that he was not going to put up with defendant's drinking, that he could not tolerate it, and that it was making him look ridiculous in the community. He also stated that under the circumstances he could not keep defendant with him and that he was going to have her leave.

Helwinkel was apparently in good health on July 23, 1960, when he and defendant had dinner at a restaurant. While returning home, he became so violently ill with stomach cramps that he was forced to stop the car and vomit. The following evening he was again ill with nausea and vomiting, and a Dr. Meade was called. Defendant told the doctor that the previous day her husband had sprayed the garden with a chemical called Dowpon. The doctor checked with a poison center in Oakland and was informed that the illness could not have been caused by any poison in Dowpon. Helwinkel continued to lose weight from vomiting, he also became dizzy and fainted. Because he had no previous history of such

101

occurrences, the doctor placed him in a hospital on July 26. During hospitalization his condition improved.

On July 30, defendant asked a neighbor, Mrs. Littler, to come to her home. When the neighbor arrived, she discovered that defendant was so drunk that she was in bed, 'real bad off.' The neighbor called a doctor at defendant's request. The doctor stated that he would have the husband released from the hospital the next morning so that he could take care of defendant. Helwinkel returned from the hospital on July 31, and defendant was drunk when he arrived home. Several days later defendant again called her neighbor, Mrs. Littler, between 10 and 12 at night. She told Mrs. Littler and her daughter, Mrs. Hall, that she did not know what she was going to do, that her husband wouldn't talk to her, and that he was going to get rid of her because of her drinking. Defendant told them that she could not take it any more. When the neighbor suggested that she leave, defendant replied that she could not as her husband had everything and that she had no place to go. During the conversation defendant confided to them that she had thought of killing her husband and herself, then added, 'I have the stuff to do it.' When the neighbor finally informed defendant that she and her daughter must be going home as they could not stay all night, defendant declared, 'Go ahead, then, nobody cares what happens, and I will go in and finish what I started. You will never see us again.' She also said, 'Well, just go on-go on home. I'm going to finish what I have started. I am going to give him the stuff and take it myself and you won't see us anymore.'

The following morning Mrs. Littler went to defendant's home to see if she was all right. When Mrs. Littler let her know that she was concerned about some of the things defendant had said the night before, defendant replied, 'Well, I still have such awful thoughts, that I still feel like killing him and killing myself.'

On August 2, Helwinkel visited his doctor and was found to be weak but fairly well. Although he was able to work August 8, he gradually began to degenerate physically. He became weaker and weaker, he lost the use of his hands and feet, and he could not climb ladders. He had difficulty operating the equipment which he had formerly manipulated with ease, he could not write in his book, he could not take a cigarette out of a package and light it, and he eventually lost the use of his hands completely. On August 22 he complained to his doctor that his hands and feet had been numb for two weeks, and that it had been necessary for him to use woolen stockings at night to keep his feet warm. His blood pressure was elevated for the first time. September 1 the doctor observed that the fingers were not only numb, but painful, and that the blood pressure was still elevated. The doctor, becoming alarmed, arranged to have Helwinkel admitted to the University Hospital. Defendant then arranged for herself and her husband to consult with an attorney, this being September 8. They kept the appointment, and wills were prepared for and executed by both of them. The day after the execution of the wills, September 9, Helwinkel was admitted to the University of California Hospital.

Following Helwinkel's admission to the hospital, defendant and her sister-in-law were discussing his condition and his illness caused by food poisoning. Although arsenic had never been mentioned, defendant said, 'You know, Elsie, arsenic can't kill a person.' On September 17, while Helwinkel was still in the University of California Hospital, defendant was stopped by police in San Jose for driving while intoxicated. She asked the officer for a break because her husband was dying and did not have much longer to live. The officer tried to encourage her by pointing out the advances made in medical science, which meant there was a good possibility that her husband would be saved. Defendant replied that she knew her husband was dying, and that the doctors could not do anything for him.

On October 5 deceased returned home, and by October 26 his condition appeared to have improved considerably. However, on November 2, his feet were burning again and bothering him at night and he stated he felt as though there was a tight elastic band around his knees, and that his feet slapped as he walked. His hands were stronger, but still numb. On November 7, a Mrs. Roberts visited defendant and deceased at their home, and had dinner with them. After dinner, deceased became ill and vomited, and did so three different times while Mrs. Roberts was there. On this occasion deceased asked defendant if she had put pepper in his salad. The following day, November 8, a doctor visited deceased, as he was suffering pains in the pit of his stomach and over his gall bladder. He also was dizzy, faint, and experienced a feeling of thirst. During the afternoon of November 9, a former fellow-employee visited deceased, and found him unable to walk without supporting himself on pieces of furniture, he was weary, his face drawn, and his skin pale. During the visit deceased suffered diarrhea and also vomited severely on one occasion.

On November 11, the doctor visited deceased, and found him complaining of nausea and weakness from vomiting for three or four days. He walked with difficulty. Defendant told the doctor that her husband complained that 'every time he eats something and gets this way, he blames it on something he's eaten just prior to the episode of nausea and vomiting.' The treatment prescribed by the doctor failed to improve his condition. On November 12, defendant called the doctor and informed him that her husband was very ill, but she demurred to the doctor's request that she take him to a hospital. At approximately 1:45 on the morning of the following day, November 13, defendant again called the doctor, who ordered an ambulance. Helwinkel was taken to the hospital; the doctor described his condition as 'very shocking.' He was writhing with pain and complained of severe pains in his abdominal region. His pulse was rapid, he was placed in an oxygen tent and given medication to raise the blood pressure, but he died shortly thereafter.

Mrs. Russo, a neighbor of defendant, arranged to have her mother stay at defendant's home the night Helwinkel died. Mrs. Russo testified that before defendant left for the hospital she gave the following instruction: 'She asked me to tell my mother not to touch anything that Lawrence might have eaten from the refrigerator.'

Defendant entered deceased's hospital room after his death, but left shortly, approached the attending physician and said, 'You are not going to order an autopsy of Lawrence after all he's been through?' Until this time there had been no suggestion by the doctor or by anyone else that an autopsy should be performed. The doctor informed defendant he was not fully convinced whether an autopsy was indicated, saying, 'Well, I just don't know what the cause of his death was and I just don't see how I can avoid it.' After this initial comment, defendant brought up the subject of an autopsy several times, and tried to convince the doctor that he should not order one.

An autopsy was performed, and it revealed as the cause of death, shock due to arsenic poisoning. Arsenic was discovered in the contents of the stomach, and in both the base and tip of the victim's toenails, in the brain, stomach wall, hair, liver, fat, heart and kidneys of the deceased. It was the opinion of the autopsy surgeon, based upon the amount of arsenic in the body and its distribution throughout the body, that the victim had continually ingested arsenic over a period of three or four months, and that a fatal dose of arsenic had been administered within hours of the victim's death. The doctor was positive that it was impossible for deceased to have been poisoned by inhalation or absorption through the skin.

Jesse Carr, M.D., a pathologist of many years' experience, whose qualifications were not questioned, testified as follows:

'Q. Now, from the facts which I gave to you, can you state whether the death was the result of acute, subacute or chronic poisoning? A. I can answer that question if I may explain the answer.

'Q. Yes. A. He actually died of all three. The immediate cause of his death on the 13th of November was acute arsenic poisoning, but in his background he also had subacute and chronic arsenic poisoning.

'Q. Now, would you explain the difference, first of all, Doctor, between chronic, acute and subacute arsenic poisoning? A. Yes. May I just refer to the words? First, chronic in a poisoning sense is a matter of months and subacute poisoning runs from, generally a month, down to a matter of a few weeks, and acute poisonings are those which terminate within twenty-four to forty-eight or at most seventy-two hours in the case of arsenic. Occasionally an acute poisoning will last as much as six to seven days. Now, to distinguish between these three: Arsenic is one of the few poisons that medical scientists get satisfaction working with because arsenic writes its own record after it is ingested or eaten or in fact any way that it may be taken, and it leaves specific evidence, so it is one of the rare things we study that we can time and that is why I say that there are all three elements here. ...'

Just a little over two weeks later, on January 28, defendant contacted another lonely hearts club, and on January 31 she reenrolled as a member of the World-Wide Group, the lonely hearts club through which she had met deceased.

On appeal defendant contends that the evidence was insufficient to support the jury verdict of guilty.

Defendant's argument, that the evidence was insufficient to support the verdict of guilty, is advanced by two arguments: (a) 'Circumstantial evidence must be irreconcilable with the theory of innocence before there is a sound basis for conviction'; and (b) 'A conviction must be reversed if it appears that upon no hypothecation whatever is there substantial evidence to support the conclusion reached in the court below.' Both arguments stem from the fact that defendant's conviction rested on circumstantial evidence.

It was said in a prior case, 'our consideration of the contention that the evidence was insufficient to justify the verdict is governed by familiar rules. The decision of the jury as to material facts, and the inferences drawn therefrom, are to be accepted as conclusive on appeal if in our judgment they are such as could have been reached by impartial and reasonable minds.

If there is room for difference of opinion among reasonable minds whether the facts impliedly found were justified by the evidence or whether the inferences drawn by the triers of fact were reasonable, we must accept their conclusions even though as triers of fact we might have reached opposite ones.

'In our analysis of the evidence we have endeavored to find a reasonable theory of appellant's innocence. If we had reached the conclusion that such a theory does exist it would only have been incidental to the further question whether it was the only reasonable theory. The jury has determined that the evidence admits of no tenable theory of innocence. That determination is based upon the evidentiary findings of fact which the verdict implies. If those findings have support in facts established, and in reasonable inferences, they are conclusive on appeal.

'If we conclude that the implied factual decisions reached have substantial support in the evidence and that the inferences which led to the verdict were reasonably drawn, it is not our function to determine whether the ultimate findings were established beyond a reasonable doubt. That lies within the exclusive jurisdiction of trial judges and juries.'

In our case the body of Mr. Helwinkel was available for an autopsy, and the autopsy revealed that poisoning by arsenic was the cause of his death. Additionally, we have a record reflecting in detail the progress of Mr. Helwinkel's four-month illness preceding death. It provides a description of his activities, of his physical degeneration, of his nausea, of his medical and hospital treatment, and of his conversations with defendant and many other witnesses. There is also before us the testimony of defendant, as well as that of many witnesses who had conversations with her and who observed her and her actions.

The record which we have heretofore related in some detail reflects ample evidence, circumstantial though it may be, to support the verdict of the jury. There is substantial evidence from which the jury could, and did, reasonably conclude that defendant had the opportunity, the means and the motive to kill her husband.

The many circumstances disclosed by the evidence not only point inexorably toward defendant as the murderess, but from the record we can perceive of no reasonable theory reconcilable with her claim of innocence. The only serious argument advanced by defendant to support her theory of innocence is that Helwinkel might have committed suicide. The instrument of death, arsenic poison, and the method by which it was administered, continual poisoning over several months, remove from the theory of suicide the probability required to bring it within the realm of reasonableness. The record shows without dispute that chronic, subacute and acute arsenic poisoning combined to cause Helwinkel's agonizing death. The poisoning occurred at intervals over a four-month period, and we find it difficult to believe that anyone bent on committing suicide would take repeated doses of arsenic and inflict excruciating pain upon himself time after time, rather than take a lethal dose and be done with it. The evidence of many episodes of vomiting and diarrhea accompanied by violent agony, the slow development of his disabling weakness, and the manner in which the use of his feet gradually became impaired until they slapped or dropped as he walked, dispel the theory of suicide.

It is equally unbelievable that a person would attempt to work and at the same time cause his body to degenerate. The deceased gradually lost the use of his hands while still on the job, getting so bad off that fellow employees had to remove his cigarettes from the pack and light them. It is significant that he continued trying to work even though he couldn't operate the machinery at the plant. This conduct is not consistent with suicide. His request for a doctor upon becoming ill, and going to the local hospital, are equally inconsistent with the theory of suicide. Nor does it appear reasonable that had he wanted to die he would have gone to the University of California Hospital for treatment by specialists when the cause of his illness could not be determined at a local hospital.

The judgment is affirmed.

H. Questions

♦ Do you think the *Helwinkel* court reached the right result when it affirmed the wife's conviction for murder? What facts support your conclusion?

- Now that you have read a case which relies in great part on circumstantial evidence, do you feel that our system correctly or incorrectly allows circumstantial evidence to be used to prove guilt? Do you think it should make any difference regarding the seriousness of the crime involved?

I. Comments

The *Hansen* case, below, has not been edited. The entire case has been included because of the wealth of information contained within the case. *Hansen* is particularly instructive on two difficult points of the law of homicide: the interrelationship between negligent conduct and homicide and intervening cause. The interrelationship is in large part controlled by "foreseeability." Pay close attention to the court's discussion of the importance of foreseeability and its role in homicide law.

On a final note, you will observe that this case does not involve murder; rather, the case centers on involuntary manslaughter. (Involuntary manslaughter is discussed more fully later on in this chapter.) At common law, had death occurring during a game of Russian roulette was considered murder under this theory that the defendant exhibited a "depraved heart" type of malice aforethought, which required extreme recklessness. As you read, consider why court did classify the defendant's actions as exhibiting a depraved heart.

J. Case

PEOPLE v. HANSEN
COURT OF APPEAL, FIRST DISTRICT, DIVISION 4
59 App.473 199

REARDON, J.

Defendant and appellant John Edward Hansen (appellant) was charged in count one with felony child endangerment while armed with a firearm which resulted in death. Count two charged involuntary manslaughter. A jury found appellant guilty as charged and alleged.

Appellant contends that the convictions are supported by substantial evidence. We affirm.

I. Statement of the Facts

On December 14, 1995, Jason Campbell, the 14-year-old-victim, was killed by a shot from a .357-caliber Magnum revolver discharged at or near the surface of the skin into his right temple. The events surrounding the death of Jason were observed by appellant and three teenage eyewitnesses: Alicia T., Johnny M. and Eric B. December 14, 1995, was one week before appellant's thirty-fifth birthday. He lived with his girlfriend and her three children. At the time of the shooting, Alicia and Eric were staying at appellant's residence. Jason was a close neighbor and resided with his mother. The teenagers were friends with each other. Before the date of the shooting, appellant had "hung out" with Jason, Eric and Johnny.

Around 10:30 p.m. on December 14, 1995, appellant, Jason and the eyewitnesses were sitting in appellant's small living room. No one else was present. All were close together and a television was playing.

Appellant was noticeably intoxicated. None of the others appeared to be intoxicated.

Alicia, Johnny and Eric testified that appellant removed a .357-caliber Magnum Ruger revolver from his jacket, placed the muzzle at his head and pulled the trigger one to four times. The gun, which held six rounds, clicked without firing. Alicia also noticed appellant clumsily load and unload the revolver. Four bullets removed from the gun were picked up by Alicia. Subsequently she threw them down a storm drain.

Alicia and Johnny heard appellant state something to the effect of would you like to play "Russian roulette," directed at the group generally. Eric heard appellant mention Russian roulette to Jason and someone asked if Eric wanted to play. A comment was made that two bullets remained in the revolver. Eric stated that he would not play Russian roulette with two out of six chances. No eyewitness could positively certify the exact number of bullets in the revolver, but each believed that at all material times at least one live round was present. Jason stated, " 'Don't take the easy way out' " or " 'That's a sucker's way to go out.' " Johnny also made the former comment.

The next person to hold the .357-caliber Magnum was Jason. Appellant handed it to him either at the request of Jason or on appellant's own initiative. Jason attempted to pass the gun to Johnny. When Johnny refused, Jason stated: " 'Don't be a chicken.' " Eric requested the gun. Jason asked appellant if he should give the gun to Eric and appellant stated no. Jason asked Eric, " 'How can you pull the trigger without making the gun go off?' " Eric explained and demonstrated with his hands how to do so. Jason carried out the procedure and handed the gun back to appellant.

Alicia observed appellant put the gun to his head, spin the barrel, pull the trigger two or three times and mention Russian roulette. The weapon clicked without firing. Johnny observed the same actions but he heard appellant again state to the group, " 'Let's play some Russian roulette.' " Eric turned his attention to the television and did not continue to watch appellant or Jason. At this point in time, Alicia, Eric and Johnny prepared to leave appellant's residence. They were going for hot chocolate and marshmallows at Jason's house. Jason was expected to join them.

As Alicia was tying her shoes, she saw Jason standing face-to-face with appellant about four inches apart. Alicia could determine that Jason and appellant were talking but she did not hear the actual words. Jason put the muzzle of the gun against his head. Alicia heard a loud noise and saw a flash. She looked toward Jason and appellant. Jason was lying up against a speaker. Appellant jumped up, threw his arms down and stated, " 'shit.' " Johnny was heading to the bathroom when he heard a gunshot, turned and saw Jason lying on the ground. Eric saw Jason holding the gun which was pointed downward. Then Eric went to the kitchen to light a cigarette and heard the gun go off. Turning toward Jason, Eric observed the flash of a gun and "Jason's eyes sticking out." Appellant and the three witnesses ran out of appellant's residence.

When the police were summoned after the shooting, they discovered two live bullets in appellant's residence. One spent cartridge was found inside the.357-caliber revolver. There were two bullets in Jason's pocket which would not fit in the revolver.

The defense presented witnesses who testified that Jason was mature for his age. Appellant and his girlfriend testified that appellant was carrying the handgun for protection because of threats to them. Due to intoxication appellant did not remember much of the circumstances of the shooting. His best recollection was that he emptied the gun and placed it to his head. The next memory is Jason shooting himself in the head. At no time did appellant mention Russian roulette. When someone else referred to Russian roulette, "almost like automatic" appellant put the gun to his own head and pulled the trigger.

II. Substantial Evidence and Intervening Cause

Appellant contends that the evidence was insufficient to support verdicts of child endangerment and involuntary manslaughter, or at minimum required an instruction on independent intervening cause. These contentions lack merit.

Section_273a, subdivision (a) provides that felony child endangerment occurs when: "Any person who, under circumstances or conditions likely to produce great bodily harm or death, willfully causes or permits any child to suffer, or inflicts thereon unjustifiable physical pain or mental suffering, or having the care or custody of any child, willfully causes or permits the person or health of that child to be injured, or willfully causes or permits that child to be placed in a situation where his or her person or health is endangered ...."

"Although ... (Penal Code section 273a...does use the word 'willfully,' the crime described is one of criminal negligence and not of malice or specific intent. [Citations.] [¶] A finding of criminal negligence is made by the application of the *objective* test of whether a reasonable person in the defendant's position would have been aware of the risk involved.... [Citation.] Criminal negligence may be found even when a defendant acts with a sincere good faith belief that his or her actions pose no risk." [Citation] (original italics.) Involuntary manslaughter may also result from criminal negligence.

"Criminal negligence 'means that the defendant's conduct must amount to a reckless, gross or culpable departure from the ordinary standard of due care; it must be such a departure from what would be the conduct of an ordinarily prudent person

under the same circumstances as to be incompatible with a proper regard for human life.' [Citation.]"

"The principles of causation apply to crimes as well as torts. [Citation.]" "It is, therefore, clear that a defendant may be liable for [criminal homicide] for a killing when his acts were the 'proximate cause' of the death of the victim, even though he did not administer the fatal wound." "Thus, in homicide cases, a 'cause of the [death of the victim] is an act or omission that sets in motion a chain of events that produces as a direct, natural and probable consequence of the act or omission the [death] and without which the [death] would not occur.' [Citations.]"

" '... [N]egligence on the part of the victim is not a defense to criminal liability.... [¶] A defendant may be criminally liable for a result directly caused by his act even if there is another contributing cause. If an intervening cause is a normal and reasonably foreseeable result of defendant's original act the intervening act is "dependent" and not a superseding cause, and will not relieve defendant of liability.... "(1) The consequence need not have been a strong probability; a possible consequence which might reasonably have been contemplated is enough. (2) The precise consequence need not have been foreseen; it is enough that the defendant should have foreseen the possibility of some harm of the kind which might result from his act. " ...' ..." [Citations]

"Thus, it is only an unforeseeable intervening cause, an extraordinary and abnormal occurrence, which rises to the level of an exonerating, superseding cause. [Citations.]"

In *Tison v. Arizona* (1987) 481 U.S. 137 [107 S.Ct. 1676, 95 L.Ed.2d 127], the United States Supreme Court cites the Model Penal Code, which refers to "shooting a person in the course of playing Russian roulette" as an example of acting " 'reckless[ly] under circumstances manifesting extreme indifference to the value of human life.' " (*Id.* at p. 169, fn. 8 [107 S.Ct. at p. 1694].) California courts have described Russian roulette as "conduct ... beyond reason" and " 'a bizarre pass-time ... courting death or severe injury'

Courts of other states have applied endangerment or homicide statutes to situations where the defendants and victim were engaged in Russian roulette and the victim shot himself.

Minor v. State (1992) 326 Md. 436 [605 A.2d 138], involved a Maryland statute providing that "... [A]ny person who [¶] 'recklessly engages in conduct that creates a substantial risk of death or serious physical injury to another person is guilty ....' " (*Ibid.*) After being found guilty in a trial by the court, defendant contended that "... the victim's act of pulling the trigger was a voluntary act of suicide that was unanticipated and, therefore, the evidence did not show that his conduct was reckless ...." (*Id.* at p. 140.) The Maryland Court of Appeals rejected the contention and held that participation in Russian roulette was substantial evidence that defendant committed the offense. (*Id.* at pp. 141-142.)

In *Commonwealth v. Atencio* (1963) 345 Mass. 627 [189 N.E.2d 223], the Supreme Judicial Court of Massachusetts affirmed a jury verdict and conviction of involuntary manslaughter for two defendants as follows: "Here the Commonwealth had an interest that the deceased should not be killed by the wanton or reckless conduct of himself and others. [Citation.] Such conduct could be found in the concerted action and cooperation of the defendants in helping to bring about the deceased's foolish act.... [¶] ... The testimony does not require a ruling that when the deceased took the gun from [defendant] Atencio it was an independent or intervening act not standing in any relation to the defendants' acts which would render what he did imputable to them.... There could be found to be a mutual

encouragement in a joint enterprise. In the abstract, there may have been no duty on the defendants to prevent the deceased from playing. But there was a duty on their part not to cooperate or join with him in the 'game.' " (*Id.* at pp. 224-225.)

Lewis v. State (Ala.Crim.App. 1985) 474 So.2d 766, involved a conviction, by a jury, of criminally negligent homicide where the 15-year-old victim shot himself while alone after the Russian roulette had concluded. The Alabama Court of Criminal Appeals reversed as follows: "A determination as to whether the conduct of a person caused the suicide of another must necessarily include an examination of the victim's free will. Cases have consistently held that the 'free will of the victim is seen as an intervening cause which ... breaks the chain of causation.' [Citation.] Therefore, the crux of this issue is whether the victim exercised his own free will when he got the gun, loaded it and shot himself. We hold that the victim's conduct was a supervening, intervening cause sufficient to break the chain of causation. [¶] ... [W]e cannot say that the appellant should have perceived the risk that the victim would play the game by himself or that he intended for him to do this." (*Id.* at p. 771.)

However, the Alabama court also stated, as explanation of its holding: "If the victim had shot himself while he and the appellant were playing Russian Roulette, or if the appellant was present when the victim was playing the game by himself, the appellant's conduct of influencing the victim to play would have been the cause-in-fact and the proximate cause of the victim's death. However, the key is the appellant's presence at the time the victim shot himself. [Citation.] ... [¶] It also seems clear that the appellant would be responsible for the victim's death if he had left the room while the victim was still playing the game because he should have perceived the result. But, the evidence reveals that the appellant had put the gun away after they finished playing the 'game.' " (*Lewis v. State, supra,* 474 So.2d at p. 771.)

We find the decisions and reasoning of the Maryland, Massachusetts and Alabama courts to be consistent with the California cases and quite persuasive. Construing the instant record most favorably to the judgment, as we must in accordance with the substantial evidence rule, the key facts are that appellant initiated Russian roulette, encouraged the victim to participate and was present when the victim shot himself while engaged in Russian roulette. The actions and words of appellant regarding Russian roulette establish that he acted in a criminally negligent manner which caused the death of Jason and constituted felony child endangerment as well as involuntary manslaughter.

We conclude that these instructions and arguments fully informed the jury of the relevant law and properly framed the superseding cause issue into layman's terms as the following question: On the evidence presented was appellant criminally liable for the death of Jason even though Jason shot himself?

The judgment is affirmed.

II. FELONY MURDER

A. Comments

In the following cases, you will see several important legal felony murder theories discussed. The first case, *Washington,* discusses whether a defendant can be convicted of first-degree murder where a cofelon is killed by the robbery victim. The conclusion that the court reaches is not a unanimous one. We have included a portion of the dissenting opinion for your review. When you read *Washington*, consider whether you think the majority or the dissent reaches the better conclusion.

B. Cases

PEOPLE V. WASHINGTON
Supreme Court of California, In Bank.
62 Cal.2d 777 1965.

TRAYNOR, C. J.

Shortly before 10 p.m., October 2, 1962, Johnnie Carpenter prepared to close his gasoline station. He was in his office computing the receipts and disbursements of the day while an attendant in an adjacent storage room deposited money in a vault. Upon hearing someone yell 'robbery,' Carpenter opened his desk and took out a revolver. A few moments later, James Ball entered the office and pointed a revolver directly at Carpenter, who fired immediately, mortally wounding Ball. Carpenter then hurried to the door and saw an unarmed man he later identified as defendant running from the vault with a moneybag in his right hand. He shouted 'Stop.' When his warning was not heeded, he fired and hit defendant who fell wounded in front of the station.

The Attorney General contends that defendant was properly convicted of first degree murder. [As support, the Attorney General cites a case in which the] defendants initiated a gun battle with an employee in an attempt to rob a cleaning business. In the crossfire, the employee accidentally killed the owner of the business. The court affirmed the judgment convicting defendants of first degree murder, which held that robbers who provoked gunfire were guilty of first degree murder even though the lethal bullet was fired by a policeman.

Defendant suggests that we [adopt the rule of other jurisdictions which hold] that surviving felons are not guilty of murder when their accomplices are killed by persons resisting the felony.

A distinction based on the person killed, however, would make the defendant's criminal liability turn upon the marksmanship of victims and policemen. A rule of law cannot reasonably be based on such a fortuitous circumstance. The basic issue therefore is whether a robber can be convicted of murder for the killing of any person by another who is resisting the robbery.

'Murder is the unlawful killing of a human being, with malice aforethought.' Except when the common-law-felony-

murder doctrine is applicable, an essential element of murder is an intent to kill or an intent with conscious disregard for life to commit acts likely to kill. The felony-murder doctrine ascribes malice aforethought to the felon who kills in the perpetration of an inherently dangerous felony. That doctrine is incorporated in section 189 of the Penal Code, which provides in part: 'All murder ... committed in the perpetration or attempt to perpetrate ... robbery ... is murder of the first degree.' Thus, even though section 189 speaks only of degrees of 'murder,' inadvertent or accidental killings are first degree murders when committed by felons in the perpetration of robbery. When a killing is not committed by a robber or by his accomplice but by his victim, malice aforethought is not attributable to the robber, for the killing is not committed by him in the perpetration or attempt to perpetrate robbery. It is not enough that the killing was a risk reasonably to be foreseen and that the robbery might therefore be regarded as a proximate cause of the killing. Section 189 requires that the felon or his accomplice commit the killing, for if he does not, the killing is not committed to perpetrate the felony. Indeed, in the present case the killing was committed to thwart a felony. To include such killings within section 189 would expand the meaning of the words 'murder ... which is committed in the perpetration ... [of] robbery ...' beyond common understanding. The purpose of the felony-murder rule is to deter felons from killing negligently or accidentally by holding them strictly responsible for killings they commit. This purpose is not served by punishing them for killings committed by their victims.

It is contended, however, that another purpose of the felony- murder rule is to prevent the commission of robberies. Neither the common- law rationale of the rule nor the Penal Code supports this contention. In every robbery there is a possibility that the victim will resist and kill. The robber has little control over such a killing once the robbery is undertaken as this case demonstrates. To impose an additional penalty for the killing would discriminate between robbers, not on the basis of any difference in their own conduct, but solely on the basis of the response by others that the robber's conduct happened to induce. An additional penalty for a homicide committed by the victim would deter robbery haphazardly at best. To 'prevent stealing, [the law] would do better to hang one thief in every thousand by lot.'

A defendant need not do the killing himself, however, to be guilty of murder. He may be vicariously responsible under the rules defining principals and criminal conspiracies. All persons aiding and abetting the commission of a robbery are guilty of first degree murder when one of them kills while acting in furtherance of the common design. Moreover, when the defendant intends to kill or intentionally commits acts that are likely to kill with a conscious disregard for life, he is guilty of murder even though he uses another person to accomplish his objective.

The judgment is affirmed as to defendant's conviction of first degree robbery and reversed as to his conviction of first degree murder.

BURKE, J.

I dissent.

The unfortunate effect of the decision of the majority in this case is to advise felons:

'Henceforth in committing certain crimes, including robbery, rape and burglary, you are free to arm yourselves with a gun and brandish it in the faces of your victims without fear of a murder conviction unless you or your accomplice pulls the trigger. If the menacing effect of your gun causes a victim or policeman to fire and kill an innocent person or a cofelon, you are absolved of responsibility for such killing unless you shoot first.'

Obviously this advance judicial absolution removes one of the most meaningful deterrents to the commission of armed felonies.

I would hold, that the killing is that of the felon whether or not the lethal bullet comes from his gun or that of his accomplice and whether or not one of them shoots first, and would affirm the judgment of conviction of murder in the instant case.

C. Comments

The second case, *Birden*, discusses two important legal concepts that apply to the felony murder rule: the merger doctrine and the natural and probable consequences doctrine.

D. Case

PEOPLE V. BIRDEN
179 Cal.App. 3d 1020
Court of Appeal, Second District, Division 4
(1986)

KINGSLEY, Acting P. J.

Over the Thanksgiving weekend in 1983, the defendant and two other individuals conspired to hold up a card game that they heard was taking place at an apartment in the Nickerson Gardens Housing Project. The apartment in question belonged to the murder victim, Elizabeth George, who was having her family over that weekend to celebrate the holidays. The defendant confessed to the police that he and another man were to approach the front door of the apartment while a third individual, Joe Page, went around to the back with a shotgun.

At about 7 that evening the defendants knocked on the door of the apartment which was answered by Beebe "James" Brewer, Elizabeth George's boyfriend.

Brewer testified that the defendants then either asked for someone or stated that this was a holdup. The defendant then pushed Brewer to the floor and held the door open.

Observing all this was Elizabeth George's daughter-in-law, Diane Haughton. When Brewer was pushed to the floor, she ran into the kitchen where Elizabeth George and some other friends and relatives were playing cards. No money was involved in the game. Diane Haughton then told everyone that someone was at the door and

had pushed James. Elizabeth George then got up, stormed into the living room and shoved the two would-be holdup men out the door. Grabbing a bottle she used as a vase, Elizabeth George reopened the door, telling the others, "I'm going to see what these mother fuckers trying to bogart my mother fucking house." A heated argument quickly ensued between Elizabeth George and one of the robbers. As she raised the bottle up over her head, Elizabeth George received one shotgun blast under the arm, which killed her. An autopsy showed she had a blood alcohol level of .08.

The defendant contends that he is not guilty of felony murder on two grounds: (1) the attempted robbery had been abandoned before the murder occurred; and, (2) that there was no causal connection between the planned robbery and the murder. These contentions are without merit.

A homicide need not occur while the underlying felony is in progress to trigger operation of the felony-murder rule. There is no requirement that the homicide take place while committing the felony, or while engaged in the felony, or that the killing be part of the felony. It is sufficient that the homicide be related to the felony and have resulted as a natural and probable consequence thereof. No technical inquiry concerning whether there has been a completion, abandonment or desistance of the felony prior to the commission of the homicide is necessary. Thus, even if there was convincing evidence that the defendant had abandoned the robbery-which there is not-he would still be liable for the murder if it resulted as a natural consequence of the attempted crime.

The defendant, however, contends that the murder was not a natural consequence of the robbery in that it was the result of an intoxicated victim attacking the robbers after they had fled and thus not causally related to the crime. This contention, however, does not change the status of the crime from a felony- murder. It is to be expected that on occasion, as was committed merely to further an intended murder, the commission of the felony does not trigger the application of the felony-murder rule. Thus, where a man breaks into the house of his intended murder victim in order to assault him-thereby committing a burglary as well as a homicide-he is not guilty of felony-murder. This doctrine can have no application here, however, unless the defendant intended to

the case here, a robbery victim may not just simply submit to his assailants but instead, may attempt to fight or pursue them, as he is lawfully entitled to do. A murder under these circumstances is no less a natural consequence of the robbery. In retrospect, it is tragically predictable. The defendant is not excused, therefore, because his victim resisted his efforts to perpetrate or flee from the crime.

The defendant also argues that his felony-murder conviction is erroneous as the robbery was an integral part of the homicide and not an independent crime. This contention seems to arise from the defendant's misapplication of the so-called "merger doctrine." When a felony is

murder Elizabeth George and the attempted robbery was somehow designed to further that end. This is hardly credible, probably legally impossible, and entirely contrary to all the evidence in this case. We therefore cannot accept the contention on appeal.

The judgment is affirmed.

E. Questions

♦ In the *Birden* case, the court states that the intoxicated attack by the victim was immaterial to the application of the felony murder rule. Do you agree? Do you think that a murder under these circumstances does or does not make the murder a natural consequence of the underlying felony?

♦ Consider *Birden's* contention that the robbery was an entirely separate offense from the homicide. Do you think the facts could reasonably be interpreted to support such an argument?

F. Comments

Finally, in the third case, *Mendoza*, you will see how felony murder and statutory degrees of murder (as set forth in the Penal Code sections, above) are harmonized by the court in *Mendoza*. The defendant's first-degree murder conviction (in the context of a felony murder factual setting) was affirmed by the California Supreme Court by a bare 4-3 decision. The unedited length of this opinion indicates the difficulty that the Court has in reaching its decision: the majority opinion is 25 pages long and the three dissenting opinions took up an additional 15 pages. This case is somewhat unusual in that each dissenting justice writes an individual dissenting opinion. The version of *Mendoza* which you will be reading is highly edited and is only a few pages long.

When reading this case and the one of the dissenting opinions which follows, pay close attention to the discussion regarding legislative intent. Legislative intent plays a pivotal role in the court's affirmance of the defendant's conviction. Legislative intent is also the basis for the dissenting opinion that follows.

F. Case

PEOPLE V. MENDOZA
Supreme Court of California
23 Cal. 4th 896 (2000)

Chin, J.

Under Penal Code section 1157, "whenever a defendant is convicted of a crime ... which is distinguished into degrees," the trier of fact "must find the degree of the crime ... of which he is guilty. Upon the failure of the [trier of fact] to so determine, the degree of the crime ... of which the defendant is guilty, shall be deemed to be of the lesser degree." Here, we consider this section's applicability under the following circumstances: (1) the prosecution's only murder theory at trial is that the killing was committed during perpetration of robbery or burglary, which is first degree murder as a matter of law (§ 189); (2) the court properly instructs the jury to return either an acquittal or a conviction of first degree murder; and (3) the jury returns a conviction for murder, but its verdict fails to specify the murder's degree. We conclude that under these circumstances, section 1157 does not apply because the defendant has not been "convicted of a crime ... which is distinguished into degrees" within the meaning of that section. Thus, the conviction is not "deemed to be of the lesser degree." (§ 1157.) We therefore affirm the Court of Appeal's judgment.

FACTS

On September 22, 1992, the Marin County Grand Jury returned an indictment accusing defendants Cruz Alberto Mendoza and Raul Antonio Valle of, among other crimes, "murder in violation of Section 187(A)," second degree robbery (§ 211), and burglary (§ 459). These charges arose out of the killing of Pastor Dan Elledge at The Lord's Church in Novato, California. As special circumstances for sentencing purposes, the indictment also alleged that defendants committed murder while they were engaged in committing robbery and burglary. (§ 190.2, subd. (a)(17).)

[T]he prosecution's only murder theory was that Valle and Mendoza shot and killed Pastor Elledge while burglarizing and robbing The Lord's Church (as one in a series of church robberies). Under section 189, all murder committed "in the perpetration of" robbery or burglary "is murder of the first degree."

In his defense, Mendoza, who admitted committing other crimes with (and without) Valle, maintained he never entered The Lord's Church and did not participate in any of the crimes Valle committed there, including Pastor Elledge's killing. In connection with the charge for that killing, Mendoza did not contend the jury could convict him of a degree or form of criminal homicide other than first degree felony murder. Nor did he ask the trial court to instruct the jury on lesser included offenses; his counsel agreed that because the prosecution had presented only a first degree felony-murder case, instructions relating to specific intent for other forms of first degree murder were unnecessary. Thus, Mendoza's counsel expressly declined to request instructions on malice aforethought and premeditation and deliberation. At other points during the discussion of the instructions, Mendoza's counsel expressed his understanding that the prosecution's only murder theory was first degree felony murder.

Consistent with these proceedings, the trial court instructed Mendoza's jury only on first degree felony murder . . . .¶ The court also gave the following instruction: "In order to find the defendant guilty of the crime of murder, . . . One, you must be satisfied beyond a reasonable doubt that, first, the crimes of robbery and burglary . . . were committed; and, second, the defendant aided and abetted such crimes; and, third, a co-principal in such crime committed the crimes of robbery or burglary . . . and, fourth, the crime of murder was a natural and probable consequence of the commission of the crimes of robbery or burglary."

In addition, [the court] instruct[ed] on the "lesser crimes" of which the jury could convict Mendoza if it found him not guilty of the charged crimes, the court did not mention any form of criminal homicide other than first degree felony murder. Consistent with these instructions, the verdict forms the court submitted to the jury did not give the jury the option to convict defendant of second degree murder or any other form of criminal homicide.

DISCUSSION

The issue here is the proper construction of section 1157, which the Legislature first enacted as part of the Penal Code of 1872. As originally enacted, section 1157 provided: "Whenever a crime is distinguished into degrees, the jury, if they convict the defendant, must find the degree of the crime of which he is guilty." In 1951, the Legislature amended this language to make

the statute apply "whenever a defendant is convicted of a crime which is distinguished into degrees ...." (Stats. 1951, ch. 1674, § 109, p. 3849.) . . . Thus, the threshold question we must consider is whether, under the facts and circumstances we have set forth above, defendants were "convicted of a crime ... which is distinguished into degrees" within the meaning of section 1157. If they were not, then the statute does not apply.

***

We begin by considering the nature of felony murder. In California, the first-degree felony-murder rule "is a creature of statute." [Citation.] When the prosecution establishes that a defendant killed while committing one of the felonies section 189 lists, "by operation of the statute the killing is deemed to be first degree murder as a matter of law." ([Citation] [section 189 "in terms makes ... a killing" committed during robbery "murder of the first degree"].) Thus, there are no degrees of such murders; as a matter of law, a conviction for a killing committed during a robbery or burglary can *only* be a conviction for first degree murder.

That such murders can only be of the first degree has several significant consequences at trial. Where the evidence points indisputably to a killing committed in the perpetration of one of the felonies section 189 lists, the *only* guilty verdict a jury may return is first degree murder. [Citation.] Under these circumstances, a trial court "is justified in withdrawing" the question of degree "from the jury" and instructing it that the defendant is either not guilty, or is guilty of first degree murder. [Citation.] The trial court also need not instruct the jury on offenses other than first degree felony murder or on the differences between the degrees of murder. [Citations]. Nor need it give [instruction that]: "Murder is classified into two degrees. If you should find the defendant guilty of murder, you must determine and state in your verdict whether you find the murder to be of the first or second degree." [Citations.] Because the evidence establishes as a matter of law that the murder is of the first degree, these procedures violate neither the right under section 1126 to have a jury determine questions of fact [citation] nor the constitutional right to have a jury determine every material issue the evidence presents. [Citations.] Finally, if, under these circumstances, a jury returns a verdict for a crime other than first degree murder, the trial court must refuse to accept the verdict because it is contrary to law, and must direct the jury to reconsider. [Citations.]

The Legislature clearly was aware of many of these principles when it enacted section 1157 in 1872. In proposing the 1872 Penal Code to the Legislature, the California Code Commission explained in its note to section 189 that where a killing occurs during commission of one of the listed felonies, the question of degree "is answered by the statute itself, and the jury have [*sic*] no option but to find the prisoner guilty in the first degree. Hence, ... all difficulty as to the question of degree is removed by the statute." [Citations.] Where, as here, "a statute proposed by the California Code Commission for inclusion in the Penal Code of 1872 [was] enacted by the Legislature without substantial change, the report of the commission is entitled to great weight in construing the statute and in determining the intent of the Legislature. [Citations.]"

In light of these principles, we conclude that where, as here, the trial court correctly instructs the jury only on first degree felony murder and to find the defendant either not guilty or guilty of first degree murder, section 1157 does not apply. Under these circumstances, as a matter of law, the *only* crime of which a defendant may be convicted is first degree murder, and the question of degree is not before the jury. As to the degree of the crime, there is simply no determination for the jury to make. Thus, a defendant convicted under these circumstances has not, under the plain and commonsense meaning of section 1157, been "convicted of a crime ... which is distinguished into degrees."

A contrary construction would violate several principles of statutory interpretation.

First, it would ignore the obvious purpose of the statute, which is to ensure that where a verdict *other than first degree is permissible*, the jury's determination of degree is clear. Applying section 1157 where jury instructions correctly permit only a first degree felony-murder conviction would do nothing to further this statutory purpose.

***

We therefore hold that the trial court properly entered judgments against defendants for first degree murder.

***

CONCLUSION

The judgment of the Court of Appeal is affirmed.

MOSK, J.

I dissent.

Penal Code section 1157 in pertinent part requires: "Whenever a defendant is convicted of a crime ... which is distinguished into degrees, the jury, or the court if a jury trial is waived, must find the degree of the crime ... of which he is guilty. Upon the failure of the jury or the court to so determine, the degree of the crime ... of which the defendant is guilty, shall be deemed to be of the lesser degree."

We have consistently, until today, taken the Legislature at its word, strictly construing Penal Code section 1157 to require an express indication by the trier of fact of the degree of the offense. [Citations.] We have specifically rejected the argument, renewed herein, that when a jury is instructed solely on first degree murder the failure of the jury to designate the degree does not trigger the default provision of the statute. "The statute applies to reduce the degree even in situations in which the jury's intent to convict of the greater degree is demonstrated by its other actions .... The key is not whether the 'true intent' of the jury can be gleaned from circumstances outside the verdict form itself; instead, application of the statute turns only on whether the jury specified the degree in the verdict form. ... [P]

... [P] ... No special exception is created for the situation presented by this case [in which the jury was instructed solely on first degree murder]." [Citation.]

Penal Code section 1157, like the statute on which it was modeled, "establishes a rule to which there is to be no exception, and the Courts have no authority to create an exception when the statute makes none. ¶ We have no right to disregard a positive requirement of the statute, as it is not our province to make the laws, but to expound them." [Citations.]

For these reasons, I would hold that the conviction of Cruz Alberto Mendoza . . . must be deemed second degree murder as a matter of law pursuant to Penal Code section 1157.

Accordingly, I dissent.

Dissenting opinions by KENNARD, J and WERDEGAR, J., omitted.

G. Question

♦ The defendant's first degree murder conviction rested on the court's interpretation of section 1157's classification of degrees of murder. Which reasoning is more persuasive as to the Legislature's intent, Justice Chin's majority opinion or Justice Mosk's dissenting opinion? Select the language from either opinion that you find most compelling.

III. VOLUNTARY MANSLAUGHTER

A. Comments

Heat of passion is a key factual consideration for courts when deciding whether an intentional killing is murder (that is, malice aforethought is present) or voluntary manslaughter (the mitigation of the killing due to certain circumstances). In both cases the victim is obviously dead. However, the *death of a victim* is not the critical issue in evaluating a defendant's guilt; it is the defendant's mental state that is often the dispositive factor. Where there is adequate provocation, the killing can be mitigated to voluntary manslaughter. In order for a heat of passion state of mind to be available as a mitigating factor, there are four tests which must be fulfilled: 1) the defendant was actually provoked, 2) a reasonable person would have been provoked, 3) the defendant's passion had not cooled, and 4) the reasonable person's passion had not cooled.

The following case analyzes heat of passion to determine whether or not the crime is first degree murder or manslaughter.

B. Case

PEOPLE V. MARTINEZ
Court of Appeal, Second District, Division 6
193 Cal.App.3d 364 (1987)

GILBERT, Associate Justice.

FACTS

Ernest Vincent Martinez, Jr. and Julie Ann R. had lived together in a studio apartment for about five weeks. On Christmas Eve, 1984, they walked to a party, which was about a mile away from their apartment. At the party they both drank beer and quarreled. Julie Ann R. became noticeably drunk. Early in the evening, Martinez left the party and visited Joseph Gonzales, a friend working at a local restaurant. Martinez invited Gonzales to visit him at home when Gonzales got off work at 12:30 that night. Martinez then left a second time at about 11:30 p.m. to buy beer.

While Martinez was out buying beer, Julie Ann R. began walking home alone, although she had difficulty because of her inebriated state. William Meyers, who had met Julie Ann R. that night offered her a ride home in his car. Julie Ann R. accepted, and brought Mcyers into the apartment she shared with Martinez. Soon they were in bed and engaged in sex. Julie Ann R. told Meyers that her boyfriend would not be home for awhile.

In the meantime, Martinez returned to the party and learned that Julie Ann R. had left with Meyers. He appeared unconcerned. He grabbed a bottle of beer and began to dance by himself. After some time, he asked for a ride home and when he was refused, he ran home.

Julie Ann R. and Meyers were in bed when they heard Martinez banging on the front door. Meyers got up and began to put on his pants as Julie Ann R. directed him to the bathroom window. But Martinez ran around the building and got to the rear window first. Seeing Julie Ann R. in the bathroom with Meyers, Martinez came in through the window as Meyers fled out the front door. Martinez grabbed the shower curtain rod and chased Meyers down the street, hitting him once or twice with the curtain rod.

Giving up the chase, Martinez returned to the apartment and found Julie Ann R. naked in an alleyway around the side of the building. He either grabbed her and caused her to fall, so that her head hit a gas meter, or he struck her and pushed her against a wall. In either event, he caused her to become semi-conscious or unconscious. A neighbor heard a faint cry from the alley, went to investigate and found Martinez standing over a body. He asked what was going on, and Martinez answered, "I caught her fucking someone else." Another neighbor heard screams from the alley and an angry voice saying, "Because you don't know what the hell you're doing."

Martinez then dragged Julie Ann R. around the building, through a courtyard and into their apartment. Along the way he beat her with his fist and pounded her head against the pavement. Once in the apartment, Martinez beat Julie Ann R. with his fists and elbow kicked her in the face, neck and vagina, broke a beer bottle over her forehead, and finally jumped on her. She died in the apartment, within minutes of the beating, of a lacerated liver.

Martinez was charged with the first degree murder of Julie Ann R., on the theory that the killing was willful, deliberate and premeditated, or was the result of torture. The defense argued that Martinez exploded in anger upon finding his girlfriend in bed with another, and so there was no premeditation. On appeal, Martinez argues, among other things, there was insufficient evidence to sustain a conviction for first degree murder.

DISCUSSION

An unjustified murder of a human being is presumed to be second, rather than first degree murder. Only where the state proves beyond a reasonable doubt that the defendant killed by means of "... a destructive device or explosive, knowing use of ammunition designed primarily to penetrate metal or armor, poison, lying in wait, torture, or by any other kind of willful, deliberate and premeditated killing ..." or during the commission of certain felonies, is the murder of the first degree. Martinez argues on appeal that the jury had before it insufficient evidence with which to convict him of first degree murder under the willful, deliberate and premeditated killing theory.

In determining whether substantial evidence exists to support the jury's determination of the degree of a crime, the appellate court views the evidence in a light most favorable to the People.

A. Willful, Deliberate and Premeditated Killing
B.

A verdict of murder in the first degree based on the theory of a willful, deliberate and premeditated killing is proper only if the defendant killed "as a result of careful thought and weighing of considerations; as a deliberate judgment or plan; carried on coolly and steadily, [especially] according to a preconceived design; ..." Our Supreme Court categorized three types of evidence which must exist in one combination or another in order to find sufficient evidence to convict the defendant of willful, deliberate and premeditated murder. These categories are: "(1) facts about how and what defendant did prior to the actual killing which show that the defendant was engaged in activity directed toward and explicable as intended to result in, the killing-- which may be characterized as 'planning' activity; (2) facts about the defendant's prior relationship and/or conduct with the victim from which the jury could reasonably infer a 'motive' to kill the victim, which inference of motive, together with facts of type (1) or (3), would in turn support an inference that the killing was the result of 'a pre-existing reflection' and 'careful thought and weighing of considerations' rather then 'mere unconsidered or rash impulse hastily executed' [citation]; (3) facts about the nature of the killing from which the jury could infer that the manner of killing was so particular and exacting that the defendant must have intentionally killed according to a 'preconceived design' to take his victim's life in a particular way for a 'reason' which the jury can reasonably infer from facts of type (1) or (2)." "Analysis of the cases will show that this court sustains verdicts of first degree murder typically when there is evidence of all three types and otherwise requires at least extremely strong evidence of (1) or evidence of (2) in conjunction with either (1) Martinez argues that here none of these three combinations appear in the record.

We disagree. There was sufficient evidence of motive and planning to sustain the conviction for first degree murder. The circumstantial evidence here provides a reasonable foundation for an inference of premeditation and deliberation, and is not merely conjecture and surmise. Here the evidence is of the type that a trier of fact could find falls within categories one and two. The record is replete with evidence that Martinez beat and killed Julie Ann R. for revenge and punishment for her sexual indiscretion, and that he had considered doing so for some time prior to the murder. Witnesses testified that in the weeks prior to the murder Martinez repeatedly threatened to kill or hurt Julie Ann R. if he ever caught her with another man. On two occasions, Martinez came to the motel where Julie Ann R. was working and told the motel manager that if he caught Julie Ann R. with the manager's son he would kill her (Julie Ann R.). Other witnesses testified that Martinez told them that if Julie Ann R. ever left him, he would kill her, and he threatened to hurt her and to "F-U-C-K her world."

Martinez' threats to kill Julie Ann R. is evidence of planning. Martinez warned Julie Ann R. that he'd kill her if she went with another man, and while beating her he paused to explain to a witness that it was because "I caught her fucking somebody else." In a phone conversation with a friend the morning after the murder, Martinez explained, "I caught Julie in the room with a man and they both was naked." A few moments later in the conversation, after describing the beating, he asked his friend, "What would you have done?"

The evidence supports the inference that Martinez, having previously formed the intent to kill Julie Ann R., if he ever caught her with another man, killed her in conformity with that preconceived plan. "'In arriving at the intention of the defendant, regard should be given to what occurred at the time of the killing, if indicated by the evidence, as well as to what was done before and after that time.' " There was also evidence to support a theory that Martinez reflected on his acts before Julie Ann R. died. He had time to consider his reaction when he first learned that Julie Ann R. had left the party with a man and when he was running home. After chasing Meyers down the street, he deliberately returned to the apartment and searched for Julie Ann R., who was by then in the alleyway. When his beating of Julie Ann R. was interrupted by a neighbor who asked what was happening, Martinez stopped, answered, and after this momentary reflection continued to brutalize her.

Once Julie Ann R. was unconscious, he struggled to drag her body into the apartment, where according to some evidence he turned on the stereo loud enough to muffle the sounds of the beating. This evidence supports a finding that Martinez killed Julie Ann R. with deliberation and premeditation.

Martinez submits that his acts were the result of an unpremeditated explosion of passion and violence. That Martinez returned home to find his girlfriend in bed with another man suggests he acted out of passion. His inviting Joseph Gonzales to visit him at home later that night suggests that by the middle of the evening, he did not plan to murder Julie Ann R. The jury nevertheless had a sufficient basis to find premeditation and deliberation. Martinez may not have planned the specific date and time of the murder, but he repeatedly warned Julie Ann R. and others of his intent to kill or harm her if he ever found her with another man.

It may seem paradoxical to discuss in the same factual setting, premeditation, with its connotation of cool detachment on the one hand, and rage on the other, but these antithetical traits may coexist when they are exhibited at different times. By planning in advance to give into rage, there is less likelihood of controlling that rage when it occurs. The evidence shows that Martinez had long predicted Julie Ann R.'s infidelity and considered his reaction to it. His behavior the night of the murder was as he planned it to be, and as he had predicted it to be.

The actual murder need not be committed in a clinical, or dispassionate manner in order for it to be first degree.

The judgment of conviction is affirmed.

G. Questions

♦ Do you agree with the court's "heat of passion" holding in this case? Is there any one fact which controls your decision? Or do you base your decision on the totality of the circumstances?

IV. INVOLUNTARY MANSLAUGHTER

A. Comments

The following case presents an interesting fact pattern which raises the applicability of the "misdemeanor manslaughter" rule. Observe the court's focus on causation when determining the applicability of the misdemeanor manslaughter rule.

B. Case

PEOPLE V. PENNY
Supreme Court of California
44 Cal App. 2d 861 (1955)

CARTER, J.

Appeal by defendant Mary Penny from a judgment of conviction of involuntary manslaughter.

Defendant was charged with a violation of section 192, subdivision 2, of the Penal Code. That section provides that manslaughter is the unlawful killing of a human being, without malice. '2. Involuntary-in the commission of an unlawful act, not amounting to felony; or in the commission of a lawful act which might produce death, in an unlawful manner, or without due caution and circumspection; provided that this subdivision shall not apply to acts committed in the driving of a vehicle.'

For seven years defendant had been engaged in 'face rejuvenation' in the city of Los Angeles. It is conceded that she had no license from either the Cosmetology Board or the Medical Board of this state; she did have a business license from the city of Los Angeles for the business of 'Face Rejuvenation.'

Defendant had a year's training with a Madame Bergeron (now deceased) in Los Angeles and approximately three months' training with one Geraldine Gorman in New York. In New York, she received the formula which she used in her work. The formula consisted of one ounce of water, a heaping tablespoon of resorcinol (of the same chemical group) and 16 drops of phenol (carbolic acid).

Kay Stanley, the victim, had consulted with defendant some seven months earlier about having her face treated to remove wrinkles and pock marks, but did not have the money to do it at that time. Around Easter time of 1953, she again asked defendant to treat her face, but defendant was to be away and could not do it then. On the morning of May 4, 1953, Kay Stanley arrived at about 10 in the morning at defendant's home where she was to stay during the treatment. Kay's face was first washed with warm water and soda; the formula was then applied with a cotton wrapped wooden applicator to Kay's cheeks, a square inch at a time. After each application, the area was pressed with sterile gauze to remove excess moisture. The entire forehead was covered as well as the eyelids, the process taking about two hours. The treated area was then covered with gauze and taped with small pieces of tape which overlapped and covered the area; regular waterproof adhesive tape was then put on over the other tape; this formed a mask over the upper portion of the patient's face. After the taping had been completed, Kay walked to an adjoining room where she had lunch, listened to the radio and looked at magazines. At approximately 6 in the evening, defendant proceeded to treat the lower half of Kay's face in the same manner as she had treated the upper portion which took about three quarters of an hour. When the treatment was completed, Kay asked defendant if she could sit up for awhile before the taping was started; she sounded sleepy. The defendant told her she could and said she would get her a glass of water. When defendant returned with the water, Kay said, 'I feel a little bit faint' and lay back as though in a faint. Defendant asked her how she felt but received no answer. When defendant tried to lift her she found she was dead weight and felt that she had fainted. Defendant tried unsuccessfully to call a Dr. Wallace and left a message for him; she then called a nurse-anesthetist who arrived at the house about 10 or 15 minutes later. Mrs. Jevne, the nurse, tried to take the patient's pulse without success; there was no respiration. She then administered Coramine, a heart stimulant by hypodermic needle, in the arm; she then gave a hypodermic injection of Metrazol, another stimulant; she then tried artificial respiration and caffeine benzoate. She told defendant to call the doctor again. Dr. Wallace arrived about an hour after Mrs. Jevne did and examined the lady whom he found lying on the treatment table. He was able to feel no pulse and there was no respiration. He noticed signs indicating death had existed for some period of time.

Defendant called her attorney who called the police.

The finding, after an autopsy had been had, was that the immediate cause of death was phenol (carbolic acid) poisoning and edema of the glottis due to 'application of phenol-containing mixture to the face and neck.' Other findings were that 5.1 milligrams of phenol per 100 grams were found in the liver and 2.9 milligrams of phenol per 100 grams were found in the blood of the victim. It was the opinion of Dr. Newbarr, prosecution witness and chief autopsy surgeon for the Los Angeles coroner's office, that these findings were the result of the application of a solution containing more than 10 per cent phenol to the face and neck of the victim. It was the opinion of Mr. Abernathy, the toxicologist, that the reddish-brown discoloration of the victim's face was a third degree burn caused by phenol, and that the normal finding of phenol in a normal human being would be practically zero.

There was evidence in the record which showed that the victim had been taking reducing pills prescribed by a Texas doctor; that in order to obtain replacement of the pills, it was necessary for her to have her heart examined and blood pressure taken by a local doctor; that prior to going to the defendant's home for the face rejuvenation treatment she had had her heart and pulse examined and her blood pressure taken and that all findings were normal.

The question which presents itself is whether defendant's lack of a license (and the fact that she was, therefore, guilty of a misdemeanor) was the cause of Mrs. Stanley's death. Section 192.2 of the Penal Code provides that a person is guilty of involuntary manslaughter if a human being is unlawfully killed 'in the commission of an unlawful act, not amounting to a felony; ...' The jury was instructed that defendant's conduct must have been the proximate cause of the death. The People argue that the law requiring licensing of those practicing cosmetology was designed to prevent injury to others and that one who violates such a law may be guilty of manslaughter if death is caused thereby. In a case factually dissimilar to the one under consideration, the court said: 'We cannot ignore the element of causation in the unlawful act necessary to connect it with the offense. In our ordinary phraseology we refer to the result of this element by saying it must be the probable consequence naturally flowing from the commission of the unlawful act.' It is extremely dubious that defendant's lack of a license had any causal connection with Mrs. Stanley's death and yet it should be noted that the statute provides that if a licensed cosmetologist uses a solution of phenol greater than 10 per cent on any human being, he, or she, is guilty of a misdemeanor. Had defendant been a licensed cosmetologist, under the evidence she would have been guilty of a misdemeanor, and, as a result, the first clause of section 192.2 of the Penal Code would have been directly applicable.

Another question which presents itself is whether defendant was guilty of an unlawful act in applying a solution containing phenol and resorcinol to the human face and neck with the knowledge that both chemicals were poisonous. The statute providing that a licensed cosmetologist may not use a solution containing greater than 10 per cent phenol without being guilty of a misdemeanor sets the standard for licensed persons in that profession or occupation. In discussing the violation of a criminal statute as a basis for a suit for civil damages, we have previously held, 'When a legislative body has generalized a standard from the experience of the community and prohibits conduct that is likely to cause harm, the court accepts the formulated standards and applies them, except where they would serve to impose liability without fault.' Is defendant, who was as a matter of law, practicing cosmetology, to be judged by the same standards as a licensed cosmetologist? The record shows that face rejuvenation, as practiced by defendant, was done to make the face look younger and fresher. The 'art of cosmetology' is defined as that which beautifies the face, or neck, by the use of 'cosmetic preparations, antiseptics, tonics, lotions or creams.' It would appear that the legislative standard set for licensed cosmetologists in the interest of the public health and safety, could, conceivably, be considered applicable to defendant

[The judgment is reversed on other grounds.]

C. Question

♦ There is an old adage in law that states, "Bad facts make bad law." Do you think the unique set of facts in this case led to an unjust result? Or do you think the result was a just one? Keep in mind that the case was reversed on *other* grounds (that is, on issues the defendant raised other than the application of the misdemeanor manslaughter rule).

V. Vehicular Manslaughter

A. Comments

Although automobiles are relatively modern inventions in the history of man, vehicular laws are not as recent as you might guess. Vehicular manslaughter laws actually had earlier counterparts in horse and buggy days. Drivers of horse-drawn vehicles could be held criminally liable for injury or death resulting from negligent operation of a horse-drawn vehicle because these laws are not stepped as much in common law tradition as other wide variation among states in the language of these laws.

The three statutes below are the primary California statutes dealing with vehicular manslaughter. Because these laws are not steeped in common law, tradition (such as ancient crimes like murder) there is a wide variation among the states in the language of these vehicular homicide laws.

B. Statutes

Gross vehicular manslaughter: Penal Code section 192 c(1)

[Gross vehicular manslaughter is defined as the] driving [of] a vehicle in the commission of an unlawful act, not amounting to felony, and with gross negligence; or driving a vehicle in the commission of a lawful act which might produce death, in an unlawful manner, and with gross negligence.

Vehicular manslaughter: Penal Code section 192 c (2)

[Vehicular manslaughter is defined as the] driving [of] a vehicle in the commission of an unlawful act, not amounting to felony, but without gross negligence; or driving a vehicle in the commission of a lawful act which might produce death, in an unlawful manner, but without gross negligence.

Misdemeanor manslaughter: Penal Code section 192 c (3)

[A defendant can be convicted for manslaughter while] [d]riving a vehicle in the commission of an unlawful act, not amounting to felony, but without gross negligence; or driving a vehicle in the commission of a lawful act which might produce death, in an unlawful manner, but without gross negligence.

VI. Self-Assessment

1. Unlike common law, California includes "fetuses" in its law of homicide.
    A. True   B. False

2. Circumstantial evidence is admissible evidence in proving murder.
    A. True   B. False

3. "Misdemeanor manslaughter" falls within involuntary manslaughter.
    A. True   B. False

4. "Heat of passion" is a purely subjective test.
    A. True   B. False

5. Crimes defining vehicular manslaughter tend to be very jurisdiction specific.
    A. True   B. False

CHAPTER TEN

Sexual Conduct &
Crimes Against Persons

Crimes against persons include both sexual and non-sexual criminal conduct This chapter includes traditional sexual crimes (such as rape) as well as modern sexual crimes (such as knowing intercourse by an AIDS victim.). Non-sexual crimes against persons include traditional common law crimes (such as assault and battery) as well as more modern crimes (such as parental kidnapping). This wide range of criminal conduct, both old and new, demonstrates the wide expanse of conduct that is subject to the law of crimes.

I. RAPE

A. Comments

At common law, the crime of rape was colorfully described as "the carnal knowledge of a woman (not the defendant's wife) forcibly and against her will." Modern law has expanded the law of rape to include spousal rape as well as to criminalize other sexually-motivated behaviors. California law provides a view to the modern day law of sexual offenders. Penal Code section 261 (below) has been highly edited. The edited statute provides you with a basic overview of the law of rape in California. You should pay particular attention to the following three provisions.

First, rape as defined in Penal Code section 261a includes both forcible and non-forcible rape. The law specifically states that sexual intercourse accomplished by either force *or* fear is sufficient to constitute rape. The "fear" language of the statute is important. It means that the victim need not resist to the utmost as common law required. It is sufficient to show that the victim's resistance was overcome by fear of the perpetrator.

Second, there are specific provisions which would criminalize what otherwise might appear to be consensual intercourse. For example, if the victim submits believing that the perpetrator is the victim's spouse, sexual intercourse would appear to be consensual on the surface. Consent cannot be freely given where it is obtained under false pretenses. (Can you think of an example of a situation were a victim would wrongly believe that the perpetrator is her spouse? Consider the scenario where a man "marries" a woman for the sole purpose of having intercourse with her, having one of his friends pose as a minister.)

Third, the act specifically provides that intercourse accomplished by the threat of public authority also constitutes rape.

The second traditional rape statute, Penal Code section 263, declares that any penetration, however slight, is sufficient to complete the crime.

B. Statutes

Penal Code section 261

(a) Rape is an act of sexual intercourse accomplished with a person not the spouse of the perpetrator, under any of the following circumstances:

(1) Where a person is incapable, because of a mental disorder or developmental or physical disability, of giving legal consent, and this is known or reasonably should be known to the person committing the act.

(2) Where it is accomplished against a person's will by means of force, violence, duress, menace, or fear of immediate and unlawful bodily injury on the person or another.

(3) Where a person is prevented from resisting by any intoxicating or anesthetic substance, or any controlled substance, and this condition was known, or reasonably should have been known by the accused.

(4) Where a person is at the time unconscious of the nature of the act, and this is known to the accused.

(5) Where a person submits under the belief that the person committing the act is the victim's spouse, and this belief is induced by any artifice, pretense, or concealment practiced by the accused, with intent to induce the belief.

(6) Where the act is accomplished against the victim's will by threatening to retaliate in the future against the victim or any other person, and there is a reasonable possibility that the perpetrator will execute the threat.

(7) Where the act is accomplished against the victim's will by threatening to use the authority of a public official. (b) As used in this section, "duress" means a direct or implied threat of force, violence, danger, or retribution sufficient to coerce a reasonable person of ordinary susceptibilities to perform an act which otherwise would not have been performed, or acquiesce in an act to which one otherwise would not have submitted.

Penal Code section 263

The essential guilt of rape consists in the outrage to the person and feelings of the victim of the rape. Any sexual penetration, however slight, is sufficient to complete the crime.

C. Questions

♦ Assume that a defendant threatens to kidnap a woman's young baby if she fails to submit to sexual intercourse. Does the defendant's conduct fall under the prohibitions of Penal Code section 261?

- Assume a 22 year-old female with a mental age of 10 recounts a rather immature explanation for her consensual intercourse with the defendant. Do you think that a defendant could be guilty of rape under this statute?

- The defendant approaches a victim who virtually "freezes" in fear of being raped and does not resist the defendant's advances. Is the defendant guilty of rape under the California rape statute?

- Assume that a defendant is impotent. He attempts to rape a victim but cannot complete penetration. If the defendant's medical doctor testifies to the defendant's impotency, can the defendant legally be convicted of rape?

D. Comments

As Penal Code section 263 above pointed out, the "essential guilt of rape consists in the outrage the person and feelings of the victim." The following case analyzes the application of rape laws to an instance where the victim has had a change of heart. When reading this case, pay close attention to the point in time at which his victim had a change part. The timing of the withdrawal of consent is a critical factor. This case has been criticized in several subsequent cases. As you read the opinion, consider why other courts may find the result in *Vela* questionable.

E. Case

People v. Vela
Court of Appeal, Fifth District
Sept. 17, 1985.

BEST, Associate Justice.

"Once penetration has occurred with the female's consent, if the female changes her mind does force from that point (where she changes her mind) constitute rape?"

On this appeal we must determine the answer to the above question. Defendant, then 19 years of age, was charged with the forcible rape of Miss M., then 14 years of age, the alleged rape occurring during the evening hours of November 20, 1982, near Bakersfield, California. The testimony of Miss M., together with other prosecution evidence, was more than sufficient to support a finding by the jury that defendant was guilty of rape by force of Miss M. However, during its case-in-chief, the prosecution presented evidence of a statement given by defendant to Deputy Eddy of the Kern County Sheriff's Department. Defendant's statement to Deputy Eddy, if believed to be true, together with all the other evidence, would have supported findings by the jury that Miss M. initially consented to an act of sexual intercourse with defendant; that during the act she changed her mind and made defendant aware that she had withdrawn her consent; and that defendant, without interruption of penetration, continued the act of sexual intercourse against the will of Miss M. by means of force.

A review of case law points out that the presence or absence of consent at the moment of initial penetration appears to be the crucial point in the crime of rape. For example, if at the moment of penetration the victim has not consented, no amount of consent given thereafter will prevent the act from being a rape. Also, a victim may give consent during preparatory acts all the way up to the moment of penetration, but the victim may withdraw that consent immediately before penetration and if communicated to the perpetrator, the act of intercourse that follows will be a rape no matter how much consent was given prior to penetration. It follows that if consent is given at the moment of penetration, that act of intercourse will be shielded from being a rape even if consent is later withdrawn during the act.

California case law and statutory law also seem to focus on the moment of penetration as the crucial moment of the crime of rape.

The essence of the crime of rape is the outrage to the person and feelings of the female resulting from the nonconsensual violation of her womanhood. When a female willingly consents to an act of sexual intercourse, the penetration by the male cannot constitute a violation of her womanhood nor cause outrage to her person and feelings. If she withdraws consent during the act of sexual intercourse and the male forcibly continues the act without interruption, the female may certainly feel outrage because of the force applied or because the male ignores her wishes, but the sense of outrage to her person and feelings could hardly be of the same magnitude as that resulting from an initial nonconsensual violation of her womanhood. It would seem, therefore, that the essential guilt of rape as stated in Penal Code section 263 is lacking in the withdrawn consent scenario.

The judgment is reversed on other grounds.

F. Questions

♦ At what point did the victim withdraw her consent?

♦ Do you think that withdrawal of consent before or after penetration should be the deciding factor in determining whether or not the defendant has committed the crime of rape?

♦ Do you think that the court's decision is in keeping with Penal Code section 263?

II. UNLAWFUL SEXUAL INTERCOURSE (STATUTORY RAPE)

A. Comments

The important points to consider in reading Penal Code section 261.5 are:

1.	the age of the victim

2.	the age of the perpetrator in relationship and to the victim (for purposes of both classification of the crime *and* punishment imposed), and

3.	the unique funding program that is benefits from the fines levied on the defendants.

B. Statute

Penal Code section 261.5

(a) Unlawful sexual intercourse is an act of sexual intercourse accomplished with a person who is not the spouse of the perpetrator, if the person is a minor. For the purposes of this section, a "minor" is a person under the age of 18 years and an "adult" is a person who is at least 18 years of age.

(b) Any person who engages in an act of unlawful sexual intercourse with a minor who is not more than three years older or three years younger than the perpetrator, is guilty of a misdemeanor.

(c) Any person who engages in an act of unlawful sexual intercourse with a

minor who is more than three years younger than the perpetrator is guilty of either a misdemeanor or a felony, and shall be punished by imprisonment in a county jail not exceeding one year, or by imprisonment in the state prison.

(d) Any person over the age of 21 years who engages in an act of unlawful sexual intercourse with a minor who is under 16 years of age is guilty of either a misdemeanor or a felony, and shall be punished by imprisonment in a county jail not exceeding one year, or by imprisonment in the state prison for two, three, or four years.

C. Questions

♦	Do you think a defendant would be guilty of unlawful sexual intercourse for having intercourse with a married woman under the age of 18 who was not the defendant's wife?

♦	In the question above, what public policy reasons do you think a court should apply in reaching a decision? Would your conclusion differ if the under-aged woman was divorced?

III. Spousal Rape

A. Comments

Some of the elements of spousal rape are similar to the general rape statute we have already studied. Omitted from the spousal rape statute below are the specific reporting requirements applicable to spousal rape.

B. Statutes

Penal Code section 262

(a) Rape of a person who is the spouse of the perpetrator is an act of sexual intercourse accomplished under any of the following circumstances:

(1) Where it is accomplished against a person's will by means of force, violence, duress, menace, or fear of immediate and unlawful bodily injury on the person or another.

(2) Where a person is prevented from resisting by any intoxicating or anesthetic substance, or any controlled substance, and this condition was known, or reasonably should have been known, by the accused.

(3) Where a person is at the time unconscious of the nature of the act, and this is known to the accused.

(4) Where the act is accomplished against the victim's will by threatening to retaliate in the future against the victim or any other person, and there is a reasonable possibility that the perpetrator will execute the threat.

(5) Where the act is accomplished against the victim's will by threatening to use the authority of a public official to incarcerate, arrest, or deport the victim or another, and the victim has a reasonable belief that the perpetrator is a public official.

IV. Assault

A. Comments

The assault statute is deceptively short. However, you need to pay careful attention to the elements of assault. In the United States, there are two distinct types of assault statutes. One way to distinguish them is to classify them either as "attempted battery assault" and "threatened battery assault" crimes.

.

There is another classification that utilizes different nomenclature to distinguish the two types of assault statutes. This alternative classification differentiates between the "present *ability*" to commit a battery as opposed to the "*apparent* present ability" to commit a battery. The majority of states allow a defendant to be convicted of assault as long as he had the *apparent* present ability to commit the battery. "Apparent" ability means that as far as the *victim* is concerned, the defendant is capable of committing the offense. Thus, under this rule, the focus is a subjective one that focuses on the victim. Under this test, the determinative test is the reasonableness of the victim's perception regarding the ability to complete the crime.

On the other hand, a minority of states permits a defendant to be convicted of assault only if the defendant has the present *ability* to complete the battery. "Present ability" assault laws focus on the *defendant*. Were the defendant's actions capable of completing the threatened crime? If the crime is frustrated because of a physical inability to complete the crime, there can be no assault under the minority view.

B. Statute

Penal Code § 240
An assault is an unlawful attempt, coupled with a present ability, to commit a violent injury on the person of another.

C. Questions

♦ Now that you have read Penal Code section 240, does California adhere to the majority rule or to the minority rule?

♦ What is the critical language in the statute that determines the California rule?

♦ Assume that a defendant is threatening to stab a victim with a knife. If the knife is not real but a very life-like looking toy, can the defendant be guilty of battery under the majority rule? Under the minority rule?

V. BATTERY

A. Comments

We have included statutes for both the traditional common law crime of battery as well as the crime of sexual battery.

B. Statutes

Penal Code § 242
A battery is any willful and unlawful use of force or violence upon the person of another.

Penal Code § 243.2

(a) Any person who touches an intimate part of another person while that person is unlawfully restrained by the accused or an accomplice, and if the touching is against the will of the person touched and is for the purpose of sexual arousal, sexual gratification, or sexual abuse, is guilty of sexual battery.

C. Questions

♦ The legislature defines the specific intent as one in which the defendant commits the act "for the purpose of sexual arousal, sexual gratification, or sexual abuse." However, the Legislature does not state whether it means the sexual arousal of the defendant or the victim. Assume now that you are a judge and are being asked to interpret the statute. How would you interpret the statute with respect to the specific intent requirement? Should it mean the sexual arousal of the defendant? Of the victim? Both? Either defendant or victim?

♦ To take this one step further, let's assume that a defendant has touched an intimate part of another person for the purpose of arousing himself. Do you think this fits the specific intent requirement? Assume instead that the defendant has touched the intimate part of another person for the purpose of arousing the victim. Should the result be the same as in the situation where the defendant commits the act for his *own* arousal?

VI. MAYHEM

A. Comments

Modernly, the crime of mayhem has been expanded beyond the narrow confines of the common law to include disfigurement. Traditional common law definitions restricted mayhem to crimes which disabled a person from fighting, such as cutting off a limb or putting out an eye. Read the California statute below to determine whether California follows the more traditional definition or the more modern definition.

B. Statute

Penal Code section 203

Every person who unlawfully and maliciously deprives a human being of a member of his body, or disables, disfigures, or renders it useless, or cuts or disables the tongue, or puts out an eye, or slits the nose, ear, or lip, is guilty of mayhem.

C. Questions

♦ Assume that a defendant slashes a person across the face with a knife, leaving a long and highly visible scar, but not injuring eyes, nose or ears. Would this be mayhem under California law? Under the common law?

VII. KNOWING INTERCOURSE BY AIDS VICTIM

A. Comments

The very name of this statute should indicate that this is a modern law. When you read this statute, decide whether you think this is a specific intent or general intent crime. Also keep in mind that this statute does not define a crime, but serves to enhance (or increase) the sentence of some specific sex offenses.

B. Statute

Penal Code section 12022.85

(a) Any person who violates one or more of the offenses listed in subdivision (b) with knowledge that he or she has acquired immune deficiency syndrome (AIDS) or with the knowledge that he or she carries antibodies of the human immunodeficiency virus at the time of the commission of those offenses, shall receive a three-year enhancement for each such violation in addition to the sentence provided under those sections.

(b) Subdivision (a) applies to the following crimes:

(1) Rape

(2) Unlawful intercourse with a female under age 18

(3) Rape of a spouse

(4) Sodomy

(5) Oral copulation

C. Comment

In *Shoemake*, the defendant challenges the enhancement to his sentence that he received under Penal Code section 12022.85. Consider the evidence the court relies on to affirm the sentencing enhancement. Based on that evidence, do you agree with the court's conclusion? Also, this statue is another example of a "wobbler" which was discussed in Chapter One.

D. Case

PEOPLE V. SHOEMAKE
Court Of Appeal Of California, Fifth Appellate District
16 Cal. App. 4th 243 (1993)

[Appellant was convicted of forcible rape and challenges the enhancement he received under Penal Code section 12022.5. Appellant challenges the basis for finding he was HIV positive, arguing that his admission that he was HIV positive was insufficient as a matter of law to support the enhancement.]

ARDAIZ, J. Appellant's . . . argument concerns the sufficiency of the evidence to support the true finding on each of the four section 12022.85 sentence enhancements. He does not dispute the sufficiency of the evidence as it relates to the underlying sexual offenses, but instead has focused his attention on what he perceives to be a shortfall in the evidence regarding his having committed the offenses with the knowledge that he had AIDS or was a carrier of the HIV virus. In this regard, appellant maintains that "proof of the truth of the section 12022.85 enhancement, on the basis of admissions by the defendant, should be deemed insufficient as a matter of law.

Our function, as an appellate court, is to determine " 'whether the evidence could reasonably support a finding of guilt beyond a reasonable doubt.' . . . '[T]his inquiry does not require a court to "ask itself whether it believes that the evidence at trial established guilt beyond a reasonable doubt." Instead the relevant question is whether, after viewing the evidence in the light most favorable to the prosecution, any rational trier of fact could have found the essential elements of the crime beyond a reasonable doubt.' " [In performing this function], we "must view the evidence in the light most favorable to the prosecution ." This does not mean that we can isolate items of evidence favorable to the judgment; instead, "we must resolve the issue in light of the whole record -- i.e., the entire picture of the defendant put before the jury. . . . [In addition,] we must judge whether the evidence of each of the essential elements . . . is substantial . . ..' " must be 'of ponderable legal significance . . . reasonable in nature, credible, and of solid value.'

Based on our review of the record, we conclude the evidence presented was legally sufficient to support the true finding on each of the section 12022.85 sentence enhancements. Appellant's acknowledging that he either had AIDS or was HIV positive were admitted into evidence without objection or limitation. No evidence was presented in rebuttal.

Thus, a reasonable trier of fact could conclude that appellant either knew he had AIDS or was a carrier of the HIV virus at the time he committed the current offenses.

The judgment is affirmed.

VIII. PARENTAL KIDNAPPING

A. Comments

The descriptive title of this statute is "deprivation of custody of child or right to visitation." From this title of the statute, you can correctly assume that this is another modern statute and one that was not a common law offense. This statue is another example of a "wobbler."

B. Statutes

Penal code section 278.5

Every person who takes, entices away, keeps, withholds, or conceals a child and maliciously deprives a lawful custodian of a right to custody, or a person of a right to visitation, shall be punished by imprisonment in a county jail not exceeding one year, a fine not exceeding one thousand dollars ($1,000), or both that fine and imprisonment, or by imprisonment in the state prison for 16 months, or two or three years, a fine not exceeding ten thousand dollars ($10,000), or both that fine and imprisonment.

C. Questions

♦ When do you think this crime should be punished as a felony or a misdemeanor?

♦ Can you think of different fact patterns, which should be punished as a felony? A misdemeanor?

♦ Does this crime apply only to the forceful abduction of a child? Whom does this law seek to protect? The child? The parent? Or both?

IX. Self-Assessment

1. The modern law of rape includes both forcible and non-forcible rape.
   A. True   B. False

2. "Statutory rape" is defined under the unlawful sexual intercourse statute.
   A. True   B. False

3. Parental kidnapping includes deprivation of a parent's right to visitation.
   A. True   B. False

4. "Knowing intercourse by an AIDS' victim only applies to forcible rape.
   A. True   B. False

5. "Spousal rape" was a subcategory of rape under the common law.
   A. True   B. False

CHAPTER ELEVEN

Crimes Against Property

This chapter on property offenses encompasses very old property crimes and very modern property crimes. You will see many of the traditional common law theft offenses included her. Many of them will appear to be similar to their original common law backgrounds, while others have been significantly updated.

On a final note, most texts classify robbery as a crime against property. However, California does not classify robbery as a property offense. California considers robbery a crime against a person. This classification indicates that the Legislature considers the harm that a robbery inflicts on the person as more serious than the harm to the property.

I. THEFT

A. Comments

The common law set forth distinctions between many theft related offenses. Under the common law, it was difficult to determine the distinctions between larceny, embezzlement, and obtaining money under false pretenses. A defendant who was tried under the wrong statute could escape punishment when his conviction was overturned on appeal because he was improperly convicted. For this reason, many modern statutes have abolished the distinctions between these offenses.

Consistent with the modern trend and the model Penal Code, California Penal Code section 484 combines many of the common law theft offenses into a single theft classification. Penal Code section 490a enacted in 1927 abolished these distinctions. From a practical perspective, a single theft offense obviates many of the potential problems with charging criminal defendants.

However, California does distinguish theft offenses based on their value. The difference between grand theft and petty theft is based on the market value of the purloined property. The distinction between grand theft and petty theft is important because the two crimes are punished differently, with grand theft receiving the harsher punishment.

B. Statutes

Abolition of distinctions: Penal Code § 490a

Whenever any law or statute of this state refers to or mentions larceny, embezzlement, or stealing, said law or statute shall hereafter be read and interpreted as if the word "theft" were substituted therefore.

Theft Offenses: Penal Code § 484

(a) Every person who shall feloniously steal, take, carry, lead, or drive away the personal property of another, or who shall fraudulently appropriate property which has been entrusted to him, or who shall knowingly and designedly, by any false or fraudulent representation or pretense, defraud any other person of money, labor or real or personal property, or who causes or procures others to report falsely of his wealth or mercantile character and by thus imposing upon any person, obtains credit and thereby fraudulently gets or obtains possession of money, or property or obtains the labor or service of another, is guilty of theft. In determining the value of the property obtained, for the purposes of this section, the reasonable and fair market value shall be the test, and in determining the value of services received the contract price shall be the test. If there be no contract price, the reasonable and going wage for the service rendered shall govern.

Grand Theft defined: Penal Code § 487

[Subject to certain statutory exceptions], when the money, labor, or real or personal property taken is a value exceeding four hundred dollars [grand theft is committed.]

Grant Theft Punishment: Penal Code § 489

(a) When the grand theft involves the theft of a firearm, by imprisonment in the state prison for 16 months, 2, or 3 years.

(b) In all other cases, by imprisonment in a county jail not exceeding one year or in the state prison.

Petty Theft Punishment: Penal Code § 490

Petty theft is punishable by fine not exceeding one thousand dollars ($1,000), or by imprisonment in the county jail not exceeding six months, or both.

II. Embezzlement

A. Comments

Modern statutory law has abandoned many of the common law theft crimes while retaining others. Unlike the theft statue which has drastically modified the common law, the embezzlement statute largely retains its traditional common law definition.

Penal Code section 503
Embezzlement is the fraudulent appropriation of property by a person to whom it has been intrusted.

III. RECEIVING STOLEN PROPERTY

A. Comments

When reading the California statute defining "receiving stolen property," determine whether this is a specific intent crime or a general intent crime. Pick the clause that supports your conclusion.

Observe some of the particular modern twists to this law. For example, subdivision (b) includes a provision which specifically applies to swap meet vendors. Another interesting provision in this statute is the restitution clause in the amount of three times the amount of actual damages. Once again, you will see that four hundred dollars is a critical amount triggering a potentially different punishment scheme.

B. Statutes

Penal Code section 496
(a) Every person who buys or receives any property that has been stolen or that has been obtained in any manner constituting theft or extortion, knowing the property to be so stolen or obtained, or who conceals, sells, withholds, or aids in concealing, selling, or withholding any property from the owner, knowing the property to be so stolen or obtained, shall be punished by imprisonment in a state prison, or in a county jail for not more than one year. However, if the district attorney or the grand jury determines that this action would be in the interests of justice, the district attorney or the grand jury, as the case may be, may, if the value of the property does not

exceed four hundred dollars ($400), specify in the accusatory pleading that the offense shall be a misdemeanor, punishable only by imprisonment in a county jail not exceeding one year.

A principal in the actual theft of the property may be convicted pursuant to this section. However, no person may be convicted both pursuant to this section and of the theft of the same property.

(b) Every swap meet vendor, and every person whose principal business is dealing in, or collecting, merchandise or personal property, and every agent, employee, or representative of that person, who buys or receives any property of a value in excess of four hundred dollars ($400) that has been stolen or obtained in any manner constituting theft or extortion, under circumstances that should cause the person, agent, employee, or representative to make reasonable inquiry to ascertain that the person from whom the property was bought or received had the legal right to sell or deliver it, without making a reasonable inquiry, shall be punished by imprisonment in a state prison, or in a county jail for not more than one year.

Every swap meet vendor, and every person whose principal business is dealing in, or collecting, merchandise or personal property, and every agent, employee, or representative of that person, who buys or receives any property of a value of four hundred dollars ($400) or less that has been stolen or obtained in any manner constituting theft or extortion, under circumstances that should cause the person, agent, employee, or representative to make reasonable inquiry to ascertain that the person from whom the property was bought or received had the legal right to sell or deliver it, without making a reasonable inquiry, shall be guilty of a misdemeanor.

(c) Any person who has been injured by a violation of subdivision (a) or (b) may bring an action for three times the amount of actual damages, if any, sustained by the plaintiff, costs of suit, and reasonable attorney's fees.

C. Question

♦ Can a person be convicted of receiving stolen property and of the theft of the same property? Does the statute speak to that issue? Why should a person not be convicted of both offenses?

D. Comments

As you have already seen from reading Penal Code section 496 subdivision (a) above, the defendant's "knowledge" is a critical element of the offense. However, proving the knowledge requirement of Penal Code section 496 can be difficult. *Barnes* discusses the knowledge requirement and how such knowledge is proved. Pay close attention to the type of evidence the courts accept as proving the "knowledge" element of receiving stolen property. (Make certain that you understand what the word "extrajudicial" means before you read this case.)

E. Case

PEOPLE V. BARNES
District Court of Appeal, Third District, California
Dec. 12, 1962.

SCHOTTKY, J.

The evidence discloses that a quantity of tools, plumbing supplies and other personal property were taken from buildings located at a home construction site in Fremont, California. Among the articles taken were Skil saws, a Porter Cable saw, electrical wire and cord, stepladders, cooking range hoods, garbage disposals, interior hardware, toilet bowls and tanks, toilet seats, bathtubs, Herco rings, faucets and 1,500 pounds of lead.

Five days after the burglary Self, accompanied by Ford, drove to a wholesale plumbing and electrical supply store operated by one Armolio. Self told Armolio he had various types of plumbing supplies for sale. He offered to sell 12 General Electric garbage disposals for $18 each, which was $16 under the wholesale price, and the other items 15 per cent below wholesale cost.

Barnes contacted one Eckstrom who operated a retail plumbing and electrical supply store and asked if he were interested in purchasing plumbing fixtures. Several days later Barnes brought a number of chrome brass fixtures of the same make as those taken in the burglary to Eckstrom's store. He told Eckstrom that he had about 700 to 1,000 pounds of lead, a case of chrome bathroom faucets, a case of kitchen faucets, water closets, garbage disposals and sinks.

On August 28, 1961, officers of the Lodi Police Department went to Ford's home and observed a box containing a Skil saw in the driveway. Some time later Self removed the saw to his bedroom in the house. After obtaining a search warrant, the officers entered the house and discovered the Skil saw in Self's bedroom. Ford disclaimed any knowledge of the tool. The officers searched the garage where they discovered a Porter Cable saw, a range hood, boxes of plumbing fixtures and various other items.

The Skil saw found in Self's bedroom and the Porter Cable saw were identified as items taken from the Fremont burglary. A search of Barnes' home disclosed two Skil saws which were identified as having been taken in the Fremont burglary. Other items found in the garage were similar to stolen items.

Barnes explained his possession of this property by stating he had purchased it from a stranger whom he had met in a Stockton cardroom. The man delivered it to his home. He paid $20 for each of the garbage disposals and $15 for each of the other items. He did not learn the man's name, did not obtain a receipt, and did not ask where he had gotten the goods.

Subsequent to the arrest of the three defendants they were taken to the Fremont police station. While there the defendant Ford asked Fremont Police Sergeant Albert Guest if he could speak with him alone. Ford suggested to Sergeant Guest that it would be a good business arrangement if the three defendants were released; that he would thus assure Sergeant Guest recovery of a high percentage of the stolen property. Ford offered to contact Sergeant Guest after his release and advise him where to locate the stolen property. He said it would be in such a place that no search warrant would be necessary.

Sergeant Guest later conversed with the three defendants together. They each agreed to cooperate fully in assisting the officer to recover the balance of the stolen property if they were released from custody by the Fremont Police Department and low bail was arranged for them in San Joaquin County.

Defendant Ford told the officer further that if he did not arrange for their release he would probably never see any of the rest of the stolen property.

Each of the defendants testified at the trial.
who came to his home with them and said he had been sent by Barnes. He paid approximately $469 for them. He did not notice the initials on the saws and did not know the property was stolen. He denied that he had gone to Armolio's store with defendant Self.

Defendant Self testified that he occupied a bedroom in the home of Ford. He knew nothing about Ford's possession of Skil saws or other property in Ford's garage. He removed the box containing the Skil saw from the driveway into his bedroom after he had seen it in the driveway several times. He did not attempt to sell plumbing supplies to Mr. Armolio and had not gone to his establishment.

Appellants' first major contention is that the evidence is insufficient to support the judgments. They argue that the corpus delicti of the crime of receiving stolen property was not established. We find no merit in this contention.

Appellants were convicted of a violation of section 496 of the Penal Code which provides in part: 'Every person who buys or receives any property which has been stolen or which has been obtained in

Defendant Barnes testified that he purchased the property in question from a man he met in a cardroom and paid slightly under $300 in cash for two Skil saws, a bathroom sink and fixtures, three garbage disposals and a range hood. He gave the man his address and the goods were delivered to his home in a truck which he could not describe. He did not know the man and did not learn his name. He had no knowledge that the goods were stolen. He observed the gold paint and the initials on the saws but did not give it much thought. Defendant Ford testified that he purchased the saws, range hoods, a water faucet, doorstops and other items from a stranger

any manner constituting theft or extortion, knowing the same to be so stolen or obtained, or who conceals, withholds or aids in concealing or withholding any such property from the owner, knowing the same to be so stolen or obtained, is punishable ....'
As stated in a previous case: 'The next question under such contention is whether the evidence was sufficient to support a finding that defendant knew that the property was stolen.

Extrajudicial statements of defendant were not admissible unless the People established the corpus delicti by evidence independent of such statements. 'It is the settled rule, however, that the corpus delicti must be established independently of admissions of the defendant. Conviction cannot be had on his extrajudicial admissions or confessions without proof aliunde of the corpus delicti. A prima facie showing that the property was received with knowledge that they were stolen is all that is required as a foundation for the introduction in evidence of extrajudicial statements of defendant. Prior case law teaches us that possession of stolen property, accompanied by suspicious circumstances, will justify an inference that the property was received with knowledge that it had been stolen. A sale of property at a price which is disproportionately low in comparison with the value of the property may be a suspicious circumstance.

In the case at bench the evidence discloses that Self accompanied by Ford offered to sell garbage disposals for less than the wholesale price. There was evidence that Self and Ford both had in their possession property which had been taken from the burglary. The evidence at this point is sufficient to establish a prima facie case against Self. The evidence is also sufficient to establish a prima facie case against Ford. Ford was concealing stolen property. He accompanied Self who was attempting to sell some property which had been stolen. This, too, is a sufficiently suspicious circumstance to meet the rule of the Malouf case. The evidence as to Barnes also shows concealment of stolen property and the sale of some Herco rings. The record does not disclose that this sale was at a disproportionately low price. It is fairly inferable, however, that a sale to a dealer in such merchandise must have been made at an advantageous price. If such an inference can be drawn, then a prima facie case was established and the extrajudicial statements of the defendants were admissible. Barnes explained possession of the property by stating he had purchased it from a stranger he had met in a cardroom. He did not learn the man's name, did not get a receipt, nor did he ask the stranger where he obtained them. Barnes also told Eckstrom he had made an exceptionally good purchase. Possession of stolen property accompanied by no explanation will justify an inference that the wares were received with knowledge they were stolen.

Barnes' statement as to the manner of purchase coupled with a statement to the purchaser of the Herco rings indicates receipt of stolen property within the rule of the Lopez case. One of Ford's explanations of the possession of the property was that some unknown fellow had unloaded them in his driveway and he put them into his garage for safe-keeping. This, too, fits the rule of the Lopez case.

In addition, both Barnes and Ford testified that they had purchased the supplies from a stranger. This testimony bolsters the fact that Ford and Barnes were receivers.

Self contends that there is no evidence to show that he ever had possession or concealed stolen property. A stolen saw was found in his bedroom. It is stated [in earlier case law] that 'Where property is found in the possession of a party other than its owner under suspicious circumstances a verdict of guilty of receiving stolen property is thereby justified.'

In addition, there is evidence that Self attempted to sell some of the stolen property. This is some evidence of reception and at least evidence that he aided in the concealment of stolen property. (Pen. Code, S 496, states one who aids in the concealment of stolen property is guilty.) While there is only little evidence that Self received stolen property, the evidence sustains the conviction on the theory he aided in concealing stolen property.

We conclude that there is sufficient evidence to prove that property was stolen and that it was received and concealed by Ford and Barnes. The guilty knowledge may be inferred from the circumstances of the purchase.

As to Self, the evidence is sufficient to show that he at least aided in concealing the stolen property. Guilty knowledge may be inferred in this action since Self sold some of the property at a very low price.

The judgments are affirmed.

F. Questions

♦ According to the court, does "knowledge" mean the defendant has to admit knowledge or can the surrounding circumstances be used to infer knowledge that the property was stolen?

♦ Can the court rely solely on the defendant's statement to prove that corpus delecti of a crime? What did the court say? Why you think the rule regarding proving elements has been formulated this way? Why do you think it has particular application to a crime such as receiving stolen property?

♦ What practical effect does the court's standard of proving the elements of the offense have on police and prosecutors? Does it make their job easier or harder in collecting evidence and proving a specific crime has been committed?

♦ Under the reasoning of this court, if you adopted a "Don't ask, Don't tell" approach to a bargain buy, will the court likely find you guilty of receiving stolen property

IV. Robbery

A. Comments

The elements of this crime are essentially unchanged from common law. However, California (unlike many other jurisdictions) classifies robbery as a crime against the person (because of the element of force or fear) and not a crime against property.

B. Statutes

Penal Code section 211

Robbery is the felonious taking of personal property in the possession of another, from his person or immediate presence, and against his will, accomplished by means of force or fear.

C. Comments

The case below teaches that it is the victim's possession of property (not ownership) that is a critical element of robbery. In the *Estes* case, the original taking was not forceful. However, the owner's attempt at regarding possession was forcibly prevented. The Court held this conduct sufficient to constitute robbery, a minority point of view not shared by many other jurisdictions. (Most jurisdictions require that the original taking must be accomplished by force of fear.)

Finally, the court discusses the concept of a "continuing offense." The court holds that the modern-day crime of robbery, similar to the old common law, does not end until the robber has reached a place of relative safety.

D. Case

PEOPLE V. ESTES
Court of Appeal, First District, Division 5, California.
Sep 15, 1983.

LOW, P. J.

In this case we affirm a robbery conviction for the taking of personal property owned by Sears, Roebuck & Company in the immediate presence of a security guard, using force and fear to complete the taking. Defendant Curtis Estes appeals from a judgment entered after a jury found him guilty of robbery (Pen. Code, § 211) by personal use of a deadly weapon and petty theft arising out of the theft of merchandise from a Sears department store. Defendant entered the Sears store in Larwin Plaza, Vallejo, wearing only jeans and a T-shirt and was observed by Carl Tatem, a security guard employed by Sears. Tatem next saw defendant wearing a corduroy coat of the type sold by Sears, and watched him remove a down-filled vest from a rack, take off the coat, put on the vest, then the coat, and leave the store without paying for the items. Tatem followed defendant outside the store, identified himself, and confronted him about the coat and vest in the parking lot about five feet from the store. Defendant refused to accompany Tatem to the store and began to walk away. As Tatem attempted to detain him, defendant pulled out a knife, swung it at Tatem, and threatened to kill Tatem. Tatem, who was unarmed, returned to the store for help.

Shortly thereafter, Tatem returned to the parking lot with Mel Roberts, the Sears security manager. Tatem and Roberts confronted defendant and again asked him to accompany them back to the store. Defendant still clutched the knife in his hand. After some time, defendant returned to the store with Tatem and Roberts, but denied using the knife and denied stealing the coat and vest. At the trial, defendant admitted stealing the coat and vest from the store, but again denied using force or fear against the security guard, or any other person.

Defendant argues that the property was not taken from a person since the security guard did not have the authority or control over the property. 'Robbery is the felonious taking of personal property in the possession of another, from his person or immediate presence, and against his will, accomplished by force or fear.' (Pen. Code, Section 211.)

It is not necessary that the victim of the robbery also be the owner of the goods taken. Robbery is an offense against the person who has either actual or constructive possession over the goods. Thus, a store employee may be a victim of robbery even though he does not own the property taken and is not in charge or in immediate control of the property at the time of the crime. Defendant reasons that in this case the store manager and sales clerks were the only ones with responsibility over the goods and, thus, they and not the guard, Tatem, could be the only victims.

The victim was employed by Sears to prevent thefts of merchandise. As the agent of the owner and a person directly responsible for the security of the items, Tatem was in constructive possession of the merchandise to the same degree as a salesperson. Because there were other people present in the store who also had constructive possession of the personal property is not dispositive, since more than one person may constructively possess personal property at the same time and be a victim of the same offender. Defendant further alleges that the merchandise was not taken from the 'immediate presence' of the security guard. The evidence establishes that appellant forcibly resisted the security guard's efforts to retake the property and used that force to remove the items from the guard's immediate presence. By preventing the guard from regaining control over the merchandise, defendant is held to have taken the property as if the guard had actual possession of the goods in the first instance. The crime of robbery includes the element of asportation, the robber's escape with the loot being considered as important in the commission of the crime as gaining possession of the property. A robbery occurs when defendant uses force or fear in resisting attempts to regain the property or in attempting to remove the property from the owner's immediate presence regardless of the means by which defendant originally acquired the property.

Defendant further claims that the robbery verdict cannot stand since his assaultive behavior was not contemporaneous with the taking of the merchandise from the store. Appellant's theory is contrary to the law. The crime of robbery is a continuing offense that begins from the time of the original taking until the robber reaches a place of relative safety. It is sufficient to support the conviction that appellant used force to prevent the guard from retaking the property and to facilitate his escape. The crime is not divisible into a series of separate acts. Defendant's guilt is not to be weighed at each step of the robbery as it unfolds. The events constituting the crime of robbery, although they may extend over large distances and take some time to complete, are linked by a single-mindedness of purpose. Whether defendant used force to gain original possession of the property or to resist attempts to retake the stolen property, force was applied against the guard in furtherance of the robbery and can properly be used to sustain the conviction.

The judgment is affirmed.

E. Question

♦ Do you agree with the court in its application of the law of robbery when it said it was immaterial whether the force used was to gain original possession or to resist attempts to read take possession?

♦ Do you think the determinative factor for the court was the danger to the victim regardless of whether the force was applied before or after taking possession of the property?

♦ If you think the court applied the law incorrectly, is the defendant guilty of committing any crime? If so, which one?

V. Extortion

A. Comments

At common law, the crime of extortion was a very narrowly defined crime: it applied only to public officials who illegally obtained property under the color of office. Modernly, the crime has expanded to include blackmail, where property is obtained by threat or fear of force. Modernly, states differ regarding the crime of extortion. In some states, the crime is completed on the making of the threat. In other states, however the defendant must actually obtain the property before the crime of extortion is completed. When reading the California statute below, what does the plain language of the statute require?

B. Statute

Penal Code § 518

Extortion is the obtaining of property from another, with his consent, or the obtaining of an official act of a public officer, induced by a wrongful use of force or fear, or under color of official right.

VI. Crimes against Habitation: Burglary

A. Comments

The crimes in the final portion of this chapter punish criminal activity directed at a person's home and property. The crimes selected for review in this chapter include burglary, arson, and criminal trespass. Each of these crimes has undergone significant "modernization" and differs markedly in many respects from their older common-law predecessors. As a general rule, the modern definitions are broader than their older common-law counterparts. At common law burglary was the breaking and entering the dwelling place of another in the nighttime with the intent to commit a felony therein.

The modern definition of burglary encompasses a much larger range of structures than common law burglary. Under the old common law, a defendant could not have been guilty of burglary by breaking and entering into a sealed cargo container. Harmonization of the old and modern laws occurs in the classification of degrees of the offense. As you will learn below, burglary of an inhabited dwelling home or a structure designed for habitation is first-degree burglary and is punished more seriously. (We will examine the meaning of "inhabited" in our discussion of arson immediately after this section.) All other kinds of burglary are second-degree and receive a lesser degree of punishment.

B. Statutes

Definition of Burglary: Penal Code § 459

Every person who enters any house, room, apartment, tenement, shop, warehouse, store, mill, barn, stable, outhouse or other building, tent, vessel, floating home, railroad car, locked or sealed cargo container, whether or not mounted on a vehicle, trailer coach, any house car, inhabited camper, aircraft or mine or any underground portion thereof, with intent to commit grand or petit larceny or any felony is guilty of burglary. As used in this chapter, "inhabited" means currently being used for dwelling purposes, whether occupied or not. A house, trailer, vessel designed for habitation, or portion of a building is currently being used for dwelling purposes if, at the time of the burglary, it was not occupied solely because a natural or other disaster caused the occupants to leave the premises.

Degrees of Burglary: Penal Code § 460

Every burglary of an inhabited dwelling house, vessel, which is inhabited and designed for habitation, floating home, or trailer coach, or the inhabited portion of any other building, is burglary of the first degree.

(b) All other kinds of burglary are of the second degree.

C. Question

♦ Why do you think the Legislature has included such diverse categories as mines, aircraft, and sealed cargo containers in its definition of burglary?

VII. Crimes against Habitation: Arson

A. Comments

Common law arson was the malicious burning of the dwelling house of another. The present-day crime of arson extends far beyond the traditional common-law definition in two significant respects. First, the modern crime of arson can include bare land, unlike the common law. Second, under the modern law of arson, a structure does not need to be charred for the defendant to be guilty of arson. (Under the common law, unless there was some charring of the wood, the defendant could only be found guilty of a lesser offense.)

Also note, we have included Penal Code section 450 which sets forth the definitions for the terms used in the arson statute.

B. Statutes

a. Penal Code section 451

A person is guilty of arson when he or she willfully and maliciously sets fire to or burns or causes to be burned or who aids, counsels, or procures the burning of, any structure, forest land, or property.

(a) Arson that causes great bodily injury is a felony punishable by imprisonment in the state

(b) Arson that causes an inhabited structure or inhabited property to burn is a felony punishable by imprisonment in the state prison for three, five, or eight years. of a structure or forest land is a felony punishable by imprisonment

(c) Arson in the state prison for two, four, or six years.

(d) Arson of property is a felony punishable by imprisonment in the state prison for 16 months, two, or three years. For purposes of this paragraph, arson of property does not include one burning or causing to be burned his or her own personal property unless there is an intent to defraud or there is injury to another person or another person's structure, forest land, or property prison for five, seven, or nine years.

b. Penal Code section 450

In this chapter, the following terms have the following meanings:

(a) "Structure" means any building, or commercial or public tent, bridge, tunnel, or powerplant.

(b) "Forest land" means any brush covered land, cut-over land, forest, grasslands, or woods.

(c) "Property" means real property or personal property, other than a structure or forest land.

(d) "Inhabited" means currently being used for dwelling purposes whether occupied or not. "Inhabited structure" and "inhabited property" do not include the real property on which an inhabited structure or an inhabited property is located.

(e) "Maliciously" imports a wish to vex, defraud, annoy, or injure another person, or an intent to do a wrongful act, established either by proof or presumption of law.

(f) "Recklessly" means a person is aware of and consciously disregards a substantial and unjustifiable risk that his or her act will set fire to, burn, or cause to burn a structure, forest land, or property. The risk shall be of such nature and degree that disregard thereof constitutes a gross deviation from the standard of conduct that a reasonable person would observe in the situation. A person who creates such a risk but is unaware thereof solely by reason of voluntary intoxication also acts recklessly

D. Comments

Jones is an example of a court analyzing the Legislature's intent in enacting a statute. Courts often look to the Legislature's intent to assist them in interpreting the law in keeping with that intent. One way courts ascertain legislative intent is to review the legislative history of a statute. Here, the court goes all the way back to 1850 and traces developments in the law of arson. (Note: The definition of "inhabited" is equally applicable to burglary as much as it is to arson.)

E. Case

PEOPLE V. JONES
Court of Appeal, Second District, Division 7
245 Cal.Rptr. 88 (1988)

JOHNSON, Associate Justice

Defendant was convicted of setting fire to an inhabited structure, the most serious form of arson. The house he set fire to was the one he and others had been evicted from the day before. The sole question on appeal is whether, at the time of the fire, the house was "inhabited" as defined in Penal Code section 450, subdivision (d).

FACTS

Defendant and others residing in a rented house were evicted by the county marshal after the landlord obtained an unlawful detainer judgment. The day after the eviction defendant set fire to the house. The evidence adequately establishes defendant is guilty of arson and that is not an issue on appeal. Rather, defendant contends there was insufficient evidence to show the house was inhabited within the meaning of Penal Code section 450, subdivision (d).

The evidence shows that after the eviction the former tenants were allowed to retrieve their clothing from the house then they dispersed, except for defendant. Defendant was seen leaving the house the morning after the eviction with other persons not identified as former tenants. No one testified they saw defendant remove anything from the house. Some clothing and furniture were in the house at the time of the fire but there was no testimony as to whom they belonged. Defendant was seen hanging about in the park across the street from the house during the day after the eviction. He was also seen entering and leaving the house several times that day. The house was set on fire later that same day.

DISCUSSION

I. AN "INHABITED STRUCTURE" IS ONE ACTUALLY BEING USED AS A DWELLING AT THE TIME OF THE FIRE, REGARDLESS OF THE POSSESSORY RIGHTS OF THE INHABITANT.

Defendant argues that, as a matter of law, the house was not "currently being used for dwelling purposes" because he and the other tenants had been evicted the day before, no new tenants had moved in and neither had the establish they are no longer using the premises as a dwelling. As the evidence in this case demonstrates, as soon as the evicting officers and landlord leave the tenants may re-enter the premises. If their possessions remained in the house it would be quite easy for them to go right on living there, at least until the landlord discovered them.

The fact the evicted tenants have no possessory right to the premises is of no consequence to the crime of arson. The question is whether the house was inhabited, not whether the inhabitants had a legal right to be there. For example, if an arsonist burnt the house down after the lease expired but while the tenant was still living there it would defy logic and the clear intent of the

Legislature to hold the house was not "inhabited" for purposes of section 450.

The legislative intent behind section 450, subdivision (d) can be gleaned from the history of California arson statutes which we recount here briefly. The first arson statute, enacted in 1850, made it a crime to burn "any dwelling house" but did not define the term "dwelling house." In 1856, arson was divided into degrees. First degree arson included burning "in the nighttime, any dwelling house in which there shall be at the time some human being...." Second degree arson included burning a dwelling house in which no one was present. The statute further provided, "Every house ... which shall have been usually occupied by persons lodging therein at night, shall be deemed a dwelling-house of any person so lodging therein...." Subsequent amendments did not materially alter the statute until 1929. In that year, section 447a was added to the Penal Code defining arson in part as burning "any dwelling house" but the provisions defining a "dwelling house" were repealed. Finally, the arson statute was revised in 1979 to provide, "Arson that causes an inhabited structure ... to burn is a felony...." The statute defines "structure" as a "building" and "inhabited" as "currently being used for dwelling purposes whether occupied or not." As can be seen from the review of the arson statute, the Legislature has taken various approaches to the burning of a dwelling. During some periods it has left the term without a definition. During other periods it has defined it as a building "usually occupied" or "currently being used." The present requirement that the building is "currently being used" is certainly more limiting than the mere reference to a "dwelling house" and more restrictive than the 1856 requirement the building "shall have been usually occupied by persons lodging therein...." We have not consulted an 1856 dictionary, but Webster's Third New International Dictionary (1981) defines "usually" as "by or according to habit or custom" "more often than not" "most often" and "as a rule"; it defines

152

current as "occurring in or belonging to the present time," "in evidence or operation at the time actually elapsing." If arson under section 451, subdivision (b) could be established by merely proving the defendant set fire to a "dwelling house" or a building "usually occupied" as a dwelling then, clearly, defendant's conviction would have been proper. But, the requirement the structure be "currently used" for dwelling purposes requires the People to prove at least one of the evicted tenants intended to continue living in the house after the eviction.

This conclusion is consistent with the interpretation given identical statutory language in section 459 applying to burglary. Each of these cases involved tenants who had moved out of a residence. In each case the court held that whether or not the structure was "inhabited" depended on the intent of the tenants to continue living there. Thus, in one case, the court held the house was not inhabited after the tenants moved out intending never to return even though the term of their tenancy had not yet expired and they had not completed moving all their belongings out of the house. "Where ... the residents have moved out without the intent to return, the house becomes uninhabited, i.e., it is no longer being used for dwelling purposes." On the other hand, in another case, the house was held to be inhabited even though the tenants had left for an indefinite period. The evidence showed the tenants intended to return to the house after they recovered from the shock of a murder that occurred there. The tenants did not tell their landlord they were going to vacate the premises, they did not cancel the utilities, file change address cards with the post office or remove any furniture. "[A] residence is still 'inhabited' ... even though the residents of the house are temporarily away from the premises, where they have indicated no intention to stop living there." Thus, we conclude it is the present intent to use the house as a dwelling which is determinative.

II. THERE WAS INSUFFICIENT EVIDENCE TO PROVE THE HOUSE WAS ACTUALLY BEING USED FOR DWELLING PURPOSES AT THE TIME OF THE FIRE.

Because inhabitation is an element of the crime of arson under Penal Code section 451, subdivision (b) the burden was on the People to prove beyond a reasonable doubt the house was inhabited at the time of the fire. The People failed to sustain this burden.

In order to meet this burden, the People had to show someone had the present intent to use the house as a dwelling at the time of the fire. The evidence shows that the tenants were physically evicted from the premises by the county marshal the day before the fire. They were allowed to remove their clothing from the house at the time of the eviction. No one was seen re-entering the house the day of the eviction and, except for the defendant, none of the tenants were seen again in the vicinity of the house. Defendant was seen leaving the house the next morning with three or four other people. During that day he was seen going in and out of the house and hanging around in the park across the street. There was evidence some clothing and furniture remained in the house after the eviction, but there was no testimony as to whom it belonged.

Viewing this evidence in the light most favorable to the People, it does not support a finding any of the tenants intended to continue using the house as a dwelling place. The fact some clothing and furniture remained in the premises is not determinative. There was no evidence anyone slept in the house after the eviction. The fact defendant and others, not identified as former tenants, were seen leaving the house at 8:30 or 9:00 a.m. does not support an inference any of them spent the night there. Even if defendant did spend the night in the house, setting fire to a house contravenes an intent to use it for dwelling purposes.

The judgment convicting defendant of arson of an inhabited structure is affirmed as so modified. The cause is remanded to the trial court for resentencing.

E. Questions

♦ Why do think the defendant in this case challenged his conviction when it is clear that he set fire to the structure? When considering your answer to this question, think about the punishment structure that is applied to the different degrees of arson. A simple determination that a structure has been burned does not determine the punishment that should be imposed. It is imperative that the nature of the structure be determined for the appropriate punishment to be imposed.

VIII. CRIMINAL TRESPASS

A. Comments

We have included only a small portion of the criminal trespass statute. The criminal trespass statute sets forth a staggering number of specific factual situations (as well as a dizzying array of punishment schemes) We have included less than one quarter of this statute. However, it is sufficient to give you an idea of the wide sweep of this law.

B. Statute

Penal Code § 602

Every person who willfully commits a trespass by any of the following acts is guilty of a misdemeanor:

(a) [Standing timber.] Cutting down, destroying, or injuring any kind of wood or timber standing or growing upon the lands of another.

(b) [Carrying away timber.] Carrying away any kind of wood or timber lying on those lands.

(c) [Injury to or severance from freehold.] Maliciously injuring or severing from the freehold of another anything attached to it, or its produce.

(d) [Soil removal.] Digging, taking, or carrying away from any lot situated within the limits of any incorporated city, without the license of the owner or legal occupant, any earth, soil, or stone.

(e) [Soil removal from public property.] Digging, taking, or carrying away from land in any city or town laid down on the map or plan of the city, or otherwise recognized or established as a street, alley, avenue, or park, without the license of the proper authorities, any earth, soil, or stone.

(f) [Highway signs, etc.] Maliciously tearing down, damaging, mutilating, or destroying any sign, signboard, or notice placed upon, or affixed to, any property belonging to the state, or to any city, county, city and county, town or village.

(g) [Oyster lands.] Entering upon any lands owned by any other person whereon oysters or other shellfish are planted or growing.

(h) [Fences, gates and signs.] Willfully opening, tearing down, or otherwise destroying any fence on the enclosed land of another, or opening any gate, bar, or fence of another and willfully leaving it open without the written permission of the owner, or maliciously tearing down, mutilating, or destroying any sign, signboard, or other notice forbidding shooting on private property.

(q) [Skiing in closed area.] Knowingly skiing in an area or on a ski trail which is closed to the public and which has signs posted indicating the closure.

(r). [Hotels or motels.] Refusing or failing to leave a hotel or motel, where he or she has obtained accommodations and has refused to pay for those accommodations, upon request of the proprietor or manager.

C. Questions

♦ Were you surprised at any of the provisions of Penal Code section 602? For example, had you previously considered that knowingly skiing in area that was posted as closed to the public constituted a misdemeanor under California law?

IX. Self-Assessment

1. The modern law of theft offenses consolidates many of the old common-law offenses.
   A. True   B. False

2. The crime of embezzlement involves a violation of trust.
   A. True   B. False

3. "Receiving stolen property" is a specific intent crime.
   A. True   B. False

4. Robbery is a crime against ownership, not possession.
   A. True   B. False

5. The modern-day crime of extortion applies only to public officials.
   A. True   B. False

CHAPTER TWELVE

Crimes Against Public Order & Morals

This probably the "quirkiest" area of law that you have studied thus far. Crimes against public order and morals often criminalize "man's inhumanity to man." When certain types of "inhumanity" overstep acceptable limits in the public's eye, those acts are criminalized and punished accordingly.

Perhaps no other chapter in this book reflects a geographic region as much as this. The enactments of these laws (and their subsequent interpretation by the courts) often bear the unmistakable mark of their origin. Legislative enactments of public order and morals laws often reflect community values. Furthermore, lawmakers are sensitive to the impact that their actions have on voters.

I. THE POWER OF PUBLIC OPINION

A. Comments

A California Example

An episode involving judicial recall demonstrates the strength of public opinion toward court decisions perceived as morally unacceptable to society. During the 1980s Chief Justice Rose Bird headed the California Supreme Court. Under her leadership, the California Supreme Court reached some unpopular and (by some standards) rather radical decisions in the area of business law. However, the California Supreme Court's undoing was its death penalty reversal rate. The Bird Court reversed approximately 90 percent of death penalty sentences. During a 1986 confirmation election, the public (outraged by this attitude of insensitivity to its collective conscience) ousted the Chief Justice and two other Supreme Court justices who were seen as closely allied with Chief Justice Bird.

As you can see from this example, it was the Court's reversal of capital sentences that was the death knell for the liberal court. Although the Court's revamping of business law was the talk of the business community, the average voter was not moved. Instead, it was the Court's denial of the right of retribution as expressed in the death penalty law that brought the Court to its knees. The ousting of these justices led to their replacement with conservative justices who affirmed capital sentences in nearly all death penalty appeals.

On a Final Note

One more introductory note before we begin. When reviewing crimes relating to public morality, the *date* of a decision is extremely important. Crimes involving public morality can change greatly over time. Whereas many laws defining common law felonies have undergone very little modern alteration, laws involving public morality can appear or disappear as societal attitudes change. For example, the definition of murder has not changed that drastically since the days of Henry VIII. However, community values have certainly changed and the morality of certain kinds of conduct is different. As an example of changed attitudes, we need look no further than attitudes toward spousal abuse. Wife beating used to be a commonly accepted practice. The expression, "rule of thumb," derives from the old English and American laws that allowed husbands to chastise their wives with a rod no bigger than their thumb. Today, however, such conduct is not acceptable to society and constitutes criminal conduct.

II. BIGAMY

A. Comments

The statutory definition of bigamy closely follows the common law definition. You will also see when you read the *LaMarr* case below that the statutory definition also has not changed in 50 years since the court decided *LaMarr* . (The bigamy statute in effect at the time of the *LaMarr* case is included in the Court's opinion.)

B. Statute

Penal Code section 281
Every person having a husband or wife living who marries any other person [absent specific exceptions] is guilty of bigamy.

C. Comment

When you read this case, pay close attention to what specific issue the defendant challenges. How does the court respond to his challenge?

D. Case

PEOPLE V. LAMARR
Supreme Court of California
20 Cal.2d 705 (1942)

EN BANC

Defendant appeals from a judgment convicting him of the crime of bigamy under section 281 of the Penal Code. The pertinent facts developed at the trial are as follows: On May 24, 1929, defendant married one Wally Meyer LaMarr in San Francisco, California; on March 20, 1935, he married Selma LaMarr in Ventura, California, while his marriage to Wally Meyer LaMarr was still in effect; and on November 23 or 24, 1938, he married Josephine LaMarr at Yuma, Arizona, neither of the two earlier marriages having been theretofore annulled or dissolved by divorce or death of a contracting party. The three wives were present in court and testified at the trial. Section 281 of the Penal Code provides that 'Every person having a husband or wife living, who marries any other person, except [in certain situations not existing here], is guilty of bigamy.'

The amended information, upon which defendant was convicted, alleged 'That the said REGINALD RAYMOND LaMARR on or about the 23rd day of November, 1938, ... did knowingly, willfully and feloniously marry one Josephine Roney, said defendant being then and there the lawful husband of another person, to wit: Mrs. Selma LaMarr, then and there living, the marriage of said defendant and said Mrs. Selma LaMarr not having been annulled or dissolved and said defendant and said Josephine Roney having thereafter cohabited together as husband and wife in the County of Los Angeles, State of California. ...' It was not until the trial that, by the testimony of defendant and of defendant's witness, Wally Meyer LaMarr, the fact of defendant's marriage to Wally Meyer LaMarr previous to his other two marriages was disclosed. Although some question is raised in the appeal briefs of the parties as to whether the trial court accepted the testimony of defendant and of Wally Meyer LaMarr concerning their marriage to each other, and as to whether the court may have drawn an inference of a divorce between them before defendant contracted his next

marriage, to Selma LaMarr, we find no indication in the record as to the relative weight given by the trial court to the testimony of the various witnesses or as to the inferences deducible therefrom, and so proceed on the basis of the facts as set forth above.

Defendant contends, chiefly, that he could not be convicted under the allegations of the amended information for the reason that at the time of his marriage to Selma LaMarr, alleged in the information to be the lawful marriage, he was legally married to Wally Meyer LaMarr. This contention cannot be sustained. It is to be noted that defendant makes no claim to having been divorced from Wally Meyer LaMarr at any time, and on the contrary the evidence produced by him established without contradiction that he was still her husband at the time of his third marriage.

The essential things for the pleading and proof to show are (1) the previously established status of the defendant as a married person and (2) his additional marriage during perdurance of that status. It is the additional marriage which identifies the particular crime. The name of the person with whom, and to some extent the place where, and the date when, the additional or bigamous marriage took place are important to identify the crime and protect the defendant against being placed in jeopardy more than once for that offense, but the name of the person with whom and the place where and the time when the marriage establishing the status was consummated have no significance in identifying the particular crime and are important only to the extent that the defendant be not misled and prejudiced in preparing his defense on the facts tending to establish such status.

Judgment affirmed.

E. Questions

♦ What is the court saying about bigamy? Is it more important to determine *who* was the specific spouse or simply that there was *another* spouse prior to remarriage?

♦ Is the court's interpretation consistent with the definition of bigamy as defined in the statute?

III. OBSCENITY

A. Comments

The following statute derives in large part from United States Supreme Court decisions. Because issues involving "obscenity" touch on First Amendment freedoms, the Legislature has incorporated a great deal of the United States Supreme Court's language. Our purpose in including this material for your review is so that you can see the detail with which the Legislature sets forth in a statute which touches on constitutional First Amendment freedoms.

When you read the statute, observe that the interpretation of what is obscene material is based on a statewide standard, not a nationwide standard. This is consistent with the United States Supreme Court's dictates in a famous case called *Miller v. California*. In *Miller*, the United States Supreme Court held "obscenity" was to be measured by community standards, not national standards. Under a "community standards" test, the public's concept of the inherent "rightness" or "wrongness" of a defendant's conduct is crucial. As this "community standards" test implies, laws regulating obscenity indirectly touch on issues of public morality. Furthermore, because the determination of "obscenity" is based on a community standard, it is important to note the specific community involved. What may be considered obscene in Billings may not be considered obscene in Los Angeles.

Finally, when reading the statute consider carefully what types of material can be construed as "obscene." Must the material always be visual?

B. Statute

Penal Code section 311

As used in this chapter, the following definitions apply:

(a) "Obscene matter" means matter, taken as a whole, that to the average person, applying contemporary statewide standards, appeals to the prurient interest, that, taken as a whole, depicts or describes sexual conduct in a patently offensive way, and that, taken as a whole, lacks serious literary, artistic, political, or scientific value.

159

(2) In prosecutions under this chapter, if circumstances of production, presentation, sale, dissemination, distribution, or publicity indicate that matter is being commercially exploited by the defendant for the sake of its prurient appeal, this evidence is probative with respect to the nature of the matter and may justify the conclusion that the matter lacks serious literary, artistic, political, or scientific value.

(3) In determining whether the matter taken as a whole lacks serious literary, artistic, political, or scientific value in description or representation of those matters, the fact that the defendant knew that the matter depicts persons under the age of 16 years engaged in sexual conduct is a factor that may be considered in making that determination.

***

...(b) "Matter" means any book, magazine, newspaper, or other printed or written material, or any picture, drawing, photograph, motion picture, or other pictorial representation, or any statue or other figure, or any recording, transcription, or mechanical, chemical, or electrical reproduction, or any other article, equipment, machine, or material. "Matter" also means live or recorded telephone messages if transmitted, disseminated, or distributed as part of a commercial transaction.

IV. "FIGHTING WORDS"

A. Comments

Penal Code section 415 sets forth several instances of different criminal conduct which can fall afoul of the law. However, we have provided only one of the statute's clauses. The specific provision we have set forth applies to the category, "fighting words."

B. Statute

Penal Code section 415

Any person who uses offensive words in a public place which are inherently likely to provoke an immediate violent reaction [is guilty of violating Penal Code section 415.]

C. Comments

In this case, your studies are coming full circle. Early on in the text (in Chapter Two), you studied issues discussing the interaction between constitutional law protections and the law of crimes. In this case, you will examine an issue of "public morals and order" in the context of "fighting words." The court examines the defendant's conduct in light of the law regarding "fighting words." In order to dispose of the constitutional issues, the court must also determine the offensiveness of the defendant's statement to decide if it constitutes "fighting words" under the statute.

In reaching its decision, the court refers to a United States Supreme Court case entitled *Cohen v. California*. This was a very famous case that began in the California courts and eventually worked its way up to the United States Supreme Court. The case took place during the Vietnam War and involved a young man who was convicted of disturbing the peace when he walked into courthouse with a jacket bearing the statement, "Fuck the Draft." The United States Supreme Court decided that his conviction infringed his freedom of speech under the First Amendment and reversed his conviction.

D. Case

IN RE JOHN V. V. STATE OF CALIFORNIA
Court of Appeal, Fourth District, Division 1
167 Cal.App.3d 761(1985)

WIENER, Acting Presiding Justice

It is an interesting phenomenon in our society that frequently the most pedestrian events can achieve constitutional status. In the "Fuck the Draft", free speech case of Cohen v. California (1971) 403 U.S. 15, 91 S.Ct., Justice Harlan said: "This case may seem at first blush too inconsequential to find its way into our books, but the issue it presents is of no small constitutional significance." We have similar feelings in this case where we are asked to determine whether John Dominic V.'s act of calling his neighbor a "fucking bitch" violated [the law which] makes it a misdemeanor for a person to use offensive words in a public place which are inherently likely to provoke an immediate violent reaction.

Sixteen-year-old John and Nancy W. are neighbors. John screamed "fucking bitch" at W. as she drove past his house, about 15 to 25 feet away. W. was startled. She felt fear and shock. When she arrived home she was angry. Her anger then turned to fury. She became incoherent, enraged and humiliated. John had been screaming at her and calling her obscene names for about three years. Included within his

repertoire of epithets were "whore," "fucking bitch," "bitch," and "fucking liar."

Police Officer Rebecca Bigbie responded to W.'s telephone call. John admitted to Bigbie he had a big mouth; he needed to learn to control it.

At trial John admitted hollering "fucking bitch" at W. because "she flipped me off as she was going by." Although W. conceded giving him a vulgar gesture ("the finger") on previous occasions she denied doing so on this day. On an earlier occasion John's obscene language made W. so angry she swung at him with a baseball bat. She missed and hit her boyfriend.

John contends the [fighting words law] is unconstitutionally overbroad and vague. He says [it] violates his rights under the First Amendment of the United States Constitution and violates his right to due process of law.

In California it is well established that the First Amendment does not protect words specifically addressed to another spoken under circumstances which create a clear and present danger that violence will imminently erupt. "[T]he mere use of a vulgar, profane, indecorous, scurrilous, opprobrious epithet cannot alone be grounds for prosecution.... The context in which the words are used must be considered, and there must be a showing that the words were uttered in a provocative manner, so that there was a clear and present danger violence would erupt." Although protected conduct may begin with the expression of opinion, it must stop with the perpetration of violence.

Unless we are prepared to reject the "fighting words" exception to the First Amendment we must accept the premise that there are certain words in our society which when directly communicated to a person under certain circumstances will in fact provoke an immediate violent reaction. As infrequent as that situation may be we are satisfied it occurred in the case before us. We are hard pressed to think of a more volatile situation than the one here when John decided to provoke W. once again by calling her a "fucking bitch."

We understand "fuck" is now a ubiquitous term frequently heard in movies or songs or overheard in essentially every social environment. We are also aware Cohen explained "the particular four-letter word being litigated here is perhaps more distasteful than most others of its genre, it is nevertheless often true that one man's vulgarity is another's lyric. But our concern is not with improving the auditory ambiance of the community by excising certain words which some may think are offensive. Rather it is with the right of the Legislature to assure public peace by proscribing conduct which causes violence. The statute as now rewritten with what we believe is the narrow specificity necessary to withstand constitutional scrutiny validly serves that purpose. As applied here it gave fair notice to John what he could not lawfully say to W. in a public place.

John is no stranger to either using or understanding vulgar words. He intentionally directed selected epithets at W. to provoke her. In light of the relationship between the parties his last recitation of these words in a public place created the clear and present danger that violence would immediately erupt. There is no basis to conclude the court applied the wrong legal standard. There is ample evidence to support the court's finding.

As difficult as it is to determine what is meant by "fighting words" at least this determination is legally and factually possible. It is virtually impossible to do the same with conduct. The Legislature simply decided to limit the scope of the law to words rather than undertaking the impossible task of including conduct. On this basis alone the distinction is rational. [We reject John's arguments and affirm the order.]

E. Question

◆ The court does not directly address the underlying issue of "public morals." However, the court does make reference to what is considered socially acceptable and what is not. Where do you find that in this opinion?

V. MISCELLANEOUS

A. Comments

Here are some examples of miscellaneous statutes that touch on public morals. It is unlikely that you are familiar with all of them. This eclectic collection of laws demonstrates the broad range of activities that can be criminalized under the category of "public morals and order." For example, as you might have already guessed, these laws can vary greatly depending on jurisdictions. Consider whether or not you think Nevada has a law identical to Penal Code section 330, the gaming law.

B. Statutes

Gaming: Penal Code section 330

Every person who deals, plays, or carries on, opens, or causes to be opened, or who conducts, either as owner or employee, whether for hire or not, any game of faro, monte, roulette, lansquenet, rouge et noire, rondo, tan, fan-tan, seven-and-a-half, twenty-one, hokey-pokey, or any banking or percentage game played with cards, dice, or any device, for money, checks, credit, or other representative of value, and every person who plays or bets at or against any of those prohibited games, is guilty of a misdemeanor, and shall be punishable by a fine not less than one hundred dollars ($100) nor more than one thousand dollars ($1,000), or by imprisonment in the county jail not exceeding six months, or by both the fine and imprisonment.

Touting: Penal Code section 337.1

Any person, who knowingly and designedly by false representation attempts to, or does persuade, procure or cause another person to wager on a horse in a race to be run in this state or elsewhere, and upon which money is wagered in this state, and who asks or demands compensation as a reward for information or purported information given in such case is a tout, and is guilty of touting.

Scalping: Penal Code section 346

Any person who, without the written permission of the owner or operator of the property on which an entertainment event is to be held or is being held, sells a ticket of admission to the entertainment event, which was obtained for the purpose of resale, at any price which is in excess of the price that is printed or endorsed upon the ticket, while on the grounds of or in the stadium, arena, theater, or other place where an event for which admission tickets are sold is to be held or is being held, is guilty of a misdemeanor.

C. Questions

Scalping" is a widely used term in American society and is commonly accepted by many people in society as a legal (albeit) sharp practice. Is always illegal? Look at the following situations and determine whether or not the conduct would be illegal under Penal Code section 346. In reaching your conclusion, carefully consider the precise fact or facts which are critical to your decision.

Before you begin, make certain that you have enumerated the specific elements of the offense of scalping, as set forth above. Then pick a specific fact to support each element of the offense. If you are missing any elements of the offense, the defendant has not committed the crime. If the factual evidence is incomplete at this point, what additional evidence would you need to make a determination if the defendant has committed the crime?

The following questions are intended to be thought provoking without necessarily having a "right" or "wrong" answer. These questions guide you in exploring how the law may or may not apply to likely real-life situations.

♦ You buy a ticket intending to go to a concert, but can't go because your grandmother is very ill. Your friend goes to the concert and near the sales office, tries to sell your ticket for $20 more than you paid for it. He did not get your permission before trying to sell the ticket. Are you or your friend guilty of a violation of Penal Code section 346?

♦ You buy a ticket with the intention of trying to sell the ticket for $20 more than you paid for it. You intend to sell the ticket outside the ticket office. Is this a violation of Penal Code section 346? If you are uncertain, what additional facts that you would need to answer this question?

♦ This time you buy the tickets intending to put an ad in the paper to sell the tickets for $20 more than you paid for them. Is this a violation of Penal Code section 346?

♦ You buy a ticket intending to go to the concert to see Band X. Instead, you find out that you made a mistake when you heard about the band, and in reality, it is Band Y that is going to be there. You stand outside the sales office at the concert and ask for $30 for the ticket, the price you paid for it. Is this a violation of Penal Code section 346?

VI.   Self-Assessment

1. "Obscenity" is based on a community standard, not a national standard.
    A.   True   B.   False

2. Crimes against public morals often apply to conduct which oversteps society's view of acceptable conduct.
    A.   True   B.   False

3. The modern-day crime of bigamy and the common-law crime of bigamy both prohibit either a husband or a wife from marrying more than one person.
    A.   True   B.   False

CHAPTER THIRTEEN

Crims Against the State

At common law treason was a crime punishable by death. In fact, in England, where the death penalty has largely been abolished, the death sentence is still permissible for a conviction of treason, indicating the seriousness of the offense. Like its common law ancestor, the modern day crime of treason focuses more on crimes against the national government. Because crimes against governmental sovereignties focus on the federal government, the material at the state level is sparse.

The traditional crime of treason has, however, been expanded beyond its conventional scope to include acts of warfare. Modern technology has broadened the ability of seditious persons to wage war against the state, including agents of biological or chemical warfare, accounting for the expansion in the law.

I. TREASON

A. Comments

Treason is not a common crime, especially at the state level. In fact, only one case has interpreted the following California treason statute. It is a case from the 1800s, a case that has been called into question by subsequent legal commentaries.

In reading this statute, notice the possibility of a death sentence is included within the definition of the crime itself, indicative of the grave harm this crime poses to society. The drafting of the statute is worthy of comment for another reason: it specifically includes evidentiary issues regarding the testimony of two witnesses. (We have seen this evidentiary issue before regarding the requirement of the testimony of two witnesses. Do you recall when?)

B. Statute

Penal Code section 37

(a) Treason against this state consists only in levying war against it, adhering to its enemies, or giving them aid and comfort, and can be committed only by persons owing allegiance to the state. The punishment of treason shall be death or life imprisonment without possibility of parole. The penalty shall be determined pursuant to Sections 190.3 and 190.4.

(b) Upon a trial for treason, the defendant cannot be convicted unless upon the testimony of two witnesses to the same overt act, or upon confession in open court; nor, except as provided in Sections 190.3 and 190.4, can evidence be admitted of an overt act not expressly charged in the indictment or information; nor can the defendant be convicted unless one or more overt acts be expressly alleged therein. .

II. BIOWARFARE

A. Comments

California has enacted an anti-terrorism act, the Hertzburg-Alarcon California Prevention of Terrorism Act. The Act is most notable for its inclusion of a list of items that fall under the purview of terrorist instrumentalities.

B. Statutes

Penal Code section 11417

The Hertzberg-Alarcon California Prevention of Terrorism Act

§ 11417. Definitions

(a) For the purposes of this article, the following terms have the following meanings:

(1) "Weapon of mass destruction" includes chemical warfare agents, weaponized biological or biologic warfare agents, restricted biological agents, nuclear agents, radiological agents, or the intentional release of industrial agents as a weapon, or an aircraft, vessel, or vehicle . . . which is used as a destructive weapon.

(2) "Chemical Warfare Agents" includes, but is not limited to, the following weaponized agents, or any analog of these agents:

(A) Nerve agents, including Tabun (GA), Sarin (GB), Soman (GD), GF, and VX.

(B) Choking agents, including Phosgene (CG) and Diphosgene (DP).

(C) Blood agents, including Hydrogen Cyanide (AC), Cyanogen Chloride (CK), and Arsine (SA).

(D) Blister agents, including mustards (H, HD [sulfur mustard], HN-1, HN-2, HN-3 [nitrogen mustard]), arsenicals, such as Lewisite (L), urticants, such as CX; and incapacitating agents, such as BZ.

(3) "Weaponized biological or biologic warfare agents" include weaponized pathogens, such as bacteria, viruses, rickettsia, yeasts, fungi, or genetically engineered pathogens, toxins, vectors, and endogenous biological regulators (EBRs).

(4) "Nuclear or radiological agents" includes any improvised nuclear device (IND) which is any explosive device designed to cause a nuclear yield; any radiological dispersal device (RDD) which is any explosive device utilized to spread radioactive material; or a simple radiological dispersal device (SRDD) which is any act or container designed to release radiological material as a weapon without an explosion.

(5) "Vector" means a living organism or a molecule, including a recombinant molecule, or a biological product that may

be engineered as a result of biotechnology, that is capable of carrying a biological agent or toxin to a host.

(6) "Weaponization" is the deliberate processing, preparation, packaging, or synthesis of any substance for use as a weapon or munition. "Weaponized agents" are those agents or substances prepared for dissemination through any explosive, thermal, pneumatic, or mechanical means.

(7) For purposes of this section, "used as a destructive weapon" means to use with the intent of causing widespread great bodily injury or death by causing a fire or explosion or the release of a chemical, biological, or radioactive agent.

(b) The intentional release of a dangerous chemical or hazardous material generally utilized in an industrial or commercial process shall be considered use of a weapon of mass destruction when a

person knowingly utilizes those agents with the intent to cause harm and the use places persons or animals at risk of serious injury, illness, or death, or endangers the environment.

(c) The lawful use of chemicals for legitimate mineral extraction, industrial, agricultural, or commercial purposes is not proscribed by this article.

(d) No university, research institution, private company, individual, or hospital engaged in scientific or public health research and, as required, registered with the Centers for Disease Control and Prevention (CDC) pursuant to Part 113 (commencing with Section 113.1) of Subchapter E of Chapter 1 of Title 9 or pursuant to Part 72 (commencing with Section 72.1) of Subchapter E of Chapter 1 of Title 42 of the Code of Federal Regulations, or any successor provisions, shall be subject to this article.

Water Code section 13375
Prohibited discharge of chemical, etc., warfare agents into waters
The discharge of any radiological, chemical, or biological warfare agent into the waters of the state is hereby prohibited.

C. Questions

♦ Why do you think there is a separate statute protecting water?

♦ Do you think the Hertzberg-Alarcon California Prevention of Terrorism Act is over inclusive? Under inclusive?

III. Self-Assessment

1. Acts of treason or more commonly prosecuted at the federal level than at the state level.
    A.   True   B.   False

2. Conduct constituting treason has remained unchanged since early times.
    A.   True   B.   False

3. Acts constituting treason must be aimed directly at a specific governmental body or person.
    A.   True   B.   False

Appendix A

Self-Assessment Answers

A=True B=False

Chapter 1:   1. B   2. A   3. A   4. A   5. B

Chapter 2:   1. B   2. B   3. A   4. B   5. B

Chapter 3   1. B   2. B   3. A

Chapter 4   1. A   2. B   3. B   4. A   5. A

Chapter 5   1. A   2. A   3. A   4. A   5. A

Chapter 6   1. B   2. A   3. B   4. B   5. B

Chapter 7   1. B   2. A   3. A   4. B

Chapter 8   1. B   2. A   3. A   4. B   5. B

Chapter 9   1. A   2. A   3. A   4. D   5. A

Chapter 10   1. A   2. A   3. A   4. B   5. B

Chapter 11   1. A   2. A   3. A   4. B   5. B

Chapter 12   1. A   2. A   3. A

Chapter 13   1. A   2. A   3. B

Appendix B

Text Correlation chart

Tozzini, *California Criminal Law*, 3rd ed.	Samaha, *Criminal Law*, 8th ed.	Boyce et al, *Criminal Law & Procedure*, 9th ed.	Bonnie, et al, *Criminal Law*, 2nd ed.
Chapter 1	Chapter 1	Chapter 1	Chapter 1
Chapter 2	Chapter 2		
Chapter 3	Chapter 3	Chapter 1	Chapter 6
Chapter 4	Chapter 4	Chapter 2	Chapter 7
Chapter 5	Chapter 5	Chapter 7	Chapter 6
Chapter 6	Chapter 6	Chapter 3	Chapter 6
Chapter 7	Chapter 7	Chapter 5	Chapter 9
Chapter 8	Chapter 8	Chapter 5, 6	Chapter 8
Chapter 9	Chapter 9	Chapter 8	Chapter 2
Chapter 10	Chapter 10	Chapter 4	Chapter 2
Chapter 11	Chapter 11		Chapter 3

Chapter 12	Chapter 12		Chapter 5
Chapter 13	Chapter 13		

Appendix C

Table of Cases